Ex Libris

Hillspeak Bookplate 83-C

THE ANGLICAN SPIRITUAL TRADITION

THE ANGLICAN SPIRITUAL TRADITION

John R. H. Moorman

Templegate Publishers/Springfield, Illinois

First published in 1983
by Darton, Longman and Todd Ltd.
89 Lillie Road, London SW6 IUD

Published in 1983 in the United States
by Templegate Publishers
P.O. Box 5152
Springfield, Illinois 62705

ISBN 0-87243-125-8

CONTENTS

FOREWORD

Anglicanism has a great tradition of spirituality, different from Roman Catholic or Protestant traditions. It began at the time of the Reformation when Anglicanism, as such, really came into existence; and it has continued right down to the present day. This book is an attempt to tell the story, from the time of the First Prayer Book onwards, to show how people loved and served God with deep devotion.

I am extremely grateful to Canon McDermott for reading the manuscript and making a number of valuable suggestions; and to Dr Robert Wright of New York for information about the Church in America. Also to Miss Dorothy Cummins, who has very kindly typed the manuscript.

JOHN R. H. MOORMAN
Durham
June 1981

ACKNOWLEDGEMENT

The Scripture quotations in this publication are from the Revised Standard Version of the Bible, copyrighted 1971 and 1952 by the Division of Christian Education of the National Council of the Churches of Christ in the USA.

PROLOGUE

THE REVEREND JAMES WHYTE

James Whyte [a purely fictitious character] was born in the city of Colchester in 1499, in the reign of King Henry VII, the son of Richard Whyte a saddler and his wife Elizabeth.

He was educated at the ancient grammar school where he did well, being a serious-minded and intelligent youth, far more interested in books than in saddlery. Like many of his schoolfellows he had no doubt that he was meant to be a priest; so, when he left school, he gave what help he could at his local church, and, in due course, received minor orders. From these he proceeded to subdeacon and deacon, and he was ordained priest in 1524 at the age of twenty-five. Ten years later he acquired a benefice in his home county of Essex, then part of the diocese of London.

James was aware that there was a good deal of loose talk going on in the area in which he lived. Essex was the county where Lollardy had long been supported in a clandestine way, and the place into which Protestant literature from Germany had been smuggled. Ships coming into Harwich often carried copies, or loose sheets, of Tyndale's English translation of the New Testament, and there were known to be little groups of people who met from time to time behind locked doors to read and study the Scriptures. All this was strictly illegal and was much frowned upon by the church authorities, who carried out a visitation in 1527 and confiscated a number of books which were publicly burned.

James Whyte heard rumours of all this, but he was not really interested. His concern was with his parish and his people. All he wanted to do was to build them up as faithful members of the Catholic Church. But in the year of his appointment to this parish something of great importance had happened: Parliament had passed a number of acts which had separated the Church in England from its old attachment to the rest of Western Christendom of which the Pope, the Bishop of Rome, was the acknowledged head. No doubt this was regrettable, but it made very little difference to the lives of the people in an Essex village. Up in London there was considerable excitement and much talk; but down where James Whyte lived, things went on much as before. None of his parishioners seemed to mind very much, or even to be aware of what had happened.

The first change which affected him was four years later when he was told that he must get a copy of the whole Bible in English and set it up in his church so that people could come and read it. This surprised him a good deal, for he remembered well the days when to possess even a single sheet of an English Bible was forbidden, and people were sent to prison for breaking the law. Now you could be punished if you didn't possess an English Bible. James was certainly mystified by the changes which were taking place, but he did not allow them to worry him. Anyhow, there weren't many people in his parish who could read at all; so it wasn't going to matter much either way. But a Bible was procured, and James got Ralph, the village carpenter, to set up a small lectern to which the Great Bible could be attached; and occasionally he found William, the clerk, standing there with a group of villagers to whom he read passages of Scripture. This was all very well. James was perfectly content that his people should have some of the Bible read to them in English. But once, when he came into the church, he found William reading the fourth chapter of the Epistle to the Ephesians; and when he got to the words, 'he set some to be apostles, some to be prophets, some to be Evangelists, some to be shepherds and teachers', he stopped and said: 'You see, there's nothing there about priests, is there?' James, of course, intervened at this point, and told William, pretty firmly, that, whereas he was permitted to read the Bible in public, he was not entitled to comment on it. It was the vicar's job to do that, not William's. William, as a faithful servant, naturally desisted in future, but James was troubled. Heresy was a poisonous and deadly thing. There had already been trouble in Essex with people who said that priests were unnecessary, or not part of God's will; but here was someone, in his own church, putting the same wrong ideas into people's heads. He must watch out. There was danger afoot.

However, in the following year, 1539, Parliament passed an Act which gave James great encouragement. It was called The Statute of Six Articles, and it showed that the King, who initiated it, was not intending to change the religious life of the people. It was described as 'An Act abolishing diversity in Opinions', and it declared that any who spoke in favour of certain opinions would be guilty of crimes punishable with imprisonment, forfeiture of goods and, in some cases, even death. The false opinions which it condemned included doubt of the real presence of the natural Body and Blood of Christ in the most blessed Sacrament of the Altar, the belief that the wine as well as the bread should be given to the people, that priests might marry, that private masses should not be allowed and that auricular confession should be brought to an end. James approved of this Act. He had always taught his people to believe in what was called 'transubstantiation'. It had never occurred to him that there was any necessity to administer the chalice to the laity. As for the marriage of the clergy, he knew that celibacy was a discipline which every ordained man accepted as part of his self-dedication to the service of Christ; and as for auricular confession, this was the basis of the pastoral and spiritual help which he gave to his people.

So, for the next few years, James Whyte was a happy man. He said his Mass regularly, offering the sacrifice for the living and the dead; he taught his people about heaven, hell and purgatory and warned them of the pains and torments which would fall upon them if they did not conform to the teaching of the Church; he told them about the saints – especially the Virgin Mother and the local worthy, St Osyth – who were praying for them and for their loved ones in purgatory; he heard their confessions and gave them their Easter communion; and he taught them to live good lives, not only by keeping the Commandments, but also by consistent attendance at church, by regular payment of their tithes and by giving alms for the relief of the poor.

So in 1547, at the age of forty-eight, James Whyte could be described as a contented and well-established parish priest, on good terms with his parishioners, and with no apprehension about the future. The Church of England had survived the crisis of breaking away from Rome, but all those liberal views which had been brought over from the Continent were not, apparently, going to get very far.

But at the end of January of that year news reached him that the King, Henry VIII, had died. James sang a solemn Dirge for him on the evening of 8 February, and a Requiem

Mass on the following morning. He also wondered very much what difference this would make in the life of the people, especially of the Church, as the King's heir was a boy of nine who would obviously have to give way, for the next few years, to the advice of older men called 'protectors'. The first thing that happened was the arrival of some 'visitors' who asked James and his churchwardens a lot of questions about the parish and what went on there. These were followed by a number of 'Royal Injunctions' which obviously had to be taken seriously. Many of them dealt with the use of English in the services of the Church. The Epistle and Gospel were to be read in English at Mass, the Bible was to be read at Mattins and Evensong, an English Litany was provided, and so on. These presented no great problems; but the command to read a set sermon, known as a Homily, every Sunday morning, was less acceptable. Aware of the ignorance of many of the laity and of the inability of most of the clergy to teach them, Convocation had been presented, in 1543, with a Book of Homilies written by notable preachers such as Cranmer, Bonner and Latimer. James procured a copy of these Homilies and read them through. The first one, 'A Fruitful Exhortation to the Reading and Knowledge of Holy Scripture', was all right, in spite of its references to 'the stinking puddles of men's traditions' which he thought a rather rude way of referring to much of the most solemn teaching of the Church on matters not touched on in the Bible. But some of the Homilies were disastrous, especially those which dealt with the question of Faith and Works, which James regarded as smacking of Protestantism. And he was now ordered to read these twelve Homilies, one by one, each Sunday morning. This he very much disliked doing, since he was one of those priests who was quite competent to preach to his people. But these Injunctions had the force of law. If he failed to observe them he might get into serious trouble.

But more was to come; for, in the following year, 1549, the whole form of worship to which James had been accustomed for nearly fifty years was swept away. The Latin Mass, which he had been saying daily for twenty-two years was now made illegal. So were the offices for baptism, marriage and burial which he had used. There was now no form of service for hearing confessions (except in the Visitation of the Sick), no invocation of saints, no mention of purgatory, no system of indulgences.

James Whyte obtained a copy of 'The booke of common prayer and administracion of the Sacramentes, and other rites and Ceremonies of the Churche: after the use of the Church of England' and read it with some dismay. It was published in the month of May and ordered to be used on Whitsunday, 1 June. There was, therefore, no time for James to prepare his people for the changes which were being forced upon them, for 'any manner of person, vicar or other whatsoever minister' who refused to use the new forms on that Whitsunday was punishable by a heavy fine and six months in gaol 'without bail or mainprize'.

As he read it through, however, he realized that things were not as bad as they might have been. The Mass was, of course, like everything else, in English; but the shape of the liturgy had been preserved and James was allowed to wear his customary vestments. He noticed also that there was now much more for the laity to do. In the old Mass they could do very little; but in the new service the worship was intended to be much more corporate, and there was far more dialogue between the priest and his people. It was also more edifying, as a sermon had to be preached or a Homily read, at every Mass.

So, on Whitsunday 1549, James Whyte led his people through the first celebration of the Mass in English. On the whole things went well, even at the administration of the Sacrament when, for the first time for 300 years or so, people were expected to drink from the chalice, though the wafer was still put not into their hands but straight into their mouths. Discussing the matter afterwards with his more intelligent parishioners, James found most of them confused and apprehensive. They had had no proper preparation for so radical a change in their customary worship, and they wondered what would happen next. At the same time, there were some among them who saw the advantages of the new rite and were prepared to see this as a step forward.

Another innovation which happened in the same year was an Act making it lawful for priests to marry. James Whyte was somewhat shocked by this. He knew that St Peter had a wife, and he thought it possible that some other of the apostles might also have been married. But for centuries the celibacy of the clergy had been part of the discipline of the Church, and James had accepted this without hesitation. But a neighbour of his, called Silverside, married a woman named Agnes Downes whom James had known as a girl many years before.

Neither James Whyte nor his parishioners knew much about what was going on in London. They knew nothing of the fall of Protector Somerset in October 1549 nor of the character of and the influence now exerted by the Earl of Warwick, who came to be known as 'the thunderbolt and terror of the papists'. Nor did they know that by the time the English Prayer Book came out, Cranmer was already at work on a liturgy which would be expressive of far more Protestant views. In their ignorance they thought that the Prayer Book of 1549 was to be the standard book for the future, for the new 'national' Church which Henry had brought into being. So they went Sunday by Sunday to their parish church, looking just as it had always looked, with the Mass celebrated in a manner not unlike that with which they were familiar.

But in 1550 a great blow struck them. In this year an Act was passed which said, first of all, that all the books which had been used in the past – missals, processionals, manuals, ordinals, etc. – were to be completely destroyed, whether they were the property of the church or were owned by private people, and, secondly, that all images or statues in the churches were to be defaced and destroyed. Thus there began the great 'Spoliation of the Churches' in which books were burnt, and statues of the Virgin and other saints, and roods, with their figures of the Crucified, supported by his Virgin Mother and his Beloved Disciple, were taken down and broken up for firewood. In some churches the ancient glass in the windows was removed, especially if it contained pictures of the saints. Failure to observe this statute carried with it the threat of heavy fines and unspecified imprisonment.

What could James Whyte and his churchwardens do? They loved their church and the things which it contained, many of them given by present and past parishioners in memory of their parents or children who had died. But they dared not disobey, or punishment would soon follow. Nor was there any chance of being overlooked; for, as soon as the Act was passed, Ridley, the new Bishop of London, sent out officials to see what was being done. Poor James had to go to Colchester with six of his parishioners, where he and they were put through a searching examination from which there was no escape. And, having got all the information he required, the Bishop issued a set of Injunctions which forbade the clergy to have candles on the altar or to continue with many of the little ceremonies, such as the elevation of the Host, the lavabo and the ringing of the sanctus bell, to which they had long been accustomed. They were also required to set up a wooden table to be used in future instead of the old stone altar.

James had to be away for some weeks during this summer; but when he came back he was appalled at what he saw. The church he loved, with all its beauty and colour, was now bare and ugly. The walls, which had been covered with paintings, were now white. The rood was nowhere to be seen. Even the little alabaster crucifix, before which he had so often said his prayers, had disappeared, no one knew where. James was horrified for he had always believed that the church was designed to be a foretaste of heaven, with its richness and colour and with the reminder, in painting and in sculpture, of those who would be our fellow-citizens in the household of God. But all this had gone. Not only was the church ruined; but his whole position as a parish priest seemed to have changed. He had always thought of himself as one who stood between God and his people. Each day he had felt that he was offering the Sacrifice of the Mass on their behalf; and in his teaching, whether in the pulpit or in the confessional, he believed that it was his task to prepare their souls for heaven. But now all was changed. The church looked like a barn, and he was forbidden to say his Mass with all the little symbolic gestures which had meant so much to him and to his people.

But worse was to come; for in 1552, a new Prayer Book was published, backed up by a new Act of Uniformity. James, who was now fifty-three, read it with dismay. The first English Prayer Book had been bad enough, but this new book was appalling, both in its directives, its language and its theology. James was not much of a theologian, but he realized that what faithful Catholic priests like himself were now required to accept was the theology and practice of a lot of German Protestants who had come over to this country to enforce their views on a feeble and complacent Anglican hierarchy. Not only had his church been transformed, but his services were now being shorn of all that had made them beloved by his people. No longer was he allowed to wear the traditional vestments; no longer was he allowed to make the sign of the cross when he consecrated the bread and wine; no longer was he allowed to tell people that what he was giving them was no less than the Body and Blood of Christ; no longer could he place the christening robe on the child he baptized, or anoint with oil the man he prepared for death. It seemed to him that a terrible blight had settled down on the Church, and he saw no way of getting back what he, and many others, so greatly loved. But the new forms and regulations had the force of law; and James made a great effort to see what was good in them and put up with the rest.

This went on for about a year; but on 6 July 1553, Edward VI died, and, after some skirmishing, the throne went to his elder sister Mary, the daughter of Henry's first wife, Catharine of Aragon. One of the first things done in the new reign was to forbid all preaching, so James had no opportunity of explaining to his people what was happening. Then, in September, several of the reforming bishops were deprived of their sees, including James's own bishop, Ridley, Bishop of London. After this an Act was passed repealing many of the Acts laid down by Edward VI and his government, and ordering all services after 20 December to be in the form used in the last year of King Henry VIII (1547).

This, to the more conservative clergy, may have been a relief, but it presented them with a number of problems. In accordance with the legislation of the previous four years they had, under threat of imprisonment, destroyed the books necessary to conduct the Latin services, broken up the altars, sold the vestments to make ladies' dresses, got rid of crosses, candlesticks and much of the paraphernalia of Catholic worship, and turned their churches into whited sepulchres. What hope was there to get things together again in a matter of a few months so that the Christmas Mass could shine forth in its old glory?

James went to talk things over with the local builder and the local joiner. Yes, said the former, he could build a stone altar of some sort, and the joiner undertook to set up a beam across the entry to the chancel and put a wooden cross on it, though he drew the line at carving either a crucifix or statues of Mary and John. Meanwhile, a wealthy lady in the parish promised, with the help of some of her friends, to make a set of eucharistic vestments out of a piece of rich brocade in her possession. Finally a small Roman missal, printed in Paris in 1506, was found from which James could say his Mass.

All, therefore, was in preparation for the Latin Mass to be sung in the church on 20 December with the old ceremonial and as much as possible of the old fittings and furniture. Most of the congregation felt quite happy to go back to the old ways. The only people who were totally lost were the younger children who couldn't understand what their parish priest was doing or why he was talking in a strange language. But that didn't matter. They would soon learn.

So, all that had been done in the last six years was swept away. The experiment had failed, and the reformers had been stopped. English people are naturally conservative in religious matters, and most of James's parishioners were quite happy to feel that there would be no more change and confusion. They had had to change their form of worship three times in five years, and surely that was enough.

And it was obvious that the Queen and her government meant business. Edmund Bonner, who had been deprived in 1549 in favour of Nicholas Ridley, had now been restored as Bishop of London with every intention of putting his diocese in order and seeing that his clergy obeyed his instructions. In 1554 he held a visitation which caused both clergy and laity to be put through a searching examination. This was followed up in 1555 by his Injunctions, in which he ordered the clergy to see that all the old ceremonies were reintroduced and to start again to wear the tonsure. He also insisted upon their reading, in place of the Homilies, his own book called 'A profitable and necessary Doctrine with certain Homilies adjoined thereto'.

James Whyte accepted this quite happily. He had been through a very difficult time with all these changes; but he was glad to get back to the ways in which he had been brought up and in which he had served his parish and his Lord for twenty years or more. Of course, the reformers had had some good ideas. He was quite happy saying all the church services in English and preaching to his people more than he had done in the past. And perhaps some of the little ceremonies were without much significance. But the desecration of the churches had troubled him, and he was bothered by new ideas about the priesthood and the Mass.

But now that things had returned to normal, James became saddened by the rigidity of the Queen and her government, at the ruthlessness with which their opponents were silenced, and at the savage way in which a large number of misguided and more or less ignorant people were put to death. In October 1555 James's former bishop, Nicholas Ridley, was burnt to death in Oxford, followed in March 1556 by his former archbishop, Thomas Cranmer. At the same time news came to him of a large number of people who had been burnt in his own county of Essex, many of them farm labourers and apprentices who could hardly be expected to understand why it was so wicked to doubt what their clergy had taught them about transubstantiation and what exactly happened on the rare occasions when they went to church to receive the Holy Communion.

It so happened that on 1 August 1557 James found himself in Colchester where he had gone to visit some old friends. He found the city in a state of great excitement as ten people were to be burnt the next day, six in the morning and four in the afternoon. Among them was his old friend Agnes Downes, who had married a priest called Silverside from whom she had no doubt learned a lot of Protestant ideas; so much so that, when examined by the bishop's officer, a man called Boswell, she had declared that the sacrament of the altar was but bread and wine before it is received, and had admitted that she no longer went to church either for Mass or Confession. Boswell, in his report to Bonner, had described her as a 'forward, obstinate heretic, and willing to burn her old rotten bones'. James saw Agnes, with three men and two women, led to a space outside the town wall where the stakes and faggots had been prepared. Here the victims were bound with chains which were nailed to the stakes, and the fires were lit. As the six slowly burnt to death, James could see them clapping their hands with joy, while the bystanders cried out: 'The Lord strengthen them! The Lord comfort them!'

James came away from this terrible scene a very unhappy man. Agnes had been his friend in his childhood, and several of the other five were people whom he had known in the past. Of course they were wrong in holding such evil ideas. Heresy was a very wicked thing, and it had long been an accepted fact that the proper punishment for obstinate heretics was for them to be burnt to death. But it was one thing to know that this was being done, and another thing altogether to see old friends going through this agony in one's own home town. Of the ten people burnt that day, five were women, one of them a servant girl aged twenty. Of the men, two were over sixty; one was a labourer aged thirty-four, a widower with three small children; and one a young man of twenty. It was obvious that the present government intended to enforce its religious views at all costs, even by torture and death, sparing neither sex nor age.

James went back to his parish and continued his work. He would have liked to tell the people what he had seen, and perhaps even pray for Agnes and her companions who had perished in the flames. But he dared not do so. Any sign of sympathy with heretics might lead to imprisonment and torture. So James kept silent; but his heart was troubled.

Then, a little over a year later, Mary and her accomplice, Reginald Pole, whom she had made Archbishop of Canterbury, both died; and Mary's half-sister Elizabeth, aged twenty-five, succeeded to the throne. She had suffered a good deal from the treatment her sister had meted out to her; and there was not much doubt that she would turn her back on Mary's Romanizing policy and restore the country to something like what it had been five years ago.

The religious problem was settled in 1559 by two Acts of Parliament, the Act of Supremacy and the Act of Uniformity, which together undid the reactionary work of Mary's reign and finally declared that the Church of England should be a 'Protestant' Church, not recognizing the jurisdiction of the papacy, using an English Prayer Book and restoring the liberties which had been given to it in the reign of Edward VI.

So James, and all the other 9000 clergy in England, had once more to change their way of life. Again the ornaments and furnishings, restored with so much difficulty five years ago, had to be removed from the churches. Again the missals and manuals had to be taken away and supplanted by an English Prayer Book not unlike that of 1552. James was now sixty years old and had had enough. In ten years he had had to face four major changes which had affected the forms of public worship, the appearance of his church and the theology which he had tried to teach his parishioners about the Eucharist and the future life. In spite of everything, he prayed that he would now be left in peace. After all, change had to come; and although much had been lost, there were things to be thankful for. One was the English Bible and the other was the Book of Common Prayer. With the help of these he could tell his parishioners the story of God's work and of man's redemption, and he could lead them in forms of worship which they could understand and in which they could take part.

The ten years from 1549 to 1559 had been difficult years

to live through – years of restlessness, constant change, uncertainty, apprehension and emotional turmoil. Yet it was out of these strained and unhappy years that the Church of England and its long spiritual tradition had been born.

1

'THE OLD ORDER CHANGETH, YIELDING PLACE TO NEW'

The English Bible

The English Bible has played such an immensely important part in the Anglican spiritual tradition that it is something of a surprise to learn that, until 1536, the possession of such a book could, in the last resort, result in one's being burnt to death.

The reason for this is that, for a long time, the Church had been convinced that uncontrolled access to the Bible on the part of people without the necessary qualifications was dangerous and liable to undermine the authority and stability of the Church. This belief was based on three things.

First: the Bible can very easily be misunderstood or deliberately misinterpreted. Even those who could read the Latin (of which, by the sixteenth century, there was an increasing number) could be led into error. It was, therefore, the responsibility – and monopoly – of the Church to tell people what they ought to know about God: his nature, his mighty acts, and his will. This was part of the *magisterium* given by Christ to his Church, something in the possession of the church authorities whose interpretation must be accepted. Once freedom of access to the Scriptures is allowed, then unorthodox and unacceptable notions are bound to appear. The Church felt very strongly about truth – or what it believed to be truth. Heresy was a sin of enormous gravity since it was bound to corrupt other people and so rob them of salvation. That was why heretics had to be burnt, totally destroyed, reduced to ashes. The Church must keep a tight hold on what was taught. If it failed to do so, all was lost.

Second: ever since the fourth century the Church had accepted the Vulgate as the standard text of the Bible, though revisions had taken place from time to time. The fact that only Latin Bibles were approved meant that the Church knew exactly what text scholars and teachers were using, while, at the same time, it would prevent the great mass of the laity from reading the Bible and making their own interpretations. As time went by, and the danger of heresy grew more alarming, the Church had tightened up its rules about translating the Bible into the vernacular. So far as England was concerned, the Psalms and the Gospels had been translated into Anglo-Saxon by Bede and others, and no less a person than King Alfred had translated part of the Book of Exodus. But in the later Middle Ages, especially after the appearance of English Bibles put out by Wycliffe and his followers in the fourteenth century, the Church became seriously alarmed and passed the necessary laws to make the possession of such a Bible a criminal offence.

For this the Church had some excuse. There is an Italian proverb, *Traduttore traditore*, which means that a 'translator' is almost certain to be a 'traitor', for it is virtually impossible for him to turn a text from one language into another without introducing some error. When it comes to translating the words of Scripture the danger is even greater, as the translator can so easily introduce his own ideas as to what the text is trying to say. One has only to look at recently produced English Bibles to see how easily this can be done, even by fully accredited scholars.

In the fifteenth century the Church in England was well aware of this danger; and when Lollard translations were known to be in circulation, a Provincial Council was held in 1407 at which a resolution was passed that 'no one shall in future translate on his own authority any text of holy Scripture into the English tongue . . . Nor shall any man read this kind of book, booklet or treatise, now recently composed in the time of John Wycliffe, or later, or any that shall be composed in the future'. Anyone disobeying this order was to be treated as a heretic. The final punishment for holding heretical opinions was death by burning.[1]

Third: the Church firmly believed that, in addition to the written Bible, she was also in possession of certain 'unwritten traditions which were received by the Apostles from the lips of Christ' and which had just the same authority as the

---

1 M. Deanesly, *The Lollard Bible* (1920), p. 296. For the decrees of the Council of Oxford in 1408 see W. Lyndewode, *Provinciale, seu Constitutiones Angliae* (1679), App., pp. 65–6.

Scriptures.[2] No one outside the hierarchy could know precisely what these traditions were; though when required, they could be used as a powerful weapon in the armoury of the *magisterium*. So long as the Church made this claim, and declared that the traditions were to be given 'equal pious affection and reverence' as was given to the Bible, the written Scriptures were bound to be regarded as only a part of the divine revelation. This was something abhorrent to the Protestants. To them the Scriptures were unique, for they were the means of communication between God and man. Everything necessary to salvation and to the knowledge of God was to be found there, and nothing could be added, whether from tradition, antiquity or reason.

This doctrine of *Sola Scriptura* was eventually adopted by the Church in England; but in the early years of the sixteenth century the Church was still thinking in medieval terms, and was determined that no English translations of the Bible should be allowed. It is known that there were English Bibles in some people's houses, as Sir Thomas More, in his *Dialogue against Heresies*, written in 1528, said that he had seen English Bibles in the homes of some of his friends; but these are thought to have been manuscripts of Anglo-Saxon translations.[3] The evidence of wills, however, shows that Wycliffe Bibles or Testaments were not uncommon.[4] But the Bible was still unread by the vast majority of English people, partly because English versions were rare, expensive and dangerous, and partly because so many lay people were unable to read anything. This, however, does not necessarily mean that English people were ignorant of all that the Bible contained. Those who went to Mass every Sunday would hear considerable portions of the New Testament read as Epistle or Gospel, while some at any rate of the more picturesque parts of the Old Testament – the Fall, the Flood, the Plagues of Egypt, or the exploits of King David – would be familiar to them either from sermons or from wall paintings and coloured windows. In addition there was an increasing number of

2 This was laid down at the Council of Trent in 1546; see *Conciliorum Oecumenicorum Decreta*, ed. J. Alberigo *et al.* (Herder 1962), p. 639. English translation in H. Bettenson, *Documents of the Christian Church* (1943), p. 365.

3 M. Deanesly, op. cit., pp. 1–12.

4 Ibid., pp. 392–8.

well-educated lay people who could read the Vulgate and find things out for themselves.

Although extensive reading of the Bible was denied to the great majority of the people, there were men, such as the scholars Erasmus and Colet, who would very much have liked to see vernacular versions of the Bible, or at least of the New Testament, so long as these were licensed by the Church. Even Cranmer was not very keen on people reading the Bible to themselves. The Bible, he said, belonged to the Church, and its treasures should be imparted to mankind in the context of worship.[5] All in authority knew perfectly well that unofficial versions were almost certain to be sectarian, erroneous, controversial and tendentious.

And, indeed, the early versions were all of this. The first attempts to translate the Bible, or parts of it, into English in the sixteenth century were made by William Tyndale. Because of the ecclesiastical prohibitions Tyndale had to do most of his work abroad, under conditions of great hardship which ended in his being burnt to death somewhere near Brussels in 1536. But, from about 1525 onwards, copies or individual sheets of his version were being smuggled into England where they were quickly snapped up by people anxious to read the text of the Scriptures for themselves.

Tyndale was, from the start, suspected of propagating heretical ideas. In this he went a good deal further than the Wycliffe translators, changing the word 'church' into 'congregation' and writing highly controversial marginal comments and prefaces into which he put some of his criticisms of the Church and its rulers.

Tyndale was succeeded by Miles Coverdale, a much more orthodox person who wanted to see reform come from within the Church and not by pressure from outside. He revised Tyndale's version and added greatly to it, so that, by 1535, a complete English text was available.

These men had run certain risks; but they probably knew that the climate of opinion was changing. Henry VIII was in favour of allowing the sale and distribution of English Bibles, prompted no doubt by his adviser, Thomas Cromwell, who had 'a positive desire to establish a religion based upon the Bible, a religion eschewing on the one hand blind trust in ecclesiastical tradition, and, on the other, the brawling of

5   J. S. Marshall, *Hooker and the Anglican Tradition* (1963), p. 14.

self-appointed expositors'.[6] So it came about that, in 1536, for the first time for many centuries, anyone who could read at all and who had access to a copy of the Bible in his or her mother tongue, could study it at will. And, two years later, orders were given that a copy of 'the whole Bible of the largest volume, in English' should be set up in every parish church and that the clergy should 'discourage no man privily or apertly from the reading or hearing of the said Bible, but shall expressly provoke, stir, and exhort every person to read the same'.[7] Thus, with a stroke of the royal pen, a policy which the Church had strenuously pursued for many centuries, was completely overthrown. Not everyone approved of this. Many of the clergy disliked it intensely, and parents were known to drag their children away from public readings of the Bible and chastise them severely.[8] But the long struggle put up by the church authorities in favour of their monopoly of the Scriptures had been lost. Those in favour of free access had won their cause with the help of two laymen – a layman calling himself 'supreme head of the Church of England' and his lay steward.

From now onwards English versions became common. During the reign of Edward VI (1547–53) many New Testaments and whole Bibles were published in England, though, early in the reign of Elizabeth, most of these were replaced by the Calvinistic Geneva Bible, much loved by the Puritans. Even so, by the early years of the seventeenth century there were so many versions in circulation that James I himself appointed fifty-four scholars to prepare a new edition which would replace all others and become the authorized version for both private and public reading. The sole survivor of the old Coverdale version still in use is the translation of the Psalms attached to the Book of Common Prayer.

As soon as it became clear in 1537 that the Bible in English was to be generally used, attempts were made to see that the clergy became fully acquainted with it, not only by regular and prolonged reading but also by learning long passages of it by heart. In 1538 Shaxton, Bishop of Salisbury, gave orders

6 A. G. Dickens, *The English Reformation* (1964), p. 135.
7 Gee and Hardy, *Documents Illustrative of the History of the English Church* (1921), pp. 275–6.
8 B. F. Westcott, *A General View of the History of the English Bible*, ed. W. Aldis Wright (1905), pp. 81–2.

that his clergy were to 'con' certain books of the New Testament and commit to memory one chapter each fortnight.[9] If they did this they should, after three years, know by heart all the four Gospels, and, by the end of ten years, know the whole of the New Testament (260 chapters). Bonner, in 1542, ordered every priest in the diocese of London to study, with gloss or commentary, one chapter of the New Testament each week, and to learn passages by heart.[10] This idea of not only reading the Bible but also of learning much of it by heart finds an echo in the exhortation still delivered by the bishop to those about to be ordained priest when he exhorts them to be studious in 'reading and learning' the Scriptures.[11] The Ordinal of 1550 also adopts the Protestant doctrine of *Sola Scriptura* when the bishop makes sure that the candidates are 'persuaded that the holy scriptures contain sufficiently all doctrine required of necessity for eternal salvation through faith in Jesus Christ', so ruling out any belief in the value of the traditions.

So far as the clergy were concerned, Bible-reading became a very important part both of their ministry and of their private devotions. From 1549 onwards all clergy were required to say Mattins and Evensong daily. This meant that, in the course of a year, they would read virtually the whole of the Old Testament once and the New Testament (with the exception of the Apocalypse) three times. How thoroughly this was carried out it is impossible to say; but when we read the writings of the reformers it is astonishing to see how familiar they were with the Bible. Thomas Becon's *The Flower of Godly Prayers* occupies fifty-seven pages in the Parker Society edition of his works. In this booklet nearly 2000 texts are quoted or referred to, drawn from sixty out of the seventy-seven books of the Bible; and this at a time when there were few English concordances[12] and when the English Bible had been in circulation for not more than a few years.

As soon as it became legal to read and possess an English

9   W. H. Frere and W. M. Kennedy, *Visitation Articles and Injunctions of the Period of the Reformation*, ii (1910), pp. 55.

10 Ibid., p. 83.

11 This occurs in the Ordinal of 1550, though the word 'learn' is probably taken nowadays to mean 'discover the meaning of' rather than 'learn by heart'.

12 John Merbecke, the musician, published a Concordance to the Bible in 1550.

Bible there is no doubt that the literate laity did their best to obtain one. The demand was, in fact, so great that the government had to control the price at which they could be bought. In 1552 a New Testament in quarto, unbound, was to cost not more than twenty-two pence, while an octavo edition could be bought for twelve pence and a still smaller one for nine pence which would then be roughly a day's wage for a better-class workman.[13] Even this meant that only people with a certain amount of money could buy Bibles, and attempts were made to see that only noblemen and gentlemen, substantial merchants and gentlewomen were given permission to read the Scriptures alone.[14]

Those not in possession of a Bible had to depend either upon hearing long passages read at Morning and Evening Prayer or upon reading the Great Bible which was set up in their church. Nevertheless, Henry's action in 1537 set on foot the reading of the Bible which is a practice at the root of all Anglican religious custom. Many people now made Bible-reading a systematic and valuable exercise, starting at the first chapter of Genesis and working steadily through to the end. In so doing they became familiar with the domestic and military exploits of generations of tribal chieftains who had operated in the Middle East some thousands of years ago. The character and fortunes of people like Ehud and Abimalech were better known than those of people in the next parish. And, of course, everything written in the Bible was regarded as historically and factually true. Adam and Eve, the sun moving backwards, the total inundation of the whole world – all was taken for granted if it was written in the 'lively oracles of God'. Even obvious contradictions (for example, how long the Flood lasted) were ingeniously reconciled, while the moral and ceremonial laws in Leviticus were often quietly overlooked or explained away. Any fact recorded in the Bible must be true, and any command must be obeyed. There could be no argument about this. The Bible was the Word of God, infallible and incontrovertible.

13 H. S. Bennett, *English Books and Readers, 1475 to 1557* (1952), p. 230.
14 A. G. Dickens, *The English Reformation* (1964), pp. 189–90.

The Book of Common Prayer

Having got their English Bible in 1537 the reformers turned their attention to an English Prayer Book to replace the Latin Missal, the Breviary and other books. But for this they had to wait thirteen years, as the Supreme Head of the Church turned out to be also Defender of the Faith. Henry VIII had no wish to see changes in the forms of worship or in the theology which went with them; and any hope of progress which may have been engendered in the reformers' breasts was crushed in 1539 by the Act of Six Articles which, among other things, came down firmly in favour of transubstantiation, communion in one kind, private masses and auricular confession. This came as a great blow to those who had been studying the new theology which was coming from overseas, since the new Act would stifle any liturgical change for many years. It was not until the death of the King in 1547 that anything new could be introduced, but when this happened, the reformers had already given considerable thought to forms of worship which would be in keeping with the theology which they had imbibed.

There were three things here which needed attention. The first was the question of language. Latin must go. How could people worship God in a language which they could not understand? In future all worship was to be in English; and, by a stroke of providence, they had in Cranmer a genius in the production of fine liturgical prose, a gift which has not often been vouchsafed and has seldom been available when most needed.

The second necessity was greater lay participation in the worship of the Church. Hitherto the laity had been able to play only a very minor part in public worship, being obliged to put up with 'the blessed mutter of the Mass' which was virtually inaudible and largely unintelligible. Of course, many of them knew more or less what was going on. If they could not hear what was being said they could generally see what was being done, and adjust their devotions accordingly. For the Church, which had broken off verbal communication between the sanctuary and the nave, had introduced a number of actions or gestures which took the place of words – the kneelings and crossings, the elevation of the Host, the ringing of bells, the movements of the priest and of the ministers who stood beside him. All these had been so carefully worked out that even quite simple people could be expected to know what was going on, while the not-so-simple (of which there were now growing numbers) would probably be able to join in the Latin Gloria, Creed, Sanctus and Lord's Prayer. But the reformers wanted to go much further, and create a new pattern of worship in which clergy and laity would co-operate. The use of the vernacular was, of course, of primary importance. It was also important that the priest should make himself heard; so he was told to stand in a good position and speak up. The laity also had plenty to do, and one of them was rightly allowed to say the General Confession on behalf of the whole congregation.[15] Two aspects to be treated with close attention were those of simplification (the cutting out of unnecessary ceremonial and misleading activity), and edification (by prolonged reading of the Bible supported by the preaching of sermons and homilies).

But far more important than any of these changes was the necessity of bringing the worship of the Church into line with the New Theology which was now rampant in northern Europe. The Reformation in England began, as we all know, as 'an act of State';[16] but it very soon became a religious issue as Protestant ideas and ideals – Lutheran, Zwinglian and Calvinist – seeped into the country.

The basis of Protestant theology is belief in justification – 'the act whereby God, in virtue of the Sacrifice of Christ, acquits a man of the punishment due to his sins; and, in his mercy, treats him as though he were righteous'.[17] This finds its roots in the words of St Paul to the Romans: 'Since all have sinned and fall short of the glory of God, they are justified by his grace as a gift, through the redemption which is in Christ Jesus ... For we hold that a man is justified by faith apart from works of law.'[18] This was what Luther taught as a result of his own certainty of what God had done for him. 'His sole concern', writes James Atkinson, 'was to tell a simple world of his own experience of the great God, who

15   *The Two Liturgies ... set forth ... in the Reign of King Edward VI* (Parker Society 1845), p. 90.
16   Sir M. Powicke wrote: 'The one definite thing which can be said about the Reformation in England is that it was an act of State'; *The Reformation in England* (1941), p. 1.
17   See *The Oxford Dictionary of the Christian Church* (2nd edn 1974), p. 769.
18   Romans, 3.23–4, 28.

had shown his hand in Christ, so that man might know God's pardon and God's peace in the Living Christ, and so live in this Kingdom of God within a corrupt, sinful, hostile, but temporal world as to be received in death into God's everlasting Kingdom.'[19]

Justification decided the destiny of man; and Luther's teaching brought him into sharp conflict with certain doctrines and practices then universal in the Church. The Protestant believed that once a man had, in sure and certain faith, accepted the truth of what God had done for him through Christ, then he would, at the end of this life, pass into what Christ had called 'the kingdom prepared for you from the foundation of the world', while those who had not this faith, or who rejected Christ, were fit only for 'the eternal fire prepared for the devil and his angels'.[20]

In this he ran up against the prevalent conviction in the Church that, since many souls, at the hour of death, were fit neither for heaven nor for hell, there must be an intermediate state, a state of condign punishment for minor and venial sins or sins unconfessed, which was known as purgatory. Since this was an 'intermediate' state it must have an end; and the question arose as to whether either the Church Militant or the Church Triumphant could do anything to succour the souls enduring the pains of purgation and reduce the length of their sentence. Yes, said the Church, there are, indeed, ways in which this can be done. One was by the offering, preferably before an image in the church, of prayers to the saints, and especially to the Blessed Virgin Mary, to enlist their help in getting souls out of purgatory. Another was in the form of prayers for the same purpose, offered by the Church on earth, especially when attached to the sacrifice of the Mass. Another was by the performance of 'good works' in the form of almsgiving, building of churches or going on pilgrimage to celebrated shrines in order to win the approval and the mercy of God.

It was the last of these which the reformers found so intolerable since it so easily opened the door to commercialism. Those who wished to do something for the souls of their parents or friends could so easily be persuaded that this could be done by means of material gifts to the Church, with the

19   J. Atkinson, *Martin Luther and the Birth of the Reformation* (1968), p. 11.
20   Matthew 25.34, 41.

inevitable result that simple people believed that one could buy one's way into heaven. An enlightened, spiritually-minded, unworldly Church could have put this right; but in the early part of the sixteenth century the Church was none of these things; and, by 1514, it was openly selling indulgences to get souls out of purgatory in order to raise money for the building of St Peter's in Rome.

To the reformers this was intolerable. Man's destiny was not a matter of ducats and doubloons. They could not believe that there was any such thing as purgatory. When the soul was released from the body it went straight to heaven or to hell, to endless bliss or to eternal torment. The choice depended solely on the person's faith. Justification, salvation – call it what you will – was the free gift of God given only to those who had faith in Christ and in the redemption won for mankind by his sacrifice on the cross. This was the basic teaching of the reformers, and something which made its way into England and changed the whole nature of Anglican thought and Anglican worship.

Three other important matters, all connected with the main doctrine of justification by faith, were also involved. One was concerned with the sacrament of penance; one with the sacrifice of the Mass; and one with the presence of Christ in the eucharistic elements.

The sacrament of penance had always played an important part in the life of the Church; and, by the later Middle Ages, the whole relationship between the pastor and his flock was based on private or 'auricular' confession. The Lateran Council of 1215 had laid it down that 'everyone of either sex over the age of discretion must confess all his sins, at least once a year, to his own priest'.[21] This entitled the parish priest to conduct an annual examination of each of his adult parishioners in matters of faith and morals. Nothing was to be overlooked. 'Have you failed to return things which you have borrowed? Have you ever ridden over growing corn? Have you ever left the churchyard gate open? Have you ever dozed off during the sermon?' and so on.[22] When everything had been dragged up and confessed, then, and only then, could absolution be given.

---

21 Denzinger-Schönmetzer, *Enchiridion Symbolorum* (1965), p. 264.
22 See J. R. H. Moorman, *Church Life in England in the 13th Century* (1945), p. 87.

The reformers were opposed to the practice of auricular confession on two grounds. One was that sin was so terrible a thing that people must take their grief and shame direct to the throne of God and seek forgiveness there. No human being could decide whether someone was entitled to receive God's forgiveness: no one could come between a man and his Saviour. Secondly, the Sacrament of Penance included the demand for something in the way of satisfaction, some good work which could be taken to be a sign of contrition. This, like the granting of indulgences, could very easily be turned to the advantage of the Church, especially when it was short of money. Chaucer must always be treated as a satirist rather than as an historian, but his account of the friar who demanded a gift to his Order before he would give absolution and anyone could be regarded as 'wel y-shrive' may be a not impossible picture of the time in which he lived.[23]

Later medieval teaching about the sacrifice of the Mass was also abhorrent to the reformers. Their whole doctrine of justification depended on the 'full, perfect and sufficient' sacrifice of Christ on the cross for our redemption. That the sacrifice of Christ was unique and something which can never be repeated or added to is fundamental Christian belief. This means that the Mass can never be anything more than a representation or pleading of that sacrifice. But the Church had allowed itself to become careless in what it had taught, and 'the Mass came to be thought of as a distinct sacrifice in itself which does not derive its sacrificial character from its relation to the sacrifice of the Cross'.[24] To the reformers the Eucharist could be no more than a memorial, a solemn remembrance of the redeeming act of Christ performed for us on Calvary. Forgiveness was obtained and justification given by God alone. Nothing done by a priest at an altar could add anything to this; and the loose talk about 'the Sacrifice of the Mass' could easily lead people into false belief about the sacrifice of Christ and the nature of the Eucharist.

Transubstantiation is a medieval way of explaining how the bread and wine become, in some real way, the Body and Blood of Christ. The reformers did not deny that there was a change in the elements; what they disliked was the idea

---

23 *The Canterbury Tales: Prologue*, ll. 225–6.
24 B. J. Kidd, *The Later Medieval Doctrine of the Eucharistic Sacrifice* (1898), p. 131.

that, at the moment when certain words were said by the priest, the bread and wine cease to be bread and wine and become the Flesh and Blood of Christ without thereby changing their outward appearance. This seemed to the reformers to look like something little short of magic; and they were in no way impressed by the casuistry of the schoolmen and their arguments about 'substance and accidents'. Many were quite happy to believe that, in the process of celebrating the Lord's Supper, the elements took on a new meaning and significance; and in the English Prayer Book, even in its most Protestant form in 1552, the congregation prays that it may 'eat the flesh of thy dear Son Jesus Christ and drink his blood';[25] but anything which claimed that the natural Body and Blood of Christ could be brought down to earth was, to them, arrogant and wholly unbelievable.

When Henry VIII died in 1547, and a Protestant form of government came into being, the reformers, led by Cranmer, began to make public the Anglican liturgies on which they had been working. The first English service, a litany, had in fact been published in 1544 and had shown the beauty of Cranmer's prose. Then, in 1548, came the Order of Communion. Although the Mass was still being said in Latin, the priest, after he had made his own communion, was now allowed to introduce a short office for the communion of the people. This, of course, was in English and consisted of a penitential section, as a spiritual preparation, followed by the administration of the elements in both kinds, thereby restoring the ancient, and indeed biblical, practice which the Church had quietly abandoned in the thirteenth century. So, in this short-lived order, two barriers were thrown down – the service was in the language of the people, and to the laity was given again the right to drink the Blood of Christ as well as to eat his Flesh.

Then, in the following year, 1549, the first English Prayer Book was published. This was an attempt to introduce people to the kind of worship which the Church thought appropriate in the light of the New Theology which it was now teaching. It knew that, in matters of worship, people like to move slowly; and it was meant, therefore, to be something of a compromise, a step in the right direction. On the practical side many of the points which the reformers wanted to see were introduced. Except for the titles of the Psalms, the Canticles, and the Athanasian Creed the whole book was in English. There was far more opportunity for lay participation all through. It was firmly based on the Bible with long passages read at Morning and Evening Prayer every day.[26] It was much less complicated than the old system ('the number and hardness of the rules called the Pie'[27]). In an attempt not to offend people's habits, especially at a birth or a death, some of the medieval ceremonies at baptism (such as exorcism and the putting on of the christening robe) and at the preparation of a man for death (which included his being anointed with holy oil) were preserved. But where there was real need for doctrinal change, the reformers could not give way to popular demands; so all idea of purgatory was ruled out, and the saints' days in the calendar were reduced from 181 to twenty-five, all, except All Saints' Day from the New Testament.

The Mass retained the shape of the liturgy and included some of the old practices to which people were accustomed. The priest was to wear the customary eucharistic vestments; he was to encourage people to come to 'auricular confession'; he was told to mingle water with the wine and to put the wafers into people's mouths rather than into their hands.

Being a compromise, the book had a mixed reception. Gardiner, the conservative, approved of it as 'not far from the Catholic faith in regard to sacrifice and transubstantiation', while Hooper, the radical, called it 'defective . . . and manifestly impious'.[28] But the authors had prepared for this, and they wrote in an Appendix 'Of Ceremonies': 'Whereas, in this our time, the minds of men be so diverse, that some think it a great matter of conscience to depart from a piece of the least of their ceremonies (they be so addicted to their old customs), and again on the other side, some be so new-fangled that they would innovate all things; and so do despise the old that nothing can like them, but what is new: It was thought expedient not so much to have respect how to please and

---

26 People were expected to attend these services every day, for the Preface speaks of the 'daily hearing of holy scripture read in Church'. *Two Liturgies*, p. 17.

27 Ibid., p. 18.

28 *Original Letters*, ed. H. Robinson (Parker Society 1846), i, p. 79.

satisfy either of these parties, as how to please God, and profit them both.'[29]

So far as the doctrines of the Sacrifice of the Mass and transubstantiation are concerned, the authors would probably have told Stephen Gardiner that he had read into the book ideas which were not there. In the course of the Eucharist three kinds of sacrifice are mentioned. The first is the 'full, perfect and sufficient sacrifice, oblation and satisfaction' made by Christ on the cross; another is 'this our sacrifice of praise and thanksgiving'; and the third is the offering of 'ourselves, our souls and bodies, to be a reasonable, holy and lively sacrifice to thee'. The Mass (as they still called it) was related to the sacrifice of Christ, though more in the form of a commemoration than what a modern Catholic Catechism calls 'the very same sacrifice as that of the cross'.[30] 'To the end that we should alway remember the exceeding love of our Master, and only Saviour Jesu Christ, thus dying for us, [they wrote] and the innumerable benefits, which (by his precious blood-shedding) he hath obtained to us, he hath left in those holy mysteries, as a pledge of his love, and a continual remembrance of the same, his own blessed body, and precious blood.'[31] This is as far as they were prepared to go, and Gardiner at least thought they had given away nothing essential to the Catholic faith.

On the question of the real presence the Prayer Book of 1549 is not very clear. The authors certainly did not want to suggest transubstantiation, a theory which they had abandoned some years previously. But they refer repeatedly to the elements as the 'Body and Blood of Christ'; and, at the words 'bless and sanctify these thy gifts', two large black Maltese crosses are printed as they had been (in red) in the old missals.[32] At the same time they were anxious to make the point that, although we eat the Flesh and drink the Blood of Christ, we do so 'spiritually'. What they wanted to do was to emphasize the fact that the whole sacrament of the Eucharist was carried out in the realm of the eternal, that it was a spiritual exercise in which the worshipper was brought into an intimate, personal relationship with his or her Saviour.

29 *Two Liturgies*, p. 155.
30 *A Catholic Catechism* (School edn 1962), p. 187.
31 *Two Liturgies*, p. 80.
32 Ibid., p. 88.

The Church used the elements of bread and wine, as Christ himself had used them, to make this contact. Exactly how it was performed was not our concern, so long as people accepted his gifts in faith.

The book was intended to be something of an eirenicon, an attempt to help both sides, Catholic and Protestant, to worship in accordance with the will of God. The customs which it abolished, and the theology which it repudiated, are not stressed. In spite of the violently polemical language which was being used at that time, the pope is only once mentioned in the Prayer Book of 1549 and that is when, in the Litany, we pray to be delivered from 'the tyranny of the bishop of Rome and all his detestable enormities'. But this lapse in courtesy was corrected in the course of time. Apart from this, the book was an attempt to produce forms of worship which, while retaining all that was best from the past, would be in accordance with the new and more enlightening ideas which were coming to birth.

The following year, 1550, saw two further productions. One was the *Booke of Common Praier noted*, by John Merbecke, the organist of St George's, Windsor. This gave life and beauty to the sung services. The other was a new Ordinal which was added to the Prayer Book. The important thing about this was that the Anglican reformers showed no intention of abandoning the threefold ministry of bishops, priests and deacons. Most of the Continental reformers had got rid of this. Calvin pointed out that, in the Epistle to the Ephesians, St Paul refers to 'apostles, prophets, evangelists, pastors and teachers' and said that, as the first three had come to an end, only pastors and teachers were left. But Cranmer refused to accept this point of view, and kept to the traditional ministry which he was quite certain had been in existence since the time of the apostles.[33]

But though the old orders were preserved, the ordination services were considerably simplified. The Anglican reformers felt that the one important thing in a valid ordination was the laying-on of hands, with prayer. Other things, such as the anointing with holy oil, the putting-on of Mass vestments, the handing-over of the eucharistic vessels, were superfluous.[34] All that the candidate was now to receive was a copy of the

33 See Preface to the Ordinal.
34 The deacon was, however, vested with a tunicle.

Scriptures, out of which he would teach good, reformed doctrine.

By this time some of the bishops were anxious to forge ahead. They did not expect the Prayer Book of 1549 to last long and they wanted to carry out such reforms as they could without delay. Nicholas Ridley, Bishop of London, who had already taken down the altar at St Paul's, told his clergy, in 1550, that they were no longer to use the altars in their churches but to set up movable tables instead.[35] This he did on the grounds that 'the use of an altar is to make sacrifice upon it; the use of a table is to serve for men to eat upon'.[36] Ridley's action may have been premature; but it was supported, within a few months, by an order in Council sent to every bishop to see that 'with all diligence all the altars in every church or chapel within your said diocese be taken down, and instead of them a table to be set up ... to serve for the ministration of the blessed communion'.[37] About the same time an Act was passed ordering the total destruction of all books which had been previously in use, together with 'any images of stone, timber, alabaster or earth' all of which were to be defaced and destroyed.[38]

With all this going on, the time was drawing near when the Prayer Book of 1549 would have to be replaced by something much more Protestant. So it was that, in 1552, the second Prayer Book was given to the people. In shape it was not far different from its predecessor, but in detail it showed that the church authorities now wished to go very much further in getting rid of old ceremonies, customs and beliefs. At baptism, exorcism and the chrisom were omitted, as was also the sign of the cross at confirmation. The anointing of the patient disappeared from the office for the Visitation of the Sick. But it was in the service of the Holy Communion that the greatest changes appeared. No longer was this to be called the Mass; no longer was the priest to wear the traditional, eucharistic vestments; and although he could refer to the 'benefit of absolution' he was no longer to speak of 'au-

35 *Chronicle of the Grey Friars of London*, ed. J. G. Nichols (Camden Society 1852), p. 67.
36 Quoted by Jasper Ridley, *Nicholas Ridley* (1957), p. 217.
37 E. Cardwell, *Documentary Annals of the Reformed Church of England* (1844), i, p. 101.
38 J. R. Tanner, *Tudor Constitutional Documents* (1922), p. 114.

ricular confession'. The consecration prayer was much shorter and lacked the black Maltese crosses, while all reference to the Virgin Mary and the saints was removed. At the communion of the people the elements were no longer to be called the Body and Blood of Christ. Finally, at the wish of the Council and not that of the church leaders, a paragraph (known as the Black Rubric) was inserted to say that, although it was perfectly proper for communicants to receive the sacrament kneeling, this being 'a signification of the humble and grateful acknowledging of the benefits of Christ given unto the worthy receiver' this must not be construed to mean that there is 'any real and essential presence there of Christ's natural flesh and blood'. This was the last nail in the coffin of transubstantiation for the paragraph stated that the bread and wine 'remain still in their very natural substances'.

The Prayer Book of 1552 was a triumph for the more advanced reformers in the Church of England, but it lasted for only a few months. Edward VI died on 6 July 1553 and was succeeded by his half-Spanish half-sister Mary. Within a few weeks, the First Act of Repeal abolished both English Prayer Books and all the changes which had taken place since her father's breach with Rome in 1534. With the healing of the breach went, unfortunately, a most savage persecution, in which at least 282 people – many of them simple country lads and servant girls – were burnt to death because they clung tenaciously to the Protestant teaching which they had been given, especially on the subject of how Christ communicated himself to his followers in the sacrament of the Eucharist.

But Mary lived for only five years as Queen, and, in 1558, the reformers found themselves once more in control. Mary's reactionary legislation was now disposed of, and an English Prayer Book, similar to that of 1552, was produced.

In the ten years from 1549 to 1559 people had had to accustom themselves to four changes in their worship and to nearly as many changes in their theology. For centuries they and their forebears had known only one Church and one way of performing their religious duties; but, during that decade, everything had been overturned several times, with indescribable confusion and distress. But there was no escape. However much they might dislike and disapprove of what was taking place, people dared not stay away from church or they could be charged with heresy. To go every Sunday to church, and to pay one's statutory church taxes, was compulsory; and the church courts were just as strict as the civil magistrates.

The new Anglican forms of worship seemed to assume that, on every Sunday morning, there would be in every church a service which would begin with Mattins and Litany, and end at the Offertory in the communion service. The reason why the clergy were told to break off at this point was that the reformers so greatly abhorred the custom of non-communicating attendance. One of the Homilies printed in 1552 tells people not to 'stand by as gazers and lookers on them that do communicate'. This, it says, would be 'a contempt and unkindness unto God'.

The medieval hope had been that the laity would be present for the whole of Mass each Sunday, though they would communicate probably not more than once a year. This had not always been the custom, but it came to be thought that, so long as people were present at the elevation of the Host, this would do. But this was an anomaly that the best churchmen would have regretted. The Anglicans seem to have been uncertain what to do. Cranmer, like Calvin, liked a full communion service every Sunday, and the Prayer Books and Injunctions suggest this for, at any rate, the larger churches. Some churches also had a daily Eucharist, as the Prayer Book of 1549 allows for parts of the service to be omitted on 'workdays'.[39] In other churches Holy Communion was certainly not celebrated every Sunday, as in one of the exhortations the priest is told to inform his congregation when a 'sacrament Sunday' was approaching. There was, therefore, considerable variety. The one thing which the reformers were quite clear about was that there should be no old-fashioned Masses at which the celebrant was the only communicant.

The pattern of church attendance, therefore, did not change very much. But there was a good deal of change in the way in which worship was conducted, and even more in the appearance of the churches. The medieval church was full of colour, with wall paintings from roof to floor, coloured windows, vestments and hangings, statues and shrines. As a result of the new teaching, most of this disappeared. The wall paintings were overlaid with whitewash; the vestments and hangings were sold; the statues and shrines were broken up. And with this terrible spoliation of the churches went new

39 *Two Liturgies*, p. 95 and cf. p. 80.

teaching about so many things. The old sense of union between earth and heaven, between the living and the dead, between man and the saints, disappeared. The comfortable belief that the holy ones of all generations were actively assisting not only the living, but also the souls in purgatory, was crushed out of existence. The one thing that mattered now was faith and the responsibility of each individual to put his or her whole trust in the mercy and forgiveness of God.

Adjuncts to Worship

The preaching of the Word came to mean so much in reformed worship that it is surprising to find how seldom it is mentioned in the English Prayer Books. Mattins and Evensong, which people were encouraged to attend, contained no sermon; and the only place in the regular services of the Church where a sermon is ordered is at a celebration of the Holy Communion for, in the minds of the reformers, Word and sacrament went together. Some thought that a sacrament was scarcely valid if the Word was not preached. As Thomas Becon said: 'A sacrament without preaching of the Word is but a dumb ceremony: a glass offered to a blind man or a tale told to one that is deaf.'[40] So the Prayer Book of 1549 says that, after the Creed, a sermon or homily shall be preached in which the people shall be exhorted to 'the worthy receiving of the holy Sacrament'. The Prayer Book of 1552 says nothing about the subject of the sermon but merely that a sermon, homily or exhortation shall be preached.[41]

As we have already seen, most people attended the Holy Communion service as far as the Offertory. This meant that they would hear a discourse of some sort every Sunday. But the preparation of a weekly sermon was perhaps asking rather a lot of men who had had no training in homiletics; and Hooper, in 1551, told his clergy in the diocese of Gloucester that if they could not preach themselves, they must arrange for others to preach four sermons in their churches every three months.[42]

After the breach with Rome the clergy in some places were

40   Thomas Becon, *Prayers and Other Pieces*, ed. John Ayre (Parker Society 1845), p. 255.
41   *Two Liturgies*, pp. 79, 268.
42   *Visitation Articles and Injunctions* (1910), ii, p. 303.

ordered to preach regularly against the usurped power of the pope. Shaxton of Salisbury appears, in 1538, to have expected this every Sunday, as if it was the only topic worth preaching about. But this must have been impossible, though other bishops demanded such a sermon once a quarter.[43] At other times the clergy were free to preach what they liked; but Bonner, in 1542, issued injunctions for the clergy of the diocese of London in which he tried to revive the idea of *sermones de tempore*, that is to say, explanations of the passages of Scripture read as Epistle and Gospel in the Mass.

> They shall not rehearse no sermons [he writes] made by other men within these two or three hundred years; but when they preach they shall take the Gospel, or Epistle, of the day, which they shall recite and declare to the people plainly, distinctly and sincerely, from the beginning to the end thereof . . . In the which Epistle or Gospel ye shall note and consider diligently certain godly and devout places, which may incense and stir the hearers to obedience of good works and prayers . . . Furthermore, that no preacher shall rage or rail in his sermon, but coldly, discreetly and charitably openly declare and set forth the excellency of virtue. And to suppress the abomination of sin and vice, every preacher shall, if time and occasion will serve, instruct and teach his audience what prayer is used in the church that day [i.e. the Collect], and for what thing the Church prayeth specially that day, to the intent that all the people may pray together with one heart for the same . . .[44]

This was sound advice, based on the former practice of the Church, linking the sermon with the liturgy.[45] Bonner was by nature conservative; but on this point he is in line with the reformers who were proclaiming that the purpose of preaching was to expound the Scriptures and exhort people to live godly, righteous and sober lives. So important was the sermon that clergy in London were told that 'all curattes (what so ever) should not be at sermones nor servyce longer than ix of the

43 Ibid., ii, pp. 54, 62.
44 Ibid., ii, pp. 89–90.
45 Cf. Felicity Heal and Rosemary O'Day, *Church and Society in England: Henry VIII to James I* (1977), p. 64.

clocke, that then the curattes with the paryshes myght come to Poles crosse and heare the preachers'.[46]

It was at places like Paul's Cross, or in the presence of the King or some other notable person that the sermons of the great preachers such as Latimer, Ridley and Hooper were generally preached. Many of these were subsequently printed and are available for us to read today. What went on in the village or city churches it is impossible now to say. But the Protestant clergy were obviously preaching their doctrines with great fervour and remarkable success; for, when the examinations and burnings took place in Mary's reign the victims not only knew what they believed, but they believed it so strongly that they were prepared to give their lives for it. Some were examined about the claims of the Bishop of Rome; and that they denied these so stoutly is a sign that the quarterly sermons against the usurped power of the pope had been taken to heart. Others were examined as to their refusal to go to church or to confession. But the most striking thing about these interrogations is that the matter on which many of them felt so strongly was the nature of the Real Presence of Christ in the eucharistic elements. Whereas the Catholics taught people to believe in transubstantiation, the Protestants taught them that the bread and wine do not become the Body and Blood of Christ until they are actually received into the mouth of the believer. This seems to us a small and perhaps academic point; yet scores of people, many of them with very little education, would go to prison for long periods and even be burnt to death rather than give way on this doctrinal issue. We may know very little of how the parish clergy fulfilled the office of preaching; but the more radical of them had an enormous influence on their congregations when they proclaimed their Protestant doctrines during the reign of Edward VI. People do not give their bodies to be burned for the sake of what might be called 'a nice idea'.

There had been a long tradition of preaching in England. In 1281 John Pecham, the Franciscan Archbishop of Canterbury, had called upon the parish priests to preach regularly in English to their people. This preaching was more didactic and exhortatory than expository. The clergy were not expected to expound the Scriptures; what they were told to do

---

46 *Narratives of the Days of the Reformation*, ed. J. G. Nichols (Camden Society 1859), p. 23 Cf. *Visitation Articles and Injunctions*, ii, p. 135.

was to explain and commend the teaching of the Church as expressed in the Creed, the Ten Commandments, the Seven Sacraments, and so on. It was their job to see that people understood what these were and were exhorted to live up to them. How well they managed to do this it is impossible to say; but, when a group of parishes in the diocese of Exeter was inspected in 1301, the synodsmen gave a report on the work done by their clergy. Of the twelve groups whose reports have been preserved, seven praise their clergy for the high standard of their preaching and teaching, and another four say that their clergy have fulfilled their priestly office well. Only one group complained that they had been neglected.[47] This needs to be borne in mind when one reads of the poor quality of medieval parochial preaching. The standard may not have been very high when one considers the great sermons of the friars or of the Reformation preachers. The synodsmen of Devon had, after all, little or nothing to go by; but at least they were content with what they got. Two hundred years later, the standard of preaching may have been slightly higher, but it was still mainly didactic and lacked 'any personal insights into, or any direct contemplation of, the Scriptures'.[48]

At the great turnover in the sixteenth century, preaching underwent a very important change, so laying the foundation-stone of the preaching which has played so important a part in the Anglican spiritual tradition. In the medieval period the preachers, being concerned with the faith and teaching of the Church, looked to the Bible for texts to support them – if they searched the Scriptures at all it was to find words which could be made to convey the message which they wished to deliver. If, for example, we of today were to read in St Luke 5.3 that 'Jesus entered one of the boats which was Simon's . . . and taught the people out of the boat' we should regard this as a fact, probably not of great importance. We should not expect to be told why he chose that particular boat; but, if asked, we should say 'Perhaps it was the first one he came to', or 'It happened to be the only one ready for another trip', or 'It was the right sort of boat for what he

47   G. G. Coulton, *Social Life in Britain from the Conquest to the Reformation* (1918), pp. 260–4.
48   Peter Heath, *The English Parish Clergy on the Eve of the Reformation* (1969), p. 103.

wanted'. But the medieval preacher would scoff at this. To him there must be a concealed message. Why did he choose Peter's boat? Because it represented the Church of Rome, the 'barque of Peter'. Jesus's entry into Peter's boat from which he was to teach the people was an obvious indication that Peter's successors, the Bishops of Rome, were responsible for what the Church taught. It was all so simple if you knew the rules.

It was of this way of using the Scriptures that the reformers complained. To them the Scriptures were there to reveal the handiwork and the will of God and must be taken in the most literal sense. With typical medieval zeal for categorization, four ways of interpreting the Bible had been laid down – the tropological (or moral), the allegorical (or spiritual), the anagogical (or reassuring) and the literal – and, of these, the last was the one least employed. Tyndale saw the danger of this and declared, of the literal meaning, that the pope had 'taken it clean away' and 'locked it up' so that men could not get at it.[49]

Two quite independent movements helped to bring about the change from the allegorical to the literal interpretation of the Scriptures. One we call the Renaissance, with its scholars trying to find out the true and precise meaning of what the Bible records. The other we call the Reformation, with its emphasis upon discovering and listening to the Word of God. Thus we find the reformers using the Old Testament not for whimsical interpretations and hidden messages, but as a historical record of the mighty works of God; while the New Testament contained the very words of God as spoken by his Son and interpreted by his disciples. God, they taught, has been perpetually at work since the Creation; and modern man must look carefully at what has been said and done, be warned of the consequences of disobeying the commandments of God, and take heed of the prophetic and apostolic exhortations to virtue.

That much preaching accompanied the Reformation is well known, though it was of different kinds. Latimer, the best known of the preachers, must not be taken as typical of his age. His sermons were like those of the great friar preachers

49   J. W. Blench, *Preaching in England in the Late Fifteenth and Sixteenth Centuries* (1964), p. 1, quoting Tyndale's *Doctrinal Treatises* (Parker Society 1848), p. 303.

of the previous century – racy, entertaining, colloquial, full of references to everyday affairs. They followed no familiar or accepted form or pattern but contained plenty of polemic, whether it was an attack on Rome or on social evils at home. Other preachers were less chatty and more balanced, conforming to some kind of pattern. But the preachers were determined, at all costs, to preach what they believed to be true about such things as justification, faith, repentance, and so forth; though, in so doing, they could not resist the temptation to attack what they thought was false. John Bradford was a very holy man, and his sermon on repentance is, in some ways, a great theological tract; but he has not gone more than a page or two before he lashes out at 'the prating of the pope and his prelates' and at 'blind buzzards and perverse papists'.[50] The Reformation preachers felt so strongly that they had been miraculously brought out of darkness and error into the clear light and true knowledge of God, his nature and his will, that people must be prevented from slipping back into the old beliefs and practices which they regarded as positively evil. 'Never, since England was England [said Bradford] didst thou so manifestly reveal thy truth as thou hast done in these days.'[51] So, in the days of safety, they hammered out the truth as they saw it; and, when darkness fell and danger faced them, they continued to preach the Word in season and out of season, to reprove, rebuke and exhort with all longsuffering, even if their own longsuffering meant years of imprisonment and a terrible death.

The great Anglican tradition of preaching, based on the literal meaning of the Bible, can, therefore, be said to have been nourished by the blood (or, in this case, the ashes) of the martyrs – Cranmer, Ridley, Bradford and the rest, though, in fact, not a great many of those put to death were clergy. Of the 282 who were burnt, only twenty-one are known to have been in holy orders; but there must have been many priests who had preached the doctrines for which men and women had died. Some of the clergy must have found preaching difficult. Few had seen a Bible before 1537, and few possessed one in the palmy days of Edward VI. Commentaries were even more hard to come by. So, much of the Protestant teaching must have been given to small groups in

50 John Bradford, *Writings* (Parker Society 1848), pp. 43–81.
51 Ibid., pp. 158–9.

people's homes, some of it provided by itinerant propagand-
ists visiting parishes where they knew they would be welcome.
What actually happened in church on Sunday mornings is
another matter altogether, and Bernard Gilpin, writing about
the middle of the century, paints a dark enough picture. 'A
thousand pulpits in England [he said] are covered with duste,
some have not had four sermons these fifteen or sixteen years,
since Friars left their limitations, and fewe of those were
worthy the name of sermons.'[52]

It was, therefore, to help the clergy, and also to see that
important truths were put before the people, that Convocation, in 1542, arranged for the writing of a number of Homilies
which could be read, instead of a sermon, at the Sunday
Mass. They were not, however, published until five years
later, as Henry VIII did not like them. As soon as the King
was dead, his son issued Royal Injunctions to say that one of
these Homilies was to be read every Sunday at High Mass
when no sermon was preached.[53] There were twelve Homilies
in all, written by preachers such as Cranmer, Latimer and
Becon, and, as some of them were rather long, even by Tudor
standards, they were, in 1549, divided into thirty-one portions. They were given considerable authority by being mentioned in each of the English Prayer Books and, later, in the
Thirty-nine Articles. They could even be used as a test of
orthodoxy.[54]

Considering the type of congregation in most parishes,
these Homilies would be above the heads of most of those
who heard them. Like academics in all generations, the
writers found it difficult to write in a language which simple
people could understand. The very first Homily, 'A fruitful
Exhortation to the Reading and Knowledge of Holy Scripture', could scarcely expect much response from those who
could not read anything at all. Others refer to Origen and
Chrysostom as if these would be familiar names in the local
ale-house. Nevertheless, for those who could understand what
they were about, the Homilies contained some good material.

---

52 A sermon preached before the court in January 1552; see *The English
    Sermon*, ed. M. Seymour-Smith, i(1976), p. 107. The 'limitations' were
    the areas in which friars of a particular convent were allowed to
    function.
53 *Visitation Articles and Injunctions*, ii, p. 129.
54 Ibid., ii, p. 132.

All of it was, of course, Protestant and anti-papal. There is little mention of the Church. Religion is a personal matter, a question of faith. 'Without faith', they say, 'all that is done of us is dead before God.' There is also a good deal in favour of civil obedience and against 'contention and brawling'.

There cannot be much doubt that a good many clergy, having found neither time nor inclination to prepare sermons for Sunday mornings, fell back upon these Homilies which were to be read, one by one, in the order in which they were printed. If this was so, then the language and the teaching of these discourses must have become familiar to the laity in the process of time. But in Mary's reign they were, naturally, suppressed as containing 'heretical and damnable opinions'.[55] Bonner, now restored as Bishop of London, provided an alternative set of homilies in his book called *A profitable and necessarye doctryne, with certayne homelies adjoined thereunto*, parts of which could be read at sermon time instead of what the reformers had provided.[56] The original Homilies were restored in the reign of Elizabeth when a second book, containing another twenty-one addresses, was added to them. Some of these are practical, one being 'For repairing and keeping clean the church'; but there are also some very good discourses on the meaning of the great festivals, and (perhaps the best of all) 'Of the worthy receiving of the Sacrament'.

Of the four main constituents of Anglican worship – the Bible, the Prayer Book, sermons and hymns – English people had, by the middle of the sixteenth century, obtained the first three. But they had very little in the way of hymns; and one of the reasons for this is that so many of Cranmer's friends and advisers were Calvinists rather than Lutherans and that the exiles in Mary's reign settled at places like Geneva and Zürich rather than in Germany. And so, while Lutherans were enjoying themselves singing their great chorales, their *Feste Burg*s and *Wachet auf*s, Calvinists and Anglicans had to be content with metrical versions of the Psalms.

Thomas Sternhold, a groom of the robes at the court of Henry VIII, began putting psalms into a popular metrical form and published nineteen of them in 1548. A few years later he issued an edition containing thirty-seven psalms, to

55 Bonner, in ibid., ii, p. 353. But Bonner had himself written no. 5 on 'Christian Love and Charity'.
56 Ibid., ii, p. 361.

which John Hopkins added another seven in 1551. Then, during Mary's reign, the exiles in Geneva brought out an edition, with tunes, in 1556. The tunes, originally composed for French versions, did not fit the English words very well and were soon abandoned. This was a pity as the tunes were, aesthetically, much better than the words, as can be seen from a perusal of the *English Hymnal* of 1906.[57]

Compared with the 'well of English undefiled' on which Cranmer drew for the Prayer Book and Coverdale for the Psalms, the English metrical versions are, for the most part, uninspiring.

> O God, to me take heed of helpe I thee require,
> O Lord of hosts, with haste and speed helpe, helpe, I thee
> desire (Ps. 70)

compares badly with the immaculate rhythm of Coverdale's

> Haste thee, O God, to deliver me:
> Make haste to help me, O Lord.

Nevertheless, the metrical psalms caught on and became very popular especially when reasonably good tunes were found for them. People have always liked to sing about their religion; and, with the disappearance of the old medieval hymns and carols, something had to be provided. So the metrical psalms, poor doggerel though most of them were, were sung everywhere. An early seventeenth-century Roman Catholic writer said:

> There is nothing that hath drawne multitudes to be of their Sects so much as the singing of their psalmes, in such variable and delightful tunes. These the souldier singeth in warre, the artizans at their work, wenches spinning and sewing, apprentises in their shoppes, and wayfaring men in their travaile, little knowing (God wotte) what a serpent lyeth hidden under these sweete flowers.[58]

Having given the people some psalms to sing when they were about their business, the reformers also gave them metrical versions of parts of the Prayer Book such as the Nicene Creed, the Gloria and the Sanctus. Even the Athanasian

57   See especially nos. 114, 200, 269 and 305. Some of these were composed by L. Bourgeois.
58   H. C. White, *Tudor Books of Private Devotion* (1951), p. 44.

Creed managed to appear, though not very convincingly, in the popular form.

So we one father hold, not three,
one sonne also, not three
Only holy ghost alone, and not
three holy Ghosts to bee.

The only real hymn which was included in the liturgical experiments of 1548–52 was the translation of the old eighth-century *Veni Creator*, which appears in the usual double-common metre beginning:

Come holie Ghost eternall God
proceeding from above:
Both from the father and the sonne,
the God of peace and love.

This may have safeguarded the *Filioque* clause; but it was replaced in the course of time by a much better version, composed by John Cosin, and now printed in Anglican ordinals and sung on many occasions:

Come, Holy Ghost, our souls inspire.

Religion at Home

In the early summer of the year 1532 the English ambassador to the court of the Emperor Charles V was staying for a time in Nuremberg when he fell in love with and married a young German Protestant girl called Margaret. The English ambassador was Thomas Cranmer, a middle-aged Fellow of Jesus College, Cambridge, and a priest. In so doing he was, of course, breaking the laws both of the Church and of his own country where marriage of clergy was strictly forbidden. The marriage of Cranmer to the niece of the Lutheran Osiander, was significant in more ways than one. In the first place it meant the creation of a clerical family home – a thing unknown for a very long time, but something which became very common and very important in the history of the Church of England. Much more remarkable (and, in the end, significant) was the fact that Cranmer, though a priest of some twenty years standing, and in full communion with the See of Rome, was beginning to think of himself as being, in some ways, more in sympathy with the Lutherans than with the

Catholics. This perhaps would not have mattered very much if he had continued as a not very distinguished Fellow of Jesus College, Cambridge. What made the whole thing so important was that, within a few months, this semi-Lutheran Cambridge don became Archbishop of Canterbury.

At that time things in England were beginning to change rather rapidly; so that, by 1534, Parliament had cut, one by one, the cords that bound the *Ecclesia Anglicana* to the Western Church with its centre at Rome, and had set up an independent, autonomous Church under the leadership of an exceedingly able and strong-minded conservative King, who had been given the title of 'Supreme Head of the Church of England', assisted by an Archbishop who had, to some extent, identified himself with the reform movements in Germany and Switzerland.

So far as the political and administrative changes were concerned, these were the responsibility of the government. But what about doctrinal change? The actual breach with Rome raised questions of the nature and authority of the Church; but there was a fairly strong conservative group among the bishops who had accepted the breach only in the belief that it need make little difference to what the Church believed and taught about the Christian faith. This party probably had the support of most of the clergy who paid only slight attention to the separation from Rome and wanted to be left in peace to get on with their work as pastors and teachers. But there was also a progressive group among the bishops and the academic and parochial clergy who were attracted by Protestant ideas and all that could be described as the 'new theology'. They wanted the now established and independent Church of England to carry out a large number of reforms, in its liturgy, its ecclesiology, its soteriology, and in its whole way of life and presentation of the faith. As for the laity, it is hard to discover what most of them thought. A few strong and holy men, like Thomas More, believed that the separation from Rome was schismatic and sinful, and were prepared to suffer for what they believed. But subsequent events, in the next twenty years, showed that there was a strong Protestant influence among the laity, and that some of the new teaching was going very deep.[59]

Clearly the church authorities had to do something to help

59   See above, p. 34.

the clergy to know what to teach and the laity what to believe. The first tract to come out, called *The Ten Articles*, was issued on the King's authority in 1536. This was a rather ill-digested mixture of Catholic and Protestant theology, designed to meet the needs of both parties. It was succeeded, in the following year, by a book called *The Institution of a Christian Man*, or, more popularly, *The Bishops' Book*, which was drawn up by a large committee of forty-six bishops, archdeacons and other divines with the intention of declaring what they believed to be the official teaching of the now liberated Church of England. In their preface, the loyal subjects of the King 'give thanks unto Almighty God with all our hearts, that it hath pleased him to send such a king to reign over us, which so earnestly mindeth to set forth among his subjects the light of holy scripture';[60] and they go on to set out what they wish 'all bishops and preachers' to teach as touching the Apostles' Creed, the Seven Sacraments, the Ten Commandments, the *Pater Noster* and the *Ave Maria*, with notes on justification and purgatory. Much of this is traditional material: auricular confession is commended, as are also prayers for the dead; ceremonies such as 'creeping to the cross' are approved; the bread and wine at Mass are declared to be 'the very selfsame body and blood of Christ, corporally, really and in the very same substance exhibited, distributed and received unto and of all them which receive the said sacrament'. On the other hand, the claim of Rome to exercise universal jurisdiction over all Christians is repudiated; and, in accordance with the parliamentary events of the previous few years, a case is made out for national or particular Churches, each entirely independent of any other Church, but together forming 'the holy catholic church or congregation' which is 'the company of the elect and faithful people of God'.

The document, which runs to about 200 pages, is meant to be a handbook for the clergy, teaching them what to proclaim from the pulpits; but it is doubtful if many of them possessed either the money to buy it or the inclination to read it.[61] It was followed, in 1543, by a similar book called *A Necessary Doctrine and Erudition for any Christian Man*, which was aimed

60 *Formularies of Faith put forth by authority during the reign of Henry VIII*, ed. C. Lloyd (1825), p. 24.
61 It is interesting to note that the first two sentences of this book contain no less than 488 words.

more at the intelligent laity than at the clergy. This was known as *The King's Book*, claimed to have been written by the King himself, though it was, in fact, written by Cranmer and three other bishops. As one would expect of anything which had the royal imprimatur, this book, written some years after the passing of the Act of Six Articles, is very conservative – 'the handsomest monument to Henry's experiment in Anglo-Catholicism'.[62] But it had a short life; and, in spite of the fact that it was claimed to have come from the royal pen, it made little impression on those who were meant to read it, for they already had other literature on which they liked to feed in their private devotions.

Much the most important and beloved book was the *Primer*. At the heart of medieval religion was the *Opus Dei*, the daily round of services said at more or less regular intervals in accordance with the promise of the Psalmist: 'Seven times a day will I praise thee.' Although secular clergy were encouraged to observe this routine, those held most responsible were the members of the religious orders – monks, canons, friars and nuns. But there was, in the later Middle Ages, a growing number of lay people, deeply pious and reasonably well-educated, who felt that they would like to play their part in the regular offering of praise to God. It was to help them to do this that books known as Primers, containing such things as the Hours of the Virgin, some Psalms, the Ten Commandments, the Beatitudes, the 'fifteen O's of St Brigid', together with a good deal of other material, were produced. These books were, at first, in Latin; but, in the fifteenth century, an English Primer appeared on the scene; and, from then onwards, the Primer came to play an important part in the devotional life of the laity. As the teaching of the reformers gradually came to be accepted, the material included in the Primer changed. Less space was now devoted to the Virgin; and the *Ave Maria* disappeared, together with the *Dirige* and the *Commendations*, both of which were concerned with praying for the dead.[63]

Realizing that a number of unauthorized Primers were coming on the market, Thomas Cromwell, in 1538, ordered John Hilsey, Bishop of Rochester, to prepare a book which could be distributed with safety. This came out in the follow-

62 A. G. Dickens, *The English Reformation* (1964), p. 185.
63 H. C. White, *The Tudor Books of Private Devotion* (1951), pp. 67–95.

ing year and showed that Hilsey, like the wise man in the Gospels, had brought out of his treasure things new and old. His book supported the supremacy of the King in religious matters, and condemned papal usurpations; yet it made use of a lot of pre-Reformation material which some of the reformers would like to have seen omitted. This Primer was given royal approval in 1545; and when an Act was passed in 1550 'for the abolishinge and puttinge awaye of diverse Bookes and Images', the Primer, in English or in Latin, was the only book exempted from this destruction.[64]

As a book for the use of the laity, the Primer became of less importance after the publication of the English Prayer Book in 1549. Here could be found a form of Morning and Evening Prayer, the whole book of Psalms, a Collect, Epistle and Gospel for every Sunday and Holy Day, a Litany, a Catechism, and a number of exhortations. But the Primer continued to be printed, perhaps because the Book of Common Prayer was designed as a manual for public, rather than for private, worship. Primers were, in fact, printed well into the reign of Queen Elizabeth, containing the seven Hour Services, the English Litany,[65] the *Dirige* with a number of prayers for the dead, the whole of Psalm 119 (which it calls 'the ABC of godly love, the paradise of learning, the shop of the Holy Ghost and the school of truth')[66] and some long personal prayers. Despite, therefore, the merits of the English Prayer Books, there was obviously a continuing desire for some sort of Primer, and many copies were printed and distributed.

The church authorities naturally hoped that, once the Scriptures were available in English, there would be a great burst of Bible-reading by both clergy and laity. Whether or not this actually happened, it is hard to say. A Bible was still a fairly expensive luxury, to be acquired only by those who could afford it; but from 1538 onwards there was the Great Bible in the parish churches to which anyone could resort. To make it more easy for people to understand the Scriptures, an order was given for a copy of the *Paraphrases of Erasmus* to be set up beside it.

64 *Private Prayers put forth by Authority during the Reign of Queen Elizabeth*, ed. W. K. Clay (Parker Society 1851), pp. vi–ix.
65 Omitting the phrase about the tyranny of the Bishop of Rome.
66 *Private Prayers*, p. 68.

Erasmus wrote his *Paraphrases* in Latin, shortly after 1500, beginning with the Epistles of St Paul and proceeding afterwards to the Gospels and the Acts. 'Here', we are told, 'was no longer a crabbed, pedantic, artificial interpretation of the text, but something to tell men, for the first time in that new age, what the Bible really said and meant'.[67] These *Paraphrases* proved so useful that translations into many languages were made; and, in 1543, a group of English scholars, under the inspiration of Queen Catharine Parr, undertook to bring out an English version of the *Paraphrases* on the Gospels. Wanting, no doubt, to do something to lighten the burden of her poor step-daughter Princess Mary, in the long years of her seclusion, she invited her to undertake the translation of the Fourth Gospel.[68] In the end Nicholas Udall, dramatist and poet and, at one time, headmaster of Eton, devoted five years to a translation of the Gospels and produced his *First Tome* in 1548. Two other scholars, Miles Coverdale and J. Olde, brought out a *Second Tome* in the following year.[69]

It must have been known that these English versions were on the way, for it was the Royal Injunctions of 1547 which ordered a copy of the *Paraphrase* on the Gospels to be put in every church, while, at the same time, ordering every priest to provide himself with a copy of the New Testament in English and Latin together with the *Paraphrases*. The former decree was certainly carried out in many churches, for we find in the churchwardens' accounts of the church of St Mary-at-Hill in London: 'Item, for a boke called the paraphrases of Erasmus v^s', and, at Great St Mary's in Cambridge: 'Item for dim' ye paraffrycys of erasmy. v^s vi^d'.[70] But it is doubtful whether either the smaller churches or the poorer clergy could afford to buy books which cost the equivalent of at least a week's salary of a parish priest.

With the invention of printing in the second half of the fifteenth century had come a large output of devotional literature. Apart from service books of various kinds, Caxton, Wynkyn de Worde and others had published English versions

67 Preserved Smith, *Erasmus* (1923), pp. 187–8.
68 P. S. Allen, *The Age of Erasmus* (1914), p. 197.
69 *Cambridge Bibliography of English Literature*, i, p. 327.
70 *Medieval Records of a London City Church*, ed. H. Littlehales (EETS 1905), p. 387; *Churchwardens' Accounts of St Mary the Great, Cambridge*, ed. J. E. Foster (1905), p. 120.

of the popular history of the lives of the saints known as *The Golden Legend*, *The Mirror of the Blessed Life of Jesus Christ* (often attributed, though wrongly, to St Bonaventura), the lives of the Desert Fathers and many other works which gave great pleasure and encouragement to members of the literate laity. Walter Hilton's *Scale of Perfection* was in print from 1494 onwards, and Thomas à Kempis's *Imitation of Christ*, the most appreciated and beloved of all medieval devotional works, from 1502. By 1530 there was a great deal of material available for those who wished to improve their minds (and their souls).[71]

During these years new books were also being written, many of them showing that people were in need of a new type of book which would be considerably more practical and supply them with prayers and meditations suitable for the layman who wished to live the life of a dedicated Christian and to order his household accordingly. The books of prayers written by Erasmus and by the Spanish scholar, Vives, come into this category.

The most interesting book of this kind was *A Werke for Housholders* by Richard Whitford, which was published in 1530. Whitford was a member of the most secluded religious order, the Carthusians; but he had a very shrewd understanding of how ordinary people lived, and of the sort of things which would support and encourage them. He wrote, naturally, for the educated, but he fully realized that many who wanted to live a good Christian life would find some of the devotional literature pitched in rather too high a key for their simple minds; and he turns his attention to those who were 'unlearned with wytte, wysdom and due knowlege of the and thy laws'. So he tells them how to pray and what to pray; he gives them moral advice, especially about Sunday observance and the dangers which lie concealed in such recreations as 'cardinge, dycynge and closshynge'; he provides a compendium of the main events in the life of Christ; and he tells people that they ought to read aloud the Lord's Prayer, the Ave Maria and the Creed at every meal, or at least once a day.[72] Whitford may seem to us to demand rather a lot of a

---

71 See F. A. Gasquet, 'The Bibliography of some devotional books printed by the earliest English printers', in *Transactions of the Bibliographical Society*, vii (1904), pp. 163–89.

72 H. C. White, *The Tudor Books of Private Devotion* (1951), pp. 157–61.

busy, practical householder; but it is important to note the emphasis upon the home and the household as the unit of the Christian life. In the past, people had tended to rely on the Church, especially the religious orders, to pray for them; but they were beginning now to think more in terms of personal responsibility and of the importance of the family.

All this came out before the great changes which occurred in the life of the English Church from 1534 onwards. With the advent of Protestant thought and the widespread condemnation of Rome, the demand for these 'Romish' books was greatly reduced as other books began to supersede them. But though publication came to a rather abrupt end about this time, copies of many of the devotional classics continued to circulate; and we find republication of some of them taking place later on when things had, to some extent, calmed down.

As the New Theology became more popular, a considerable amount of devotional literature was written, though some of it was not published until after the reign of Queen Mary. One of the best writers of this period was John Bradford, a native of Lancashire, born in about 1510. He began life as a lawyer, but in the 1540s he became interested in what the Protestants were teaching and greatly concerned for the spiritual welfare of the people. So he went to Cambridge, took his degree, and became a Fellow of Pembroke Hall. Later he became a chaplain to Nicholas Ridley and a prebendary of St Paul's.

Like all Protestants he laboured under an intense feeling of unworthiness and depravity. Deprived of the wholesome gift of sacramental confession, he felt bowed down and overwhelmed by the weight of his sins. His great friend, Thomas Sampson, tells us that, every day,

> his manner was to make to himself a catalogue of all the grossest and most enorme sins, which in his life of ignorance he had committed; and to lay the same before his eyes when he went to private prayer, that by the sight and remembrance of them he might be stirred up to offer to God the sacrifice of a contrite heart, seek assurance of salvation in Christ by faith, thank God for his calling from the ways of wickedness, and pray for increase of grace to be conducted in holy life acceptable and pleasing to God.[73]

73 *The Writings of John Bradford*, ed. A. Townsend, ii (Parker Society 1853), p. xix.

This sense of perpetual guilt was something which he could not shake off. Sudden bursts of despair would come over him; and he was known, while sitting at dinner, to pull his hat over his eyes and weep plenteously into his plate.[74]

It is no wonder, therefore, that his devotional works show over and over again this sense of sin, and the need for repentance and for calling upon the saving power of Christ, who has redeemed us by his grace. Meditation upon the sufferings of Christ in paying the price of sin led to deep sorrow that man's wrongdoing had made this necessary. His long sermon on repentance gives us an account of his belief and that of the most Protestant of the reformers.

> In heaven and in earth [he wrote] was there none found that could satisfy God's anger for our sins, or get heaven for man, but only the Son of God, Jesus Christ . . . Dearly beloved, therefore abhor this abomination even to think that there is any other satisfaction to God-ward for sin than Christ's blood only. Blasphemy it is, and that horrible, to think otherwise. 'The blood of Christ purifieth', saith St John, 'from all sin.' And therefore he is called 'the Lamb slain from the beginning of the world', because there was never sin forgiven of God, nor shall be, from the beginning unto the end of the world, but only through Christ's death: prate the pope and his prelates as please them with their pardons, purgatory, purgations, placebos, trentals, diriges, works of supererogation, superabomination, etc.[75]

This sermon was completed on 12 July 1553, only six days after the death of Edward VI and one week before Mary was proclaimed Queen. Bradford, though fully aware of the dangers which lay ahead, disapproved so much of the thinking, teaching and practice of the unreformed Church that he felt he must denounce it with every ounce of energy which he could summon up, regardless of the consequences. It is natural, therefore, that, when he saw what was happening under Mary, his writing becomes more and more polemical. Though by nature a man of extreme gentleness, he felt that he must speak out: the redemption and destiny of his countrymen depended upon it. Take, for example, his Paraphrase of Psalm 79 ('O God, the heathen are come into thine inheritance'), in

74 Ibid., i (1848), p. 35n.
75 Ibid., pp. 48–9.

which he inveighs against the doctrines and practices which were now being reintroduced into the country by the papists with their 'idolatrical and antichristian' services.[76]

All this led, inevitably, to his arrest and imprisonment; but even in prison he could not keep silent while men and women were, to his absolute certainty, being deprived of salvation and condemned to endless torment in the next world. So he preached, and pleaded, and defended his convictions to his fellow-prisoners, his jailers, and his examiners – Bishops Gardiner, Heath, Day and the rest – knowing full well that this would lead to his death. A man of great courage and great holiness, he was burnt to death at Smithfield on 1 July 1555.

Thomas Becon, a more or less exact contemporary of Bradford, was also educated at Cambridge and became, in time, chaplain to the Lord Protector and a member of the domestic household of Cranmer. He also expressed his convictions in strong language, but, on the accession of Mary in 1553, he fled to Germany where he remained until 1559 when he returned to England and was made a canon of Canterbury. It was in his early writings that Becon showed his great gift for devotional and spiritual work, though even here he found it impossible to prevent himself from dropping into castigation and denunciation of the Church of Rome. Take, for example, *The Flower of Godly Prayers*, written in about 1539 in the reign of Henry VIII.[77] This is a collection of seventy prayers, some of inordinate length, designed for all occasions. Some are purely personal, some are meant for the family or household, for those in office in Church and State, for all sorts and conditions of men, even including one's enemies. Many of them are, to our ears, curiously informative, didactic and abusive. They go to great length to inform the Almighty of facts with which he must be already acquainted; they tell the Lord that a bishop is no good shepherd if he 'standeth all day whistling and calling at his sheep' when he ought to be driving them to 'sweet and pleasant pastures'; and they inform the poor that poverty, like riches, is a gift of God. Becon is also highly critical of false clergy who teach us to seek God not in heaven but in the 'cloister and the pix', or of preachers who said that Christ 'took no flesh of that blessed and undefiled

76 Ibid., p. 282.
77 *Prayers and other Pieces of Thomas Becon, S.T.P.*, ed. John Ayre (Parker Society 1844), pp. 3–70.

virgin Mary his mother'; while his ecumenical prayer for 'Uniform and Perfect Agreement in Matters of Christian Religion', with its attack not only on the recognized religious orders of the Roman Church, but on the Speculcaries, the Brothers of Purgatory and the Ninivites 'with an innumerable rabble of hypocrites more, papists, anabaptists . . . and such other dunghills of Satan' would scarcely win approval for a Week of Prayer for Christian Unity.

Becon's *Pomander of Prayer*,[78] dedicated to Anne of Cleves before she came to England in 1540, is free of vituperation and criticism, and contains a number of attractive prayers to be said by people of all kinds – magistrates, ministers of God's word, parents and children, masters and servants, husbands and wives – with prayers for 'a free and merry conscience', for faith and charity, for patience and humility, for the help of God's angels and for the glory of heaven. His *Sick Man's Salve*[79] is an immensely long death-bed scene in which four friends prepare a man called Epaphroditus for his death. In spite of its length, this was so popular that many editions had to be printed in the sixteenth century, and some people appear to have learned the whole thing by heart.[80] Poor Epaphroditus, having been preached at by his friends for several hours, and having made his will, and having exhorted his wife and family and said some kind things to his servants, is allowed eventually to die a good Protestant death in the assurance that, through the everlasting mercy of God and the remission of his sins, he will pass immediately 'out of this vale of wretchedness unto the joyful inheritance of God's everlasting kingdom'.

In the twenty-five years from 1534 to 1559, the people of England had seen a great many changes. Twice the existing service-books and church ornaments and decorations had been destroyed, and once they had had to be replaced. Ideas which had been assumed and customs which had been practised for centuries had come and gone with remarkable rapidity. All was confusion, uncertainty, insecurity.

The beginning of all this was the decision to separate the Church in England from the rest of Western Christendom.

78 Ibid., pp. 74–85.
79 Ibid., pp. 89–191.
80 D. S. Baily, *Thomas Becon and the Reformation of the Church in England* (1952), p. 68.

This was obviously something of extreme importance to those accustomed to think of the Church as 'one' as well as holy, catholic and apostolic. It would be misleading to say that the papacy was a popular institution in England in the later Middle Ages. It was just something to be accepted like land-lords, taxes and the long arm of the law. Remote, autocratic, avaricious, Rome seemed to most people to take all and give very little in return. The upper ranks of scholars and eccle-siastics knew what a breach with Rome would involve. They were aware of the famous dictum that outside the Church there is no salvation; and yet, with the exception of John Fisher, the English hierarchy put up very little opposition to Henry's determination to acquire autonomy for the Church in his realm. When the subject of the separation was under discussion the bishops were, on the whole, an elderly and conservative lot. Chichester was well over eighty; at least three (of whom Fisher was one) were over seventy; seven had held office for at least fifteen years; two were Italians, and one a Spaniard who spoke no English. Yet these were the men who gave their assent to the passing of Acts of Parliament which cut the lifeline between Canterbury and Rome, set up a layman as Supreme Head of their Church, and made the Church of England an independent body subject only to the State in deciding matters of belief and of worship. 'Seldom', it has been said, 'has so momentous a change, affecting the religious life of a whole people, been initiated so easily.'[81] Many at the time, and even more in the succeeding centuries, believed that this was right and good. Only now are we beginning to see the distortions and weaknesses of a divided Church and have begun to work for unity.

At the time when this happened, considerable areas of Europe were also breaking away from the Roman obedience. But the separation in England was different from theirs. The Continental picture is one of eminent theologians – Luther, Calvin, Zwingli and others – proclaiming a new theology which was incompatible with much of the recognized teaching and practice of the Church of Rome. This was not so in England, where the new theology came, for the most part, after the breakaway, and was not, therefore, a cause but a result of the acquisition of independence.

From this new theology came the changes which affected

81   S. E. Lehnberg, *The Reformation Parliament, 1529–1536* (1970), p. 181.

the lives of the people in town and village – the new forms of service, the appearance of the churches, the ideas of what became of the souls of the departed, the functions of the clergy, the meaning of the Mass, the conviction of sin and the comfort of the confessional. In all this change, practical and theoretical, much had obviously been lost. But there had also been gains. Free access to an English Bible, and congregational, vernacular forms of worship were clearly signs of progress. To the more intellectual, the clearing away of the muddle-headed teaching served up by many of the clergy and sometimes smacking of superstition was an obvious step forward.

Meanwhile, the more Protestant thinkers would acclaim the whole of the new theology as undoubted gain. Here was a clear issue between truth and falsehood. Their doctrine of justification by faith alone was what they had learned from the Bible, the infallible and irrefutable Word of God. They knew that they had been 'brought out of darkness and error into the clear light and true knowledge' of God. What they had been rescued from was something evil – 'the stinking puddles of Rome' – or whatever they chose to call it. They felt clean, emancipated, self-confident.

It was in this spirit of hope and assurance that the Church of England went forward. The 'old order' had changed in many ways, 'yielding place to new'; but they had no doubt that God had 'fulfilled himself in many ways'.

2

GOLDEN MEAN OR LEADEN MEDIOCRITY?

By Law Established

The death of Queen Mary on 17 November 1558, was followed, within a few hours, by that of Reginald Pole, Archbishop of Canterbury. As a result of these practically simultaneous deaths the whole religious situation in the country was thrown wide open. The new Queen, daughter of Henry VIII and Anne Boleyn, regarded by the Church of Rome as illegitimate and heretical, was now to be Governor of both the realm and the Church since no one could contemplate any possibility of separation between the two estates. Elizabeth was young, well-educated, conservative and resolute, and it soon became clear what religious policy she proposed to pursue. What she wanted to see was a Church, independent of Rome and internally reformed, but fundamentally catholic. And there were a good many people in England who were prepared to support her. But not all. Throughout her long reign there were, in fact, four parties or groups, each of which had its own plan for the Church and was prepared to work very hard to get it accepted.

The religious situation at the end of 1558 was very confused. All the clergy, and technically all the laity, were Roman Catholics until Parliament saw fit to repeal the legislation of Queen Mary's reign and bring to an end her attempt to reunite the English Church with Roman Catholicism. But what with the energy and determination of Elizabeth, the co-operation of the leading laymen of the time, the depletion of the episcopate, and the general apathy of the people, those who wished to remain in communion with Rome stood little chance of making much headway. In addition to all this, the bungling policy of the papacy and the militant opposition of Spain made the position of the English Catholics practically untenable; and the possibility of their getting control soon became negligible.

Meanwhile a large number of people, who had sought refuge in Switzerland and Germany during Mary's reign, came joyfully home, determined to bring the Church in England into conformity with the Calvinistic theology and practice which they had found so engaging in places like Geneva and Zürich. The two things of which they most disapproved were the Book of Common Prayer (with all the ceremonial that went with it) and an episcopal form of church government; and their policy was, therefore, to get rid of both of these barriers which stood in the way of their entry into the promised land. The returned exiles, together with a large number of like-minded people in England, regarded themselves as true Anglicans, and they were prepared to fight hard to ensure that the future Church of England would be wholly Protestant with no trace of what they regarded as medieval superstition and antiquated idolatry.

But there were some who wanted to go much further than that. To them a presbyterian form of church government and worship, organized from the top, was almost as bad as what the episcopalians wanted. In their eyes, the true Church was composed of a number of independent congregations, each of which had the right to control its own affairs, elect its own ministers, and regard any kind of outside interference as the work of anti-Christ.

While the Papists, the Puritans and the Separatists pursued their particular policies, the vast mass of the English people was prepared to support the Church by law established, though many of them thought that a lot of reform still needed to be done. It is impossible to draw a clear line of demarcation between the conventional Anglicans and the Puritans. Most of the leading members of the Church, including the Queen and Matthew Parker, Archbishop of Canterbury, 'not only fought to preserve what they conceived to be the truth against the constant assaults of all parties, but they from the very first addressed themselves to the task of building up a Church'.[1] It was a stiff job, for the Puritans had support in the House of Bishops, as well as among the parochial clergy, and some of the more powerful laymen. But by means of the Royal Injunctions in 1559, the Advertisements in 1566 and a whole string of Orders and Regulations[2] the conventional

---

1 H. C. White, *English Devotional Literature (Prose) 1600–1640* (1931), p. 46.
2 See W. H. Frere, *Visitation Articles and Injunctions*, iii (1910).

Anglicans struggled to enforce adherence to the Prayer Book, to raise the educational standard of the clergy, to see that some of the old medieval customs and ornaments were finally abolished, and to control extra-liturgical functions which could easily promote disunity and disloyalty.

There is no doubt that, in the early years of Elizabeth's reign, the Church was in a state of great confusion. It had passed through a period of ten years in which the form of worship had been changed four times, twice the churches had had to be despoiled, while the official teaching about such important matters as sin, justification, and life after death had been hopelessly disrupted. It is no wonder that both teachers and taught felt confused and helpless. Many of the churches fell into decay; some of the clergy were inadequately educated and perhaps not even ordained. Some took their pastoral and priestly duties very lightly, and devoted their time either to farming or to less reputable occupations. Some wearing lay dress ('great bumbasted breches, skalings and scabulonious clokes') frequented the taverns and took part in rough sports with their parishioners. Many were pluralists and absentees. Some were Romanizers at heart and clandestinely observed rites and ceremonies which were strictly illegal. Others were Calvinizers who flatly refused to obey the rubrics of the Prayer Book or the orders of their superiors. And if the clergy were so divided and unsettled, what chance had the laity of knowing what to believe or how to behave?

Helen White speaks of the Anglicans 'building up a church'; and, throughout the latter part of the sixteenth century, one sees this building in progress. The Prayer Book of 1559 set the forms of service which the State was empowered to enforce; and the bishops did their best to correct abuses and set up a reasonably high standard of behaviour both within the churches and outside them.

But there still remained the problem of what people were to believe. As early as 1536, two years after the break with Rome, a set of Ten Articles had been published, the purpose of which was 'to establish Christian quietness and unity . . . and to avoid contentious opinions'.[3] But a lot had happened since then. In 1549 Cranmer had put out a set of Forty-five Articles (later reduced to Forty-two) which were meant to

3   E. J. Bicknell, *A Theological Introduction to the Thirty-nine Articles of the Church of England* (1925), pp. 10–11.

attack both Roman doctrines (now in process of formulation at Trent) and the more extreme Protestantism emanating from northern Europe. When the coast became clear after Mary's ill-judged escapade, these Forty-two Articles were brought up for consideration in 1563 and were reduced to Thirty-nine. It is these which are still valued as an official statement of Anglican thought, at any rate on the sort of questions which had disturbed the minds of people during the period of the Reformation.

The Thirty-nine Articles were written in a spirit of charity which compared favourably with the anathemas of Trent and the denunciations of Calvinist Confessions; but they are essentially Protestant. After stating some of the fundamentals of Christian belief and acknowledging the ultimate authority of the Bible, they plunge into a defence of reformed theology on justification by faith and predestination, before going on to the controversial question of the Church and its services. In this section they are bound to express their disagreement with Rome; but, compared with the violent and inflammatory language of contemporary literature, they are remarkably mild. The 'Church of Rome' is mentioned only once (when it is said to have erred); the 'Bishop of Rome' is never condemned but merely said to have no jurisdiction in England, and 'Romish doctrine' (of purgatory) is said to be repugnant to the Word of God. At the same time many aspects of Roman Catholicism are discountenanced, especially such things as the use of Latin in worship, communion in one kind, the reserved sacrament and some of the customs associated with it, and sacrifices of the Mass. In the same way the Anabaptists or extreme Protestants are mentioned only once, though an anonymous 'they' in Article 16 and a 'whosoever' in Article 34 would seem to point in that direction.

The Articles have played an important part in the history of Anglicanism and have even been regarded as the Anglican platform of orthodoxy and the test of faith. But this is to give them more prominence than they were meant to have. As Bishop Pearson pointed out in the seventeenth century, the Articles are 'but an enumeration of some truths which, upon and since the Reformation, have been denied by some persons'.[4] Nevertheless, the fact that they came to be bound up with the Prayer Book, and that assent to them was long

4 Quoted by Bicknell, op. cit., p. 22.

required of everyone who was to hold office in the Church, has endowed them with an authority which is sometimes scarcely distinguishable from infallibility.

It was the purpose of the Articles, gently and courteously, to make sure that the Church of England was, for the most part, in step with Continental Protestantism. But their moderation, and sometimes ambiguity, has meant a variety of interpretation. The classic adventure in this field was Newman's *Tract 90* which, by subtle argument and casuistry, showed that many of the Articles could be given a catholic (if not Roman) interpretation. This sort of thing would have surprised those who drew them up. In their final form in 1571 they appeared just after the papal excommunication of Queen Elizabeth when anti-Roman feeling was running high. They were also something of a shock to the Puritans who, in the following year, presented their *Admonition to Parliament* in which they clamoured for the abolition of existing forms of worship and church government. The Articles were, therefore, to the Anglicans a 'golden mean' even if, to the Puritans, they were no more than a 'leaden mediocrity'.

Although born in a time of bitter controversy, the Articles do their best to stress the gifts of the Spirit. If we look at Article 28 on the Eucharist and remove the two sentences which condemn the doctrine of transubstantiation and ceremonies connected with the reserved sacrament, we get the following:

> The Supper of the Lord is not only a sign of the love that Christians ought to have among themselves one to another; but rather is a Sacrament of our Redemption by Christ's death: insomuch that to such as rightly, worthily and with faith, receive the same, the Bread which we break is a partaking of the Body of Christ; and likewise the Cup of Blessing is a partaking of the Blood of Christ. The Body of Christ is given, taken and eaten, in the Supper, only after an heavenly and spiritual manner. And the means whereby the Body of Christ is received and eaten in the Supper is Faith.

This emphasizes the fact that the whole operation of the Eucharist is in the realm of the Spirit and of faith, and that it is a meeting-place between Christ and those who believe in him. There is no doubt of the presence of Christ, as the bread and wine are described as his Body and his Blood. But the mind of the worshipper is not to be confused with theories as to the manner in which this change is made. This is something which must be left to God. The Eucharist traces its origin back to the Upper Room (the 'Supper of the Lord'); but it is also rightly linked with the sacrifice of Christ on the cross, so becoming the 'Sacrament of our Redemption by Christ's death'. Christ comes to us in the material form which he chose to make the contact which he desires. But, since the whole thing is a spiritual encounter, the recipient of Christ's love and grace must be in a receptive state of mind. Hence the need not only of faith but of preparation. Article 25 refers to the words of St Paul about eating the bread and drinking the cup 'unworthily',[5] and Article 28 speaks of the communicant 'rightly and worthily' receiving the gifts of Christ. The Eucharist cannot, therefore, be regarded as something automatic, or (as the theologians would say) *ex opere operato*; the worshipper has his part to play in the transaction by faith with expectation. This has, in recent years, been expressed thus:

> The sacramental body and blood of the Saviour are present as an offering to the believer awaiting his welcome. When this offering is met by faith, a life-giving encounter results.[6]

This sort of teaching put the Eucharist, or the Mass, in a new light. In the medieval Church (in which everyone over the age of twenty-five in 1571 had been brought up) it had been customary for people to attend Mass every Sunday, but to communicate only about once a year. In their minds the encounter between Christ and the worshipper was in the elevation of the elements rather than in the reception of the consecrated wafer. To Anglicans this seemed a complete misunderstanding of what the Eucharist was meant to be. What Christ said was 'Take and eat' not 'Look and adore'; hence the remark in Article 25 that the sacraments were not meant just to be 'gazed upon'. To Anglicans the Lord's Supper (or Mass) meant Holy Communion; and the Prayer Book made non-communicating attendance exceptional, and the private Mass, with no communicants, illegal.

Article 28 is careful also to stress the fellowship of the

5 1 Cor. 12, 27–9.
6 Anglican–Roman Catholic International Commission, *Three Agreed Statements* (1977), p. 11.

worshipping community. The Eucharist is 'a sign of the love that Christians ought to have among themselves one to another'. It is totally un-Anglican for a priest to talk of 'my Mass', as he must always worship with the fellowship, and share the consecrated elements with them. The men who drew up the Articles were fully aware of this, and were determined to bring to an end the custom of the priest as the only communicant, turning his back on his people, using a language which they did not understand and performing an action in which they could not share. The new conception of the Eucharist also encouraged every attempt to make the service reverent. Many episcopal injunctions impress upon worshippers the need for quietness and concentration during the services, forbidding people to come in and out while the rite was in progress, or to wander about the church to meet their friends or to transact business.

During the forty-five years of Elizabeth's reign, the Church made good progress; and it has been estimated that, by the year 1603, apart from the large per cent of the population who were more or less ignorant and indifferent, 8 per cent of those who remained were ardently Puritan, 20 per cent were Roman Catholics, and 72 per cent were keen supporters of the Establishment.[7] The churches were in a much better state of repair, the clergy were better educated, the worship was more reverent. The Prayer Book, the Ordinal, the Thirty-nine Articles, and, in 1604, the Canons, all helped to make things more settled and orderly; while the writings of men such as Hooker and Andrewes did much to show the virtues of Anglicanism to those who would wish to destroy it. James I, although he was the child of a Roman Catholic mother and had been brought up in a Presbyterian country, soon showed that his sympathies lay with neither of these, but with the Church of England as by law established.

Public Worship and Private Devotion

The Prayer Book of 1559 was essentially that of 1552, but with certain alterations to show that Anglicans were not going to give way to Puritan demands. In fact, such changes as were made were all in the opposite direction. The joining

7   A. Tindal Hart, *The Country Clergy: in Elizabethan and Stuart Times, 1558–1660* (1958), pp. 17–18.

together of the words at the administration of the eucharistic elements in the Prayer Books of 1549 and 1552 restored the declaration that these were the Body and Blood of Christ, so strengthening belief in a real presence. So did the omission of the 'Black Rubric' which had denied 'the Corporal Presence of Christ's natural Flesh and Blood'; while the removal from the Litany of the phrase about 'the tyranny of the Bishop of Rome and all his detestable enormities' could be regarded as a slight nod towards the occupant of the throne of Peter.

All these alterations were much disliked by the Puritans; but the change which annoyed them most was the introduction of a rubric which ordered that

> such ornaments of the church and of the Ministers thereof shall be retained, and be in use, as was in this Church of England by the authority of Parliament in the second year of King Edward the sixth.

This order was not very well phrased. It looked like a reference to the Prayer Book of 1549 which says that 'the priest who shall execute the holy ministry' of the Mass shall wear 'a white Albe plain, with a vestment or Cope'; and it is generally thought that this is what the Prayer Book of 1559 meant. But the second year of the reign of Edward VI ended on 27 January 1549, several months before the first Prayer Book was published. This meant that, if this rubric was to be taken literally, it would be ordering the restoration of all the vestments and ornaments which had been used in the Middle Ages. Few thought that this was intended; but no one could deny that, in the days of the first Prayer Book, it had been compulsory to wear not just a surplice but the traditional eucharistic vestments including an alb and a chasuble. This restoration of what they called the 'popish wardrobe' made the Puritans, including a number of bishops, so angry that it became impossible to enforce this rubric; and, so far as the alb and chasuble were concerned, it remained more or less a dead letter until the post-tractarian revival in the nineteenth century.

But, throughout Elizabeth's reign, the battle over the surplice was hard fought. This innocent garment was, to the Puritans, a symbol of unreformed, unscriptural worship, and, as such, was regarded as idolatrous and anti-Christian. It must, therefore, be got rid of, whatever the Queen and some of the bishops might say in its favour; and in making their stand,

and fighting for their cause, the Puritans received considerable support from Calvinist clergy abroad. But supporters of the Prayer Book were not going to be beaten; and Archbishop Parker in his *Advertisements* of 1566 ordered that

> in the ministration of Holy Communion in cathedral and collegiate churches the principal minister shall use a cope, with Gospeller and Epistoller agreeably

and

> every minister saying any public prayers or administering the Sacraments or other rites of the church, shall wear a comely surplice with sleeves, to be provided at the charges of the parish.[8]

The Puritans regarded the fight against the vestments as a matter of principle. They were convinced that the wearing of these garments supported a doctrine of the Eucharist which they were not prepared to accept. The vestment (chasuble or cope) was a relic of the unreformed Church and of unreformed theology. It emphasized the transcendence rather than the immanence of God. It encouraged thoughts of the sacrificial element in the Eucharist, thoughts which they were anxious to obliterate from people's minds. In addition to this primary objection, they disliked the use even of the surplice because it was not mentioned in the Bible and was, therefore, an invention of what was, in their view, an idolatrous Church. They also thought that any kind of clerical vesture, be it ever so humble, gave a false impression of the nature of the ordained ministry, and they saw no reason why a priest should dress any differently from a layman. But the surplice, and even the cope, continued to be worn by those who were anxious to preserve traditions which they thought acceptable.

The church authorities were able to make their intentions clear; but, in spite of endless Articles and Injunctions, the style of worship in the parishes varied enormously. There were old-fashioned priests, especially in the north of England, who, in the earlier part of the reign of Elizabeth, quietly continued to use the Roman Mass; and there were Puritans everywhere who ignored the Prayer Book to suit their wishes and ideas. They refused to use the ring in marriage or to make the sign of the cross in baptism; they taught their people

8   Frere and Kennedy, *Visitation Articles and Injunctions*, iii, p. 175.

to stand or sit, rather than kneel, at communion; they put the Holy Table where they wanted it; they wore whatever they liked.[9]

All this confusion, disobedience, disagreement and diversity arose from two opposed views of the nature of worship. The Anglicans were prepared to keep all old traditions unless they were forbidden by Scripture, while the Puritans needed positive scriptural approval for everything. Anglican worship was basically sacramental (the Mass being regarded as appropriate after weddings and churchings, and essential at ordinations, penance being encouraged in the visitation of the sick, and the laying-on of hands being required in confirmation and ordination), whereas the Puritans put all their effort into the reading and exposition of the Bible, and extemporary prayer. Anglicans liked to approach their worship from an historical point of view, making much of the Church's year with its reference to the events in the life of Christ, allocating feast days to the Virgin Mary and commemorating a number of the saints, while the Puritans were far more concerned with the present and with the battle between Christ and Satan for the soul of man. Finally, Anglican worship was organized and controlled, great efforts being made to preserve dignity and reverence; while the Puritans wanted freedom and flexibility, a more casual approach, claiming thereby a far greater sense of joy.

When James I came to the throne in 1603 all parties in the country tried to get his support; but it was the Anglicans who succeeded. The Prayer Book of 1604 was virtually the same as that of 1559 but with one important addition. In previous books the Catechism had ended with the 'desires'; but it was now extended to contain twelve questions and answers on the sacraments. These helped to support the idea that Anglican religion was essentially sacramental and that children should be made to recognize this fact. Not only do they provide a sound and convenient definition of a sacrament ('an outward and visible sign of an inward and spiritual grace') but they also declare that, in the sacrament of the Lord's Supper, 'the Body and Blood of Christ are verily and indeed taken and received by the faithful'. Meanwhile the Canons of 1603–4

---

9 See W. P. M. Kennedy, *Elizabethan Episcopal Administration*, i (1924), pp. civ–v; and H. Gee, *The Elizabethan Prayer Book and Ornaments* (1902), pp. 164–5.

supported Anglican views of worship by insisting that people should kneel during the prayers and especially at communion, that they should show 'due and lowly reverence' at the mention of the name of Jesus, that the clergy should use the sign of the cross in baptism, and that students in colleges should, like the clergy, wear surplices in their chapels.

A lot, therefore, was being done to build up a tradition of reverence and decorum in all acts of worship. If the Puritans could claim to have more joy in their worship, the Anglicans could claim to have more beauty. This showed itself in the outburst of church music of a very high quality which is one of the most remarkable features of the Elizabethan Church and which has continued throughout the centuries. At the beginning of Elizabeth's reign, church music was in a state of chaos. The Romanists of Mary's reign had put an end to the vernacular psalmody of Sternhold and Hopkins, and had tried to reintroduce Latin hymns and complicated polyphonic music; but, with the reappearance of an English Prayer Book, the metrical psalms, with other 'songs of sadness and pietie', were restored.

So far as the smaller parishes were concerned, nothing very elaborate could be attempted, though good hymn-tunes were being written by men such as Tallis and Byrd, and, in 1563, *The Whole Psalms in foure parts* was published to encourage churches to organize choirs which could sing thus in harmony. They were encouraged to do this by the work of Thomas Ravenscroft, who, in 1621, produced a psalter with a number of new tunes, many of them associated with certain towns, for example Carlisle and Dundee. This set the pattern for the singing of the metrical psalms which became the chief diet of most worshippers until the new versions of Tate and Brady and the advent of popular hymns in the eighteenth century.

But if this was the best that the ordinary parish churches could do, the cathedrals and larger churches began to introduce music of a very high quality both in composition and performance. The English Prayer Book had not yet made any reference to the singing of anthems in church; but the Royal Injunctions of 1559 laid down that

> for the comforting of such that delight in music, it may be permitted that, in the beginning or in the end of Common Prayers, either at morning or evening, there may be sung an hymn, or such-like song, to the praise of Almighty God,

in the best sort of melody and music that may be conveniently devised, having respect that the sentence of the hymn may be understanded and perceived.[10]

The Queen herself did much to provide good music in the Chapel Royal, and had sixty musicians in her service including three great composers – Tallis, Byrd and Morley, all of whom were Roman Catholics. These and many others poured out anthems and settings of great beauty and richness which have become the treasure-house of religious music for all generations of worshippers. Some of the anthems were provided with instrumental accompaniment on the sackbut, viol or recorder. The organ which, right down to the nineteenth century, was thought by some to be a popish invention, now came into its own in the larger churches and played an important part in the performance of the more complicated anthems. This great flowering of church music, some in Latin and some in English, was warmly welcomed by staunch Anglicans who had a 'delight in music' and needed 'comforting' thereby.

While the church authorities were doing their best to raise the standards of public worship, private individuals were anxious to furnish people with devotional literature for use at home. The rapid increase in literacy and the intense interest in religion together provided an extensive market for literature of this kind, and a very large number of devotional books were published in the reign of Queen Elizabeth and in that of James I. The type of book varied considerably, from translations of medieval material down to the heavily biased, but extremely popular, anti-Romanism of *Foxe's Book of Martyrs*.

The revival of pre-Reformation devotional literature is interesting as a sign that the need to satisfy spiritual hunger can override the dogmatic barriers which keep Christians in separate camps. Thus a book called *Certain Select Prayers gathered out of St Austine's Meditations* was published in 1574 and ran through five editions in the next few years. One of the most popular medieval books, *The Imitation of Christ* by Thomas à Kempis, had been translated into English and printed several times before the Reformation; but it was retranslated, and, to some extent, bowdlerized to suit Protestant taste, by Edward Hake in 1567 and thereafter widely read. Even more

10 Frere and Kennedy, *Visitation Articles and Injunctions*, iii, p. 23.

remarkable was the popularity of a work by Robert Parsons, the Jesuit missionary, whose *Booke of Christian Exercise appertaining to Resolution* was edited, and slightly doctored, by Edmund Bunny to become *Bunny's Resolution*, the book to which Richard Baxter attributed his conversion.

In addition to the books, a good many Roman Catholic prayers were introduced into what were essentially Protestant collections, regardless of their origins. Prayers written not only by St Augustine and Thomas à Kempis, but also by St Bernard, St Brigid, St Bernardino of Siena, Erasmus and the Spaniard, J. L. Vives, rubbed shoulders with the outpourings of Melanchthon, Calvin, Foxe, Bradford and Becon. One of the most popular books for private devotion was the *Book of Christian Prayers* printed by John Daye in 1578.[11] The editor of this handbook knew what his readers wanted, and chose his material accordingly. If they wanted to meditate on the sufferings of Christ, he turned to Vives's *Meditationes Diurnae* for these words:

> What man is this whom I behold all bloody, with skin all-to torn, with knubs and wales of stripes, hanging down his head for weakness towards his shoulders, crowned with a garland of thorns, pricking through his skull to the hard brain, and nailed to a cross?

and if they needed to be reminded of man's sinfulness, he offered them some words from Erasmus:

> When I perceive, from how blessed freedom of mind into how miserable thraldom I have cast myself, I condemn my own madness, and I utterly dislike myself, and my conscience is put in such terror by thine uneschewable justice, as I see nothing before me but hell-fire and despair.

It is here also that we find a translation of the medieval prayer *O bone Jesu* and a version of the *Fifteen O's* of St Brigid.[12]

The main theme which runs through the great mass of devotional literature of this period is Responsibility, both personal and communal. In the old days people had been inclined to think that so long as they obeyed the commands of the Church, their future was assured. The Church would see to that. But, in the reformed Church, people were expected

---

11 See *Private Prayers put forth by Authority during the reign of Queen Elizabeth*, ed. W. K. Clay (Parker Society 1851), pp. 429–561.

12 Ibid., pp. 493–4, 507–12.

to take far more responsibility for their lives and for those with whom they came in contact. Most collections of private devotions contain whole series of prayers to be said at regular moments during the day. This was, in some ways, an attempt to take on the monastic horarium, based on a rhythm of prayer offered to God by a community of men or of women devoted to that end. But now that monks and nuns were no more, the responsibility for continuous and organized prayer was largely placed on the shoulders of the laity. There were, therefore, prayers for 'first waking', for 'uprising', for 'putting on of our clothes', for 'first going abroad' and so on until we come to 'when we unclothe ourselves to bed-ward' and 'when we be ready to sleep'. The pious laity were expected to live every moment of their lives in the sight of God, to read three chapters of the Bible every day, and to engage in constant warfare against the sins which did so easily beset them. 'Preserve and keep holy my soul and body,' prayed Henry Bull, 'and let them not be by thine enemies defiled, spoiled nor made a dungeon of devils and wicked spirits through delectation in sin.'[13]

Realizing that people's lives differed greatly according to their work and their position in society, special books were published for schoolboys, sailors, miners and suchlike. Among these were Arthur Dent's *Plain Man's Path-way to Heaven* (1601) and *The Prentises Practise in godlinesse* (1608) by a man who signed himself 'B. P.' As the poor were almost entirely illiterate, the more fortunate were expected not only to pray for them but to help to supply their needs. John Daye prints a prayer for the poor beginning: 'They that are snarled and entangled in the extreme penury of things needful for the body, cannot set their minds upon thee, O Lord, as they ought to do: but, when they be disappointed of the things which they do so mightily desire, their hearts are cast down and quail for excess of grief.' It goes on to pray earnestly that God will relieve their misery, though, at the same time, recognizing that we, because of our 'naughtiness, niggardship and distrust' ought to see to a better distribution of God's gifts.[14]

Responsibility for self and for others applied particularly to

13   H. Bull, *Christian Prayers and Holy Meditations, 1566* (Parker Society 1842), p. 152.
14   *Private Prayers*, pp. 486–7. This is a rough translation of a prayer by J. L. Vives.

the household. Prayers for the family, joined by servants and apprentices, were now becoming common, the head of the establishment reading to them passages of Scripture, praying with them, and, on Sundays, leading them in a procession to the parish church, singing psalms on the way.[15] For such godly laity books containing a little theology, some instruction on the nature of prayer, texts and subjects for meditation, and lengthy prayers, poured from the press. Anglicans and Puritans were agreed on the importance of the Christian home, brought into being through the disciplines enforced by a godly householder.

Few books did more to help the earnest layman to fulfil his duties than *The Practice of Piety, Directing a Christian how to walk that he may please God*, written by Lewis Bayly, Bishop of Bangor, published in 1612 or earlier, and running into fifty-eight editions in little more than 100 years. The importance of this book, 'informing the religious views of middle-class English people', says C. J. Stranks, 'can hardly be overestimated.' Puritan in outlook, it pays much attention to the 'sin-haunted' and their need for God's mercy and forgiveness. It begs people to live every minute as in the sight of God who, far from being their loving Father is 'the outraged Creator of the Universe, the divine, inflexible Judge' of whose presence every living soul must be aware.[16]

All these books were written to help people to live good and holy lives; but the book which was most widely read was intended to show people the wickedness of the Church from which they had recently become separated. This book was called *Acts and Monuments of the Christian Martyrs*, but is generally known as *Foxe's Book of Martyrs*.

John Foxe had become a keen Protestant when he was a young man, and had had to go abroad in 1554 when things got too hot for him in England. While in exile he had begun to write his book, corresponding with friends at home and collecting a vast amount of material from the New Testament onwards. When he returned to England in 1559 he devoted all his energies to recording the tribulations of those who had suffered during the reign of Queen Mary. About 280 are known to have been burnt to death, including Cranmer and

15 See the delightful account of Squire Bruen in D. Horton Davies, *Worship and Theology in England*, i, p. 440.
16 C. J. Stranks, *Anglican Devotion* (1961), ch. 2.

four other bishops and a handful of priests who had preached doctrines which were regarded as heretical. But the vast majority of the victims were obscure, humble people who in some way or another had been brought to believe that it was their duty to die rather than accept teaching which they thought to be false.

To our way of looking at such qualities as justice, mercy or compassion, the burnings present an appalling picture. The rough way in which men such as Bonner and Gardiner, who were otherwise good and kindly men, could handle their captives, the prolonged imprisonments, and the terrible method of execution all helped to foster fear and hatred of the Church of Rome. Foxe goes into great detail and is careful to make it clear that the crowds who witnessed the burnings generally showed sympathy towards the victims. 'God strengthen them!', 'God help them!' they cried, when they saw young men and old women, naked, hairless and blackened out of all recognition, collapsing into the ashes.

We are not concerned here with Foxe's accuracy or honesty, though it is generally agreed that, so far as the more recent excutions were concerned, his information is reasonably reliable. What concerns us is the effect of his book on the way in which English people came to think about religion. The book, published in Latin in 1559 and in English four years later, is of immense length, nearly four times as long as the Bible. Yet it was bought and read by a great many people, and was greatly respected and loved. Nicholas Ferrar at Little Gidding ordered a chapter of the *Book of Martyrs* to be read to his community every Sunday evening; and when John Bunyan took two books to his cell in Bedford Gaol the ones which he chose were the Bible and the *Martyrs*. So these terrible stories, read with pride in every household, became a part of the English religious tradition, breeding and fostering a fear of Rome which, today, remains perhaps the last vestige of religion in some people's minds.

The Apologists

In one of his attacks on the Church of England, Thomas Harding, writing from Louvain about 1564, said:

Ye have divided the Church of God, ye have rent our Lord's nette, ye have cut his wholewoven cote, which the wicked souldiers that crucified him could not finde it in their hartes to do.[17]

This, no doubt, expressed the feelings of all Roman Catholics and possibly of a number of Anglicans who regretted the fact that the Church had once more separated itself from Rome.

What precisely was the Church of England in the time of Elizabeth I? Where did it stand and what did it believe? It was no longer part of the Roman Church, for Mary's counter-reformatory policy was swept away by the Act of Supremacy and the Act of Uniformity. But neither was it in step with the European Protestants, to whom it appeared hopelessly muddled and half-hearted. The true Anglicans were, therefore, put on the defensive and obliged to explain themselves to their opponents on both sides. Three men in particular contributed to this exercise; and it is to them that we must turn if we want to know what the Church of England thought about itself then, and how they laid the foundations of future Anglican thought.

The first of these was John Jewel, born in 1522, an able student in the humanistic tradition of Oxford, and an exile during the reign of Mary. He came home in 1559 to find that, in spite of governmental changes, Roman ideas were still strong in parts of England, fortified to some extent by the declarations and anathemas which had been issued by the Council of Trent. Jewel decided that he must publicly show why the Church in England had again broken away and where the Church of Rome was in error, both in its teaching and in its practice, especially in matters connected with the Eucharist. This he did in a sermon preached at Paul's Cross in London on 31 March 1560. Shortly after this, when he had become (rather against his will) Bishop of Salisbury, he wrote his *Apology* in defence of the Church of England.

At first sight the *Apology* looks more like an assault on Rome than a defence of Canterbury. As in the 'Challenge' sermon, his object was to show that the Church of Rome had altered so much from early days that it could no longer be regarded as part of the Catholic Church. During the first six centuries the Church had organized its life on the basis of the Scriptures, the Councils, and the writings of the Fathers, but

17   From *A Confutation of a Booke intitled An Apologie of the Church of England*, quoted in D. Horton Davies, *Worship and Theology in England*, i, p. 29.

so much had happened since then, and the Church in the West had been so steadily corrupted and led astray, that it had ceased to be the *sponsa Christi* until it had been rescued in the sixteenth century by the Reformers.

He starts with these words:

> It hath been an old complaint, even from the first time of the patriarchs and prophets, and confirmed by the writings and testimonies of every age, that truth wandereth here and there as a stranger in the world, and doth readily find enemies and slanderers amongst those that know her not;[18]

and it was his conviction that the Church of Rome, largely by ignoring the Scriptures, had 'slandered the truth' and had thereby become heretical. Roman Catholics such as Harding attacked the Church of England because it had cut itself off from the true Church of Christ. Jewel's reply was that it was Rome which had defected, and Churches such as the Church of England which remained in the apostolic succession. His attack on Rome is long and bitter. It criticizes and condemns not only her doctrines (of the papacy, of the Mass, and so on) but also the gross immorality among many in high places. Jewel saw the true Church as composed of those who were faithful to the Bible, who conformed to the teaching and decisions of the Fathers and Councils of the first 600 years, and who were prepared to judge issues by the light of reason inspired by the Holy Spirit. On many points Jewel showed that he was no Puritan, no extreme Protestant. Though he denies, for example, the doctrine of transubstantiation, he admits that 'Christe's Body and Bloude in deede and verily is geven unto us . . . We are Boones of his Boones and Fleash of his Fleash'.[19]

If Jewel seems to devote more time to attacking the Church of Rome than to defending the Church of England it is because he wanted his fellow-countrymen to see the folly of the Church from which they had so recently escaped. Over and over again he comes back to the Scriptures as the source of all truth. 'We', he wrote, 'allure the people to read and to hear God's word: they drive people from it . . . we reverence, as it becometh us, the writings of the apostles and prophets;

18 *Works of John Jewel*, ed. J. Ayre, iii (Parker Society 1848), p. 52.
19 *Replie* (1566), quoted in J. E. Booty, *John Jewel as Apologist of the Church of England* (1963), p. 175.

they burn them.'[20] In his view, a Church which preferred its 'own dreams and full cold inventions' to the Word of God could no longer be regarded as the true Church. This was the basis of his *apologia* for the Church of England.

Jewel's attack on Rome may have given satisfaction to the Anglicans, but it brought little comfort to those who lived, mentally and spiritually, in Geneva or Zürich. In their view, new Canterbury, by clinging to episcopacy and a fixed liturgy, was not much better than old Rome: and they were determined to carry through the changes which they so much desired. Knowing that they would get no support from the Queen, and having lost their Six Propositions (though by only one vote) in Convocation, they decided to turn to the country, and especially to the House of Commons, for support. This was done in the form of an *Admonition to the Parliament* which was written by two young clergymen in 1572, printed and widely disseminated, though it was never formally presented to Parliament.

Obviously something had to be done to counteract this appeal, and the person chosen to do so was John Whitgift, Master of Trinity College, Cambridge. His *Answer to the Admonition* led to a 'pamphlet war' (though one of Whitgift's 'pamphlets' fills nearly three volumes of small print)[21] which continued for some years, conducted on the Presbyterian side by Thomas Cartwright and Walter Travers, both of whom had been Fellows of the College of which Whitgift was the Master.

Whitgift's task was a heavy one. It was not just a case of answering the points put out by the Puritans; it was a case of saving the Anglican Church from shipwreck. The 'precisians', as they were now called, had a large following, and were determined to destroy the existing Church and substitute something of a different kind, based on Scripture as interpreted by them and on violent anti-Romanism. Had they succeeded, Anglicanism would have disappeared, probably for ever.

Whitgift was, by nature, a convinced Protestant and in favour of some of the reforms which the Puritans wished to carry out. But he was loyal to his Church and his Queen, wise and reasonable in his thought, a trained thinker and

20 *Works* (Parker Society 1848), iii, pp. 92–3.
21 *The Works of John Whitgift*, ed. J. Ayre, 3 vols. (Parker Society 1851–3).

theologian, temperate and tolerant. He quickly saw through the false reasoning of the *Admonition* in which, he said, 'the Scripture is most untolerably abused and unlearnedly applied', and he opposed the revolutionary aim and the rigid biblicism of Cartwright, who went so far as to say that, because God had told us to slay all false prophets, he would be prepared to put all Roman Catholic priests to death. Whitgift took the line that, although the Bible was our chief authority, and although in its pages were to be discovered the foundations of faith and morals, yet a distinction must be drawn between the legalistic language of the Old Testament and the charitable teaching of the New. It was absurd and dangerous to say, as the Puritans did, that nothing could be lawful unless some biblical text in favour of it could be found. As Whitgift said: 'That no ceremony, order, discipline or kind of government may be in the Church, except the same be expressed in the Word of God, is a great absurdity and breedeth many inconveniences.' Nor was he prepared to say that anything which had been used in 'the pope's church' was, on that account, wrong. Whitgift thought that the Bible should be treated with reverence and reason, but its teaching, especially in the Old Testament, was not always relevant to the times in which we live. Christ had promised that the Holy Spirit would guide the Church into all truth, and it was the task of Christian leaders to show, with all care and devotion, what the Spirit was saying to the Churches in their own day. This was what the precisians claimed to be doing, but in a totally arrogant and unreasonable way.

In his voluminous writings Whitgift shows up some of the inconsistencies, inaccuracies and dishonesties of the *Admonition* and its supporters, pointing out, over and over again, that, although the writers give chapter and verse for what they are saying, the texts to which they refer often bear little or no relation to the point which they are trying to make. In both his *Answer to the Admonition* (1573) and his *Defence of the Answer* (1574) Whitgift states the Anglican view about the nature of the Church, its government, its worship and its customs; and it was through the energy and skill of men like him that the Church of England gradually won its battle against Presbyterianism and could justify its claim to be catholic though reformed.

The third writer who set out to defend the Anglican citadel was Richard Hooker; and he was by far the greatest of the three. Born in Devon about the year 1555, Hooker was only a child when the Elizabethan settlement came into being; yet he grew up in a world of controversy and debate on all things to do with religion. As a young man he was supported by John Jewel, who got him a place at Oxford where he became Professor of Hebrew at the age of twenty-five. Marriage made it necessary for him to leave Oxford; and, after a year or so as a country parson, he became Master of the Temple where he was obliged to share his duties with one of the most provocative Protestants in the land, Walter Travers, whose *Explicatio* was regarded by the Puritans as the most convincing statement of their point of view.

Hooker, when still quite a young man, set out to write a book in defence of episcopacy, but this developed into a long dissertation on the nature of the Church and a detailed defence of the Church of England, especially against those who were determined to replace it by a much more Protestant institution with no priesthood and no liturgy. Books I to IV of *The Lawes of Ecclesiastical Politie* were published in 1593 or 1594, and Book V in 1597. Hooker died, at the age of forty-five, in 1600; and the remaining three books were not published until later.

Hooker, the protégé of Jewel, had been brought up to accept Protestant ways of thought; and these come out, from time to time, in his writings, especially in his *Learned Discourse of Justification*. For one thing, he found some difficulty in accepting the idea of a visible Church. 'The Church of Christ', he writes, 'which we properly term his body mystical, can be but one; neither can that one be discerned by any man'[22], though this may be no more than an attempt to justify the existence of Churches which were not in communion with Rome, which claimed to be the one and only true Church. Again, on the subject of the real presence of Christ in the eucharistic elements, he writes: 'The real presence of Christ's most blessed body and blood is not therefore to be sought for in the sacrament but in the worthy receiver of the sacrament';[23] though he explains this, a little later, by putting the following words into the mouth of Christ: 'This hallowed food, through concurrence of divine power, is in verity and

22 Quoted by Lionel Thornton in *Richard Hooker: a Study of his Theology* (1924), p. 76.
23 *E.P.* (*Ecclesiastical Polity*) V, lxvii, 6.

truth, unto faithful receivers, instrumentally a cause of that mystical participation, whereby as I make myself wholly theirs, so I give them in hand an actual possession of all such saving grace as my sacrificed body can yield, and as their souls do presently need, this is *to them and in them*, my body' – which is a long way from the doctrine of Receptionism.

Hooker had, of course, studied the writings of the reformers (Lutherans as well as Calvinists), but he was also deeply steeped in catholic literature of all ages; and he was able to show very clearly that, although the Church of England had repudiated some of the doctrines and customs of Rome, it was prepared to defend, to the last ditch, its own ways and beliefs against the criticisms fired at it from all sides. His book is an apology for, and a defence of, the Church of which he was proud to be a member; but it is much more than that. It goes to the very heart of the Christian religion, to a consideration of the whole relationship between God and man, and, above all, to the meaning and the consequences of the incarnation, the 'Word made flesh'.

To understand Hooker's thought, we cannot do better than start with chapters 50 to 56 of Book V of the *Laws of Ecclesiastical Polity*. At this point Hooker turns away from a fairly long discourse on the appearance of churches and on the form of worship expressed in Morning and Evening Prayer and makes ready to deal with the sacraments. But, between these two sections lies his dissertation on the nature of the sacraments, which takes him back to fundamental questions about the relationship between God and man and to the theology of the incarnation.

The basis of the Christian religion is the union of God with man and the power of God to bring man to eternal life. 'As our natural life', says Hooker, 'consisteth in the union of the body with the soul, so our life supernatural consisteth in our union of the soul with God.' To make this possible it was necessary that God should take to himself human nature and be born as man, for there can be 'no union of God with man without that mean between both which is both', that is, the Word made flesh.[24] Without the incarnation there could be no redemption. As the Nicene Creed says, it was 'for us men and for our salvation' that the Son of God 'came down from heaven, and ... was made man'. Redemption could be

24 *E.P.*, V, l.

achieved only through sacrifice, and so Christ, the Son of God, had to take human nature 'that by it he might be capable of death'.[25] Because Christ had died for his sins and risen again for his justification, man was brought into a new relationship with God; he became a 'partaker of the divine nature'.[26] Once this new relationship (for which Hooker constantly uses the word 'participation') has been formed, man becomes totally dependent upon grace, the gift of God to those who believe. Hooker sums this up in these words:

> Thus therefore we see how the Father is in the Son, and the Son in the Father; how they both are in all things, and all things in them; what communion Christ hath with his Church, how his Church and every member thereof is in him by original derivation, and he personally in them by way of mystical association wrought through the gift of the Holy Ghost, which they that are his receive from him, and, together with the same, what benefit soever the vital force of his body and blood may yield, yea by steps and degrees they receive the complete measure of all such divine grace, as doth sanctify and save throughout, till the day of their final exaltation to a state of fellowship in glory, with him whose partakers they are now in those things that tend to glory.[27]

This 'complete measure of divine grace' is provided by the sacraments, the channels whereby God communicates with man, giving him 'both light and life eternal'. 'They serve', he says, 'as bonds of obedience to God, strict obligations to the mutual exercise of Christian charity, provocations to godliness, preservations from sin, memorials of the principal benefits of Christ.' By them 'God doth impart the vital or saving grace of Christ unto all that are capable thereof'.[28]

Of all the sacraments, the Eucharist – the regular reception of the grace of God, in the form and by the method which Christ chose – holds first place; and it is over the nature and meaning of this sacrament that some of the most bitter disputes in the history of the Church have taken place. Hooker

25   *E.P.*, V, li.
26   2 Peter 1.4.
27   *E.P.*, V, lvi, 13.
28   *E.P.*, V, lvii, 2 and 3.

is not much interested in the points of difference and hostility, and looks to the things on which we are agreed. He writes:

Take therefore that wherein all agree and then consider by itself what cause why the rest in question should not rather be left as superfluous than urged as necessary. It is on all sides plainly confessed, first that this sacrament is a true and a real participation of Christ, who thereby imparteth himself even his whole entire Person *as a mystical Head* unto every soul that receiveth him, and that every such receiver doth thereby incorporate or unite himself unto Christ *as a mystical member* of him, yea of them also whom he acknowledgeth to be his own; secondly that to whom *the person of Christ* is thus communicated, to them he giveth by the same sacrament his Holy Spirit to sanctify them as it sanctifieth him which is their head; thirdly that what *merit, force or virtue soever there is in his sacrificed body and blood*, we freely, fully and wholly have it by this sacrament; fourthly *that the effect thereof in us is a real transmutation of our souls and bodies* from sin to righteousness, from death and corruption to immortality and life; fifthly that because the sacrament being of itself but a corruptible and earthly creature must needs be thought an unlikely instrument to work so admirable effects in man, we are therefore to rest ourselves altogether upon *the strength of his glorious power* who is able and will bring to pass that the bread and cup which he giveth us shall be truly the thing he promiseth.[29]

In the light of a statement like this, Hooker brushes aside such theories as transubstantiation and consubstantiation as 'unnecessary'. He urges people to 'meditate with silence what we have by the sacrament, and less to dispute of the manner how'.[30] 'This food', he says, 'is given for the satisfying of our empty souls and not for the exercising of our curious and subtle wits';[31] and he sums up his point of view with these words:

What these elements are in themselves it skilleth not, it is enough that to me which take them they are the body and blood of Christ, his promise in witness hereof sufficeth, his word he knoweth which way to accomplish; why should

29   *E.P.*, V, lxvii, 7.
30   *E.P.*, V, lxvii, 3.
31   *E.P.*, V, lxvii, 4.

any cogitation possess the mind of a faithful communicant but this, O my God thou art true, O my soul thou art happy.[32]

Of a book of such length, dealing with so many subjects – theological, political, legal, philosophical – it is impossible to give any sort of summary. But we are concerned here with Hooker's contribution to Anglican spirituality which was based on the following foundation: 'Thy Word was made Flesh that he might give us his life; we share his life by eating his flesh and blood, and so our own bodies are prepared for their resurrection.'[33] Life – eternal life – is what Christianity is about. 'This is the will of my Father,' said Jesus, 'that every one who sees the Son and believes in him should have eternal life.'[34] It was to give us this eternal life that God sent his Son into the world; and Hooker bases all his thought on the purpose and meaning of the incarnation. Without incarnation there could be no redemption: and without redemption there could be no life eternal. People's apprehension of this depended on their faith; but both their faith and their obedience needed to be continually strengthened by the grace which God gave them. Thus, while the Calvinists based their hope on predestination and election, Hooker, as a devout Anglican, saw the importance of a sacramental basis for his life – a regular use of the channels of grace which God had provided. 'Unless you eat the flesh of the Son of man and drink his blood,' said Christ, 'you have no life in you.'[35] Belief in the incarnation leads inevitably to belief in the sacraments. As Thornton says: 'The religion of the Incarnation consists largely in a complex relationship of persons through the media of things.'[36]

Hooker believed that of all the kinds of Christian religion which were fighting for people's souls in his day, it was the Anglican, which he regarded as a kind of purified Catholicism, which outshone all the rest. He based his conclusion, above all things, on reason, and, by so doing, he carried the whole argument about the relative value of Catholicism, Protestantism and Anglicanism on to a new dimension. It was

32   *E.P.*, V, lxvii, 12.
33   L. S. Thornton, *Richard Hooker: a Study of his Theology* (1924), p. 58.
34   John 6.40.
35   John 6.53.
36   Op. cit., p. 82.

utterly unreasonable of the Protestants to refuse to touch anything which came down from the ancient Church simply because the Church of Rome had introduced both teaching and practices which seemed to them irreconcilable with Scripture. It was equally unreasonable of Rome to refuse to reform things which clearly needed to be reformed, and to cut itself off from all dialogue or contact with other groups of Christians.

Hooker writes always in a clear, unemotional and leisurely style, free of polemic and reluctant to condemn others, but equally anxious to show them where he thought they were wrong, and to persuade them of the truth of what he was expressing. By his learning, his discernment, his charity, and what is called his 'judiciousness' Hooker shows us how to search for the truth, the truth which his master said does so often 'wander here and there as a stranger in the world'.[37]

Preachers and Pray-ers

'For the instruction of all sorts of men to eternal life,' wrote Hooker, 'it is necessary that the sacred and saving truth of God be openly published unto them. Which open publication of *heavenly mysteries* is, by an excellency, termed Preaching.'[38]

Preaching certainly played an important part in Puritan worship; so much so, that it is difficult to imagine one of their services without a sermon. Much of their preaching was theological, in support of Protestant doctrines of predestination, justification and election, as these were the 'sacred and saving truths' which were always in their thoughts and on their lips. But some of it was polemical, as they brought their guns to bear against Anglicans for clinging to what they regarded as unbiblical methods of worship and of church government, with even more powerful bombardments of the Church of Rome. Much of their preaching was also moral, attacks on what they thought particularly sinful, including such things as Sabbath-breaking, extravagance, gluttony, even attendance at the theatre, though this was sometimes condemned partly for hygienic reasons.

Meanwhile the conforming Anglicans were encouraged to preach regularly in their churches, though little was done to

37 J. Jewel, *Apologia*, i; see above, p. 71.
38 *E.P.*, V, xviii, 1.

tell them how to preach or what to preach. Some of them, no doubt, fell in with the Puritans, preaching the theology with which they were familiar. Others made the sermon an opportunity for expounding the Scriptures, with multitudinous cross-references to fill in the time. Others did their best to put before their people as high a standard of morals as they thought likely to be accepted. Yet others fell back on the Homilies, now extended by the addition of another twenty-one.[39] But, in spite of this, there is no doubt that, in many parishes, there was neither sermon nor homily. A Visitation in the Diocese of York in 1567 reveals the fact that, in parish after parish, the incumbent was a pluralist and an absentee. Even if he were resident, he very often failed to preach his quarterly sermons; and at Thorpe Arch there had been no sermon for twenty years.[40] On the other hand, Sebastian Benefield treated his congregation of Gloucestershire yokels to a series of twenty-one sermons on the first chapter of Amos in 1613. Whatever the village folk thought, this preacher was obviously pleased with his performance as he launched out on another twenty-one sermons on chapter 2 a few years later.[41] But this must have been exceptional. Many of the country clergy were ignorant and indolent. They had had no training and little experience and had seen so many changes in the turbulent years in which most of them had spent their youth.[42]

The standard and regularity of preaching in the country parishes was undoubtedly deplorable; but in the larger town parishes, in the cathedrals and at such places as Paul's Cross and the royal chapels, things were obviously much better. Henry Machyn, a London merchant and sedulous sermon-taster, records a large number of sermons which he heard from 1553 onwards. But he does not tell us much about the subject-matter of the sermons which he heard. The first sermon he mentions, which included an attack on Ridley, Bishop of London, led to what he describes as 'a gret up-rose and showtyng at ys sermon as it [were] lyke mad pepull . . . as

---

39 See above, p. 39.
40 J. S. Purvis, *Tudor Parish Documents* (1948), pp. 16–27, 138.
41 W. Fraser Mitchell, *English Pulpit Oratory from Andrewes to Tillotson* (1932), p. 204.
42 It is worth noting that those born in 1540 had lived under four sovereigns, and four very different church policies, by the time they were twenty-one.

herle-borle and casting up of caps'; and he often contents himself with information as to the size of the audience or to the dress of the preacher, as when Jewel preached at Paul's Cross on 17 March 1560, 'in ys rochett and chymmer'.[43]

A good deal is known about the sermons at Paul's Cross, the most important pulpit in the country.[44] Many of them were little more than political or patriotic speeches, or strong attacks on Rome or the Anabaptists, while some were spirited defences of the Church of England. Some of the preachers, imitating the methods of the Old Testament prophets, passed judgement on the sins of society, especially in the City of London, or warned their hearers of the evils of profaning the Sabbath, wearing smart clothes or using bad language. Not many of the preachers seemed very anxious to talk about religion, though Thomas Playfere had a good sermon in 1593 on the joys of believing in God, and Immanuel Bourne preached on the Bible and family religion in 1617.[45] This is surprising when one realizes that many of the preachers were convinced Puritans who liked to think of the sermon as a means of grace, and who should have regarded this as an opportunity for delivering a message on behalf of the Lord. But perhaps they thought that Paul's Cross was not the right place from which to preach that kind of sermon. The monthly sermons preached there were regarded as occasions when men of learning and ingenuity could address the nation; and many of the sermons were afterwards printed and sold.

Taken as a whole the preachers at Paul's Cross showed that they had a vision of a Christian country, living under a godly prince, its morals founded on the Gospels and its religion on the Pauline epistles, with its members honest, upright, disciplined and loyal. Maclure even goes so far as to say that 'the sermons at the Cross were the greatest single influence in forming the Anglican attitude and temper'.[46] This is perhaps saying too much, as a lot of preaching went on in the larger churches and cathedrals. At St Paul's Cathedral there was a lecture every day and a sermon every Sunday;[47]

43 *The Diary of Henry Machyn*, ed. J. G. Nichols (Camden Society 1848), pp. 41, 228, 332.
44 See M. Maclure, *The Paul's Cross Sermons, 1534–1642* (1958).
45 Maclure, op. cit., pp. 218, 238.
46 Ibid., p. 170.
47 Horton Davies, *Worship and Theology in England*, i, p. 232.

and, at Winchester, in 1562, the bishop ordered a lecture in divinity to be given twice a week and a sermon preached every Sunday, though he somewhat restricted the preacher by saying that the subject of the sermon was to be loyalty to the Queen and repudiation of the Pope.[48] Perhaps more important as a means of instructing and exhorting the people were the sermons in the larger parish churches, delivered by what were called 'painful preachers' to 'solid middle-class people [who] sat comfortably and appreciatively, Sunday after Sunday, under menacing clouds of damnation'.[49] Many of the preachers took a great deal of trouble over the preparation of their sermons. John Donne, immediately after delivering his sermon in St Paul's, started preparing for the following Sunday and devoted most of the week to this labour. 'It is a late time of meditation for a sermon', he once said, 'when the Psalm is singing';[50] and preachers like him had no use for the charismatic, extemporary preachers of whom it was said that 'they onelie turne the cocke and let the water runne'.[51] One preacher of this school is reported to have said: 'I preach until they wake up.'

The laity, especially in the country parishes, complained a good deal about not getting their sermons; but one wonders how many bothered to come and listen to the 'parson's saw'. Even those who came and listened did not always take much notice of what was said. 'The state of England', said Thomas Drant, 'is lyke to chyldren, sitting rechlesse in the market steede. We playe and pipe to them, but they relent not . . . They believe Lawiers in lawe matters and follow them: Phisitians, and follow them: Councellors, and follow them: they heare Preachers, but they doo not follow them.'[52] This is perhaps not altogether surprising when one remembers that sermons were of considerable length. Thomas Cheaste in 1611 spoke of his 'two houres labour in the Lord's Harvest'[53] and this seems to have been accepted as the normal length of a sermon. Thomas Playfere was kind enough to cut down his

48 Frere and Kennedy, *Visitation Articles and Injunctions*, iii, pp. 134–5.
49 Maclure, op. cit., p. 144.
50 E. M. Simpson, *A Study of the Prose Works of John Donne* (1924), p. 237.
51 Maclure, op. cit., p. 147.
52 Quoted in Blench, *Preaching in England in the Late 15th and 16th Centuries* (1964), p. 309.
53 Maclure, op. cit., p. 232.

sermon to one hour when he preached before Prince Henry in 1604; but the Prince was, after all, only ten years old.[54] On the other hand, John Donne preached before the boys of Christ's Hospital for two and a half hours in 1622.[55]

To hold the attention of an audience, possibly sitting out of doors or in a cold church, for two hours was a considerable feat, even in those days when the sermon took the place of what are now called the media; and it is no wonder that preachers cultivated a style which they thought would appeal to the people. Some introduced a large number of quotations from classical and other authors. Preachers of the greatest solemnity were capable of telling a merry tale or two, like the friars of old. Some enjoyed allegory and the invention of 'characters' in which vices and virtues were personified. Thomas Adams was one who favoured this idea. He said:

> There stalkes *pride* with the face of a souldier but habit of a Courtier; striving to *adde to her owne* stature: fetherd on the crowne, cork'd at the heeles, light all over: stretching her legges and spreading her wings like the Ostrich.[56]

Language of this sort would help to pass the time; but how far did it drive home the gospel message which the preacher was called to deliver? Henry Smith implored the clergy to preach simply, which, he said, 'is not to preach rudely, nor unlearnedly, nor confusedly, but to preach plainly, that the simplest man may understand what is taught'.[57] But this, of all things, was the most difficult to achieve, especially in an age which looked for ingenuity and what they called 'conceit'.

Smith was a Puritan and a Calvinist who must have wanted to drive home the theological ideas to which he was committed. But his sermons abound in allegories and quotations, many of which must have been unintelligible to many more than 'the simplest man' in his congregation. For, in the early years of the seventeenth century, a homiletic style known as 'witty', meaning intellectual or learned, had got hold of many of the preachers, who gave out their texts in Latin, introduced Greek and Hebrew words, and spattered their sermons with quotations from the Fathers. The greatest of these were men

54 Mitchell, *English Pulpit Oratory*, p. 27.
55 Evelyn Simpson, *John Donne, Selected Prose* (1967), p. 216.
56 Mitchell, op. cit., p. 217.
57 Ibid., p. 117.

such as Andrewes and Donne, who are often called Anglo-Catholics because they believed in 'a purified catholic Church, the old, historic, visible, familiar household of faith, healed of its wounds and returning to its higher, earlier self.'[58]

Lancelot Andrewes was a more or less exact contemporary of Richard Hooker. Born in 1555, educated at Cambridge, a Fellow of Pembroke College, he became vicar of St Giles, Cripplegate, in London, one of the translators of the Authorised Version of the Bible, Bishop of Chichester (1605–9), of Ely (1609–19) and of Winchester (1619–26). He was, as his writings show, immensely well read, familiar with a large number of languages, and in possession of a phenomenal memory. He was also a man of peace, who refused to get involved in disputes over matters which seemed to him of little importance, and, above all, a man of prayer: 'a spiritual nature of unusual purity and intensity'.[59]

Many of Andrewes's sermons have survived as he was highly thought of as a preacher and was much in demand at court and on great occasions elsewhere, which naturally led to the printing of many of his sermons in his own lifetime. Much has been written about his style, which is unlike that of most notable preachers. Some have poured scorn on it, Thomas Birch writing in the middle of the eighteenth century that 'the great corruption of the oratory of the pulpit may be ascrib'd to Dr Andrewes' and 'the vicious taste introduced by him'.[60] But, in recent years, Andrewes has received high praise, T. S. Eliot assuring us that his prose is not inferior to that of any sermons (with the possible exception of Newman) and that he occupies 'a place second to none in the history of the formation of the English Church'.[61] His sermons are not easy to read. He cannot be rushed. Every word counts, and often he 'takes a word and derives the world from it; squeezing and squeezing the word until it yields a full juice of meaning which we should never have supposed any word to possess'.[62]

But, in a study of Anglican spirituality, what matters is not the style but the substance, the instruction and exhortation which every sermon should contain. Andrewes, in spite of

58 D. Macleane, *Lancelot Andrewes and the Reaction* (1910), p. 2.
59 *Lancelot Andrewes: Sermons*, ed. G. M. Story (1967), p. xxiv.
60 Quoted by C. E. Smyth in *The Art of Preaching* (1940), p. 106.
61 T. S. Eliot, *For Lancelot Andrewes* (1930), p. 32.
62 Ibid., pp. 24–5.

what looks sometimes like mere ingenuity or 'conceit', was fully aware of what has been called 'the awful import and unearthly sanctity of the message to be conveyed'.[63] Andrewes preached on the great themes of the Christian religion – the incarnation, the death and resurrection of Jesus Christ, the power of the Holy Spirit – from which flow our faith and our life. He preaches from the Bible, making people stop to look carefully, even microscopically, at what the Scripture is saying to us. But his sermons were not, like those of some Protestants, just a concatenation of texts. Texts appear in the most unexpected places; but they are always apposite and appropriate. He can also take a scene from the Gospels, and, by meditating on it, and squeezing every word of the narrative, as it has come down to us, draw out some special message. Here is a passage, slightly abbreviated, from his 'Sermon 12 of the Nativitie' preached on Christmas Day 1618, when he wants to draw out the wonder of the incarnation.

> *Verbum infans* the *Word* without a *word*; the *aeternal Word* not able to speake a *word*; 1. A wonder sure. 2. And *swadled*; and that a *wonder* too. *He* that (as in the 38 of *Job* he saith) *taketh the vast bodie of the maine Sea, turns it to and fro, as a little child*, and *rolls it about with the swadling bands of darkness*; He, to come thus into *clouts*, himselfe! 3. But yet, all is well; All children are so: But, *in presepi*, that is it, there is the wonder: *Children* lye not there; He doth: There lieth He; the *Lord of glorie*, Instead of a *Palace*, a *poore stable*; of a *cradle* of state, a beasts *cratch*; No pillow, but a lock of hay; No hangings, but dust and cobwebs; No attendants, but in *medio animalium*.[64]

The picture here given – so unlike the hygienic-looking Christmas cards with which we are familiar – gives us some idea of the poverty and humility of Christ. A learned discourse on the self-emptying of Christ, based perhaps on Philippians 2.8, might have been forgotten. But no one could forget the picture of the Son of God in his clouts, lying among the dust and cobwebs.

Or take a sermon on the resurrection, Sermon 14 for Easter, 1620.[65] The text here is verses 11–17 of John 20, and it con-

63 Mitchell, op. cit., p. 141.
64 *Lancelot Andrewes: Sermons*, ed. G. M. Story, p. 85.
65 Ibid., pp. 192–217.

cerns Mary Magdalene's encounter with the risen Lord at the sepulchre. On verse 11 Andrewes wants to show, as an example to us all, the intense love of Mary Magdalene for the Lord. This he does by taking the finite verbs one by one and drawing out their meaning. She *stood*, as she had stood in loving sympathy at the foot of the cross when others had fled. She *wept*, as Jesus had wept at the tomb of Lazarus, showing how much he loved him. She *looked* twice into the tomb, showing that love 'never thinks it hath looked enough'. But her love was very human, the love that can make mistakes. First to the angels as to the disciples Mary says: 'They have taken away the Lord'; but when the man whom she supposed to be the gardener asks her what she is doing there, she is immediately suspicious, saying: 'If you have taken him away.' So Andrewes goes on:

> To *Christ* she seemes somewhat more harsh, than to the *Angels*. To them she complains of others, *They have taken*. *Christ* she seemes to charge, at least to suspect of the fact, as if He looked like one that had beene a breaker up of graves, a carrier away of corpses out of their place of rest. Her *if* implies as much. But pardon love: as it feares where it needs not, so it suspects oft where it hath no cause.[66]

In both these passages we see that it is the detail which counts, the actual conditions of the nativity of Christ, the precise movements and words of Mary Magdalene. This was Andrewes's particular gift; yet he can pack a lot of Christian teaching into a small space. If, for example, we take a whole sermon like 'Sermon 1 of the Nativitie',[67] we shall see that it contains the whole of the Christian message. Starting with the love of God and his intense desire to apprehend, or take hold of, man, it goes on to explain the meaning of God taking upon him the whole nature of man. This he did in order to deliver man, a deliverance which he could achieve only by his death, and 'Dy he could not except he were mortall'. We, then, because of the incarnation are one flesh and one blood with the Son of God; and, as he took our flesh and blood, so now, in the Eucharist, which was about to take place, we take his Flesh and Blood.

Andrewes lived in a world of ideas. Everything he said was

66   Ibid., p. 211.
67   Ibid., pp. 1–21.

based on prolonged thought and meditation. He believed strongly in the ultimate harmony of all things, and saw the incarnation as the final, irrefragable truth which governed the life and destiny of man. It is no wonder, then, that the basis of his preaching is the coming together of God and man and of the spiritual with the material. It was this that made the Eucharist, where the material bread and wine become the spiritual Body and Blood of Christ, the very heart of Christian worship.

Andrewes's sermons soon went out of fashion, and none were printed between 1661 and 1851. Yet they left their mark on Anglican spirituality – its intense interest in the life and words of Christ as of greater importance than the theological speculations of St Paul, and its devotion to the Bible as of greater importance than the teaching of the Church – thus marking the *via media* between Geneva and Rome.

Whereas Andrewes had been nourished in the more or less Calvinistic theology of the Elizabethan Church, John Donne was brought up as a staunch Roman Catholic, his mother being a great-niece of Sir Thomas More and his uncle leader of the Jesuit mission to England.

After some years of study at the universities he entered Lincoln's Inn as a young lawyer and became involved in the somewhat dissipated and riotous life of London youth. But he was a thoughtful young man and, during these years, he found that he was deriving little satisfaction from the teaching of the Roman Catholic Church; as a result, he lost his churchmanship though not his faith. In 1601 he married Ann, the daughter of Sir George More, and took on a number of diplomatic and academic jobs. In spite of a happy home, with seven children round about his table, he fell into a depression so great that he even contemplated suicide. But he managed to survive, though in considerable poverty and, at times, illhealth, eventually finding his spiritual home in the established Church into which he was ordained priest in 1615. The benchers of Lincoln's Inn continued to support him, and made him their Reader in Divinity in 1616, a post which he held until 1621 when he became Dean of St Paul's. He died at the Deanery in 1631 at the age of fifty-nine.

Donne was a poet, a mystic, a thinker, a correspondent and a writer of controversial tracts; but it is as a preacher that we find him laying bare his soul and wrestling with the problems of faith and the spiritual life. Many of his sermons were preserved and now occupy ten stout volumes. They were said, by no less a critic than Quiller-Couch, to contain 'the most magnificent prose ever uttered from an English pulpit, if not the most magnificent prose ever spoken in our tongue';[68] but no one can say that his style is easy to understand. His sermons, which normally took an hour or two to deliver, are very concentrated. Some of his sentences are very long,[69] and some of his observations very obscure. When he proclaimed that 'the World is a great volume and man the Index of that Booke',[70] he was, no doubt, saying something very profound, but it is not the sort of thing which a London citizen would instantly understand. Nevertheless, behind the barrier of his peculiar style lies truth of great depth. Donne used to spend many hours working on a sermon, drawing on his vast erudition; and his sincerity and earnestness were so great that people were immensely moved by his message. His friend Isaak Walton calls him

> a preacher in earnest, weeping sometimes for his auditory, sometimes with them; always preaching to himself, like an angel from a cloud, but in none; carrying some, as St Paul was, to heaven in holy raptures, and enticing others by a sacred art and courtship to amend their lives; here picturing a vice so as to make it ugly to those that practised it; and a virtue so as to make it beloved, even by those that loved it not; and all this with a most particular grace and an inexpressible addition of comeliness.[71]

Donne, like most of his audience, had known the bondage of sin, as he knew also the glorious liberty of the children of God. The sense of sin was, to him, deep and constant, as is shown in his poem 'An Hymn to God the Father' which begins:

> Wilt thou forgive that sin where I begun,
>   Which was my sin, though it were done before?
> Wilt thou forgive that sin through which I run,
>   And do run still, though still I do deplore?

68· A. Quiller-Couch, *Studies in Literature*, 1st Series (Pocket edn 1923), p. 100.
69 One at least runs to 485 words: *John Donne, Selected Prose*, chosen by Evelyn Simpson (1967), pp. 220–1.
70 Ibid., p. 281.
71 Quoted by Augustus Jessopp, *John Donne* (1897), p. 136.

> When thou hast done, Thou hast not done,
>   For I have more.[72]

But he knew that he was forgiven, and that God's mercy and pardon were available to those who sought him and loved him.

> To him that beleeves aright, and overcomes all tentations to a wrong belief, God shall give the accomplishment of his fulnesse, and fulnesse of joy, and joy rooted in glory, and glory established in eternity, and this eternity in God; to him that beleeves and overcomes God shall give himself in an everlasting presence and fruition. Amen.[73]

So, into his sermons, he poured his deepest thoughts and aspirations, the intensity of his own spiritual experience, his love for Christ and his yearning for people's souls, giving his sermons a quality not often to be found in the preachers of his generation. In the face of God's mercy and loving-kindness, people were driven to their knees in penitence and in contemplation of their own unworthiness. He said:

> Humiliation is the beginning of sanctification; and as without this, without holinesse, no man shall see God, though he pore whole nights upon the Bible, so without that, without humility, no man shall heare God speake to his soule, though hee heare three two-houres Sermons every day. But if God bring thee to that humiliation of soule and body here, hee will emprove, and advance thy sanctification *abundantius*, more abundantly, and when he hath brought it to the best perfection, that this life is capable of, he will provide another *abundantius*, another manner of abundance in the life to come; which is the last beating of the pulse of this text,[74] the last panting of the breath thereof, our anhelation, and panting after the joyes and glory, and eternity of the Kingdome of Heaven.[75]

In 1623 Donne passed through the experience of great pain and sickness which nearly brought his life to an end and

---

72 John Donne, *Complete Poems and Selected Prose*, ed. J. Hayward (1929), pp. 321–2.

73 Quoted by Helen C. White in *English Devotional Literature (Prose) 1600–1640* (1931), p. 57.

74 The text was John 10.10.

75 *John Donne, Selected Prose*, p. 362.

concentrated his thoughts more than ever upon death and what the death of the body really meant, physically, mentally and spiritually. He almost gloated on the concomitants of death – corruption, putrefaction, vermiculation and inciner- ation[76] – yet he always looked beyond this to the eternal life which was promised to those whose faith was sound and their love sincere. All this comes out in what is probably the best known of his sermons, the one to which has been given the title 'Death's Duel'. It was preached on 25 February 1631, only a month before his death. He was so ill, so feeble, so emaciated, that many of his audience wondered if he would get through. Isaak Walton, who was probably present, wrote: 'Many that then saw his tears, and heard his faint and hollow voice, professing they thought the text prophetically chosen[77] and that Dr Donne had preached his own funeral sermon.'[78] He begins by emphasizing that we are born to die, and that life is only a series of deaths. 'How much worse a death than death is this life, which so good men would so often change for death?' he asks. He then plunges into his usual morbid contemplation of what happens to the body after death, and contrasts this with the incorruptible body of Christ who will come again in his glory to raise us from death to life ever- lasting. So, he says, no man need fear death. 'Whether the *gate* or *my prison* be *opened* with an *oyld key* (by a gentle and *preparing sicknes*) or the gate bee *hewen downe* by a *violent death*, or the gate bee *burnt downe* by a *raging* and *frantique feaver*, *a gate into heaven I shall have*, for *from* the *Lord* is the *cause* of *my life*, and *with God the Lord are the issues of death*.' But, as this is a Lenten sermon, he bids people think of Christ in his suffer- ings and cease to worry about their own death. 'To us that speake dayly of the *death* of *Christ* (he was *crucified*, *died* and *buried*) can the memory or mention of our owne *death* bee yrksome or bitter?' he asks. Then, after recalling the last few hours of Christ's life, and putting this forward as a subject for meditation during Lent, he ends:

> There wee leave you in that *blessed dependancy*, to *hang* upon *him* that *hangs* upon the *Crosse*, there *bath* in his *teares*, there

76 Ibid., p. 380.
77 The text was Psalm 68.20: 'Unto God the Lord belong the issues of death'; or, in the Prayer Book version, 'God is the Lord by whom we escape death'.
78 Quoted in A. Jessopp, *John Donne*, p. 213.

suck at his *woundes*, and *lye downe in peace* in his *grave*, till he vouchsafe you a *resurrection*, and an ascension into that *kingdome*, which hee hath *purchas'd for you*, with the *inestimable price* of his incorruptible blood. AMEN.[79]

Within a month he himself was dead.

The penetrating force of the sermons of men such as Andrewes and Donne came from the depth of their own spiritual life. They were men of God, men of prayer, whose colloquies with God occupied a considerable part of each day.

Andrewes's private devotions are well known, as the book which he compiled in Greek, Latin and Hebrew for his own daily use has been preserved, translated into English, often printed and meditated upon. It was said that he spent five hours every day on his knees, and his book of prayers, which he gave to William Laud, was described after his death as 'happy in the glorious deformity thereof, being slubbered with his pious hands and watered with his penitential tears'.[80] To fulfil all the requirements of the *Preces Privatae* would certainly occupy many hours each day. The Morning Prayers for each day of the week begin with a commemoration of the days of Creation and thoughts rising therefrom. They go on to acts of penitence, deprecation (praying against) and comprecation (praying for), which are followed by acts of faith and hope, long and comprehensive intercessions in which no one is forgotten, and a final blessing, commendation and thanksgiving. There are also lengthy prayers to be said at the Holy Mysteries, forms of Confession, and Evening Prayers to end the day. It has been said that his prayers are 'a representative book of the true tone and character which the English Church aims at forming in her children: largeness of sympathy, self-restraint, soberness, fervour, the spirit of continuous but not unhopeful penitence'.[81] In these copious notes Andrewes drew much from the Bible, especially the Psalms; but there are also quotations from ancient Liturgies, medieval prayers, even prayers from the worship of the Jewish synagogue and the writings of the rabbis. There is, in these prayers, a wonderful

79 The full text of the sermon will be found in *John Donne: Selected Prose*, ed. E. Simpson (1967), pp. 373–92; *John Donne, Complete Poetry and Selected Prose*, ed. J. Hayward (1929), pp. 738–60; and elsewhere.

80 This was said by Richard Drake who brought out an edition of the Prayers in 1648; R. L. Ottley, *Lancelot Andrewes* (1894), p. 179.

81 R. L. Ottley, op. cit., p. 180.

wholeness, a feeling that the man who prayed them had a deep sense of the unity and harmony of all things, and that he fully understood the meaning and purpose of prayer.

Donne did not leave us any personal, daily, devotional notebook. What he left was an account of the thoughts and prayers which occupied his mind during a severe illness which nearly brought him to the grave in 1623.[82] These are divided into twenty-three sections, each representing one stage in the course of his illness from 'the first grudging of the sicknesse' to 'the fearefull danger of relapsing'. Each section is then divided into three parts: Meditation, Expostulation and Prayer. Donne was a man of intense introspection, a tortured spirit always examining the movement of his thoughts and debating the ways of the Almighty. The *Devotions* are extremely personal, telling us much of the physical nature of his disease as well as its effect upon his mind and his soul, yet Donne decided to publish them, or, as he said, 'to put the meditations had in my sicknesse into some such order as may minister some holy delight'.[83] But it is doubtful if these strange and complicated expostulations could give much delight to the unmetaphysical mind of the average Englishman who would certainly have derived more help from the simple, comprehensive prayers of Bishop Andrewes.

Hooker, Andrewes and Donne added much to the credibility, character and self-confidence of the Church of England, so fortifying it for the troubles which lay ahead. Rome condemned it because it was not in communion with the Holy See, and Geneva was angry with it because it had never completed its reformation. But the leading writers and preachers of this period, men of great learning and wisdom, showed that the English Church was something which could not be brushed aside as a mediocrity, a deformed Catholicism or a half-hearted Protestantism. Its theology was sound, its devotional life was deep; and it was educating a laity who were prepared not only to sanctify the Lord God in their hearts, but also to give an answer to every person that asked a reason of the hope that was in them.[84]

---

82 These he called *Devotions upon Emergent Occasions*.
83 *John Donne: Selected Prose*, ed. E. Simpson, p. 156.
84 Cf. 1 Peter 3.15.

3

CHARLES STUART AND SONS

Catholic but Reformed

The sixteenth century was an age of debate, legislation and polemic; but in the seventeenth century the climate became more tense, and men fought and killed each other in order to get the kind of government, in Church and State, which they supposed to be in accordance with the will of God. In a period of less than half a century we see the monarchy destroyed, reinstated and then thrown away. We see the Church suppressed and many of the clergy driven away from their homes for fifteen years until they were able to come back and drive out those who had supplanted them. We see a King and an Archbishop of Canterbury both publicly executed, Christian ministers mutilated and tortured, and devout laymen arrested and imprisoned for going to church on Christmas Day. We see brawls in churches, ornaments and furnishings broken up and the use of the Prayer Book made illegal. We see a hard line drawn between churchmen and dissenters which has never been erased.

Yet, while all this was going on, we see some of the finest religious literature of all time, the work of the Caroline divines and the Cambridge Platonists; of Baxter, Fox and Bunyan; of Milton, Herbert and Vaughan. The thirty-six years (1642–78) produced Thomas Browne's *Religio Medici* (1642), Thomas Fuller's *Holy and Profane State* (1642), Richard Baxter's *Saints' Everlasting Rest* (1650), Jeremy Taylor's *Holy Living and Holy Dying* (1651), John Milton's *Paradise Lost* (1667) and John Bunyan's *Pilgrim's Progress* (1678). In spite of the violence and disturbance we find a large number of peaceful and devout homes where prayers were said regularly, the Bible was read and the sacraments were respected. These were the homes where books such as those mentioned above were bought and studied, and where their exhortations for leading a life of deep devotional discipline were obeyed.

During this period the association of the Church with the Crown was close. The preceding five monarchs, from Henry VIII to James I, had all played an active part in the fortunes of the Church; and James's son, Charles, was to carry this on. Charles was a sincere Anglican who found the High Church conservative party his strongest support in spreading the doctrine of the Divine Right of Kings; and his death at the hands of his enemies in 1649 was regarded by many as a martyrdom, his 'feast day' being given a place in the Church's calendar until Queen Victoria had it removed in 1859. But Charles's two sons had different views. His elder son, Charles, was eighteen, and his younger son, James, was fifteen when their father was executed. Both spent the next eleven years mostly in France under the influence of their strong-minded Catholic mother. Charles, though an Anglican, tended to regard Romanism as the creed of all civilized courts and was eventually received into the Church of Rome. James made no secret of his adherence to the papal cause, and did his best to impose his religious principles upon the country.

All through this period there were various types or schools of religious thought and practice fighting for control over the people of England. It was a bitter and prolonged conflict since toleration, which we now regard as an axiom of civilization, was not yet seriously considered by any of them.

The religious protagonists can be divided into four groups, two of which were Anglican. There were the conservative churchmen, often called Arminians, who stood for the traditional form of an episcopal Church and who wished both theology and worship to be in conformity with the Book of Common Prayer and with the formularies which accompanied it – the Ordinal, the Thirty-nine Articles, the Canons of 1604 and some Acts of Parliament, Royal Proclamations and such like documents. They believed such a Church to be truly catholic and reformed, something which was not to be found anywhere else in the world since Rome, though catholic, they regarded as unreformed, while the other reformed Churches were, in their opinion, no longer catholic.

Then there were the Calvinistic Anglicans, who formed a large section of the community. They belonged to the Church of England, but they disapproved of its form of church government and its methods of worship. These were the people who regretted that the Reformation in England had stopped short; and they wanted to get control of the Church so that they could bring it into line with the reformed Churches on the Continent, especially at Geneva. Several of the bishops, many of the clergy, and most of the laity belonged to this school of thought.

Outside the Anglicans were two groups, one of which contained the more extreme Protestants who saw no need for any visible Church, and who wanted to make the congregation, the local Christian fellowship, the autonomous unit of church life. To these must be added others outside the mainstream – Baptists, Quakers and the smaller and less significant sects who called themselves Seekers, Levellers, Fifth Monarchy, and so on.

Finally there were the Roman Catholics, still lamenting the collapse of Mary's Counter-Reformation, and hoping and working for the total destruction of Anglicanism and the introduction of post-tridentine Roman Catholicism. They had considerable support from Henrietta Maria and from one at least her two sons when they came to the throne. But the stupidity of James II and the underground activities of the Jesuit priests turned the English people against them and completely destroyed any possibility of their achieving success in their mission.

For much of the century religion was at the heart of everything. It influenced people's thought and their lives more than anything else, and it even drove them to fratricide and murder. But while people quarrelled over the form which their religion was to take, no one was free to withdraw from the religious life of the country. Religious pluriformity existed, but it was regarded as wholly unacceptable. Nonconformity was looked upon by many as a sin and a crime.

Behind the differences in thought and practice lay a religious way of life which was common to all, with the exception of the Roman Catholics. The basis of this was the Bible, the religion of Christians. By the 'Religion of Protestants', said Chillingworth, 'I do not understand the Doctrine of Luther, or Calvin, or Melanchthon . . . no, nor the Harmony of Protestant Confessions, but that wherein they all agree, and which they all subscribe with a greater harmony, as a perfect rule of their faith and actions; that is, the BIBLE. The BIBLE, I say, the BIBLE only, is the Religion of Protestants.'[1] Religious

---

1 From *The Religion of Protestants: A Safe Way to Salvation*, quoted in More and Crosse, *Anglicanism*, pp. 103–4.

writers and speakers searched the Bible for texts to support their theories, often wrenching them out of their contexts and making them mean very much what they wanted them to mean. The Scriptures formed people's daily nourishment, to some the only book they ever thought of opening.

The Bible told people everything: what to think and what to do. This meant that, for most people, life was taken very seriously and seen against the terrifying backcloth of what are called The Four Last Things – death, judgement, heaven and hell. As people battled their way through life they believed that the forces of good and evil were in bitter conflict for the possession of their souls. 'For both Anglicans and Puritans', wrote J. S. McGee, 'Christian life was a sojourn, a pilgrimage, a wayfaring between this world and the next, a warfaring between the forces of good and evil which buffeted the soul trapped in its coffin of flesh.'[2] Life on earth, which, for many, was 'nasty, brutish and short', was of little value. Of what account were a few years here compared with an eternity of either indescribable bliss or unimaginable torment? The one important thing was to live a life pleasing to God, and hope to be one of the elect whom God had already chosen to be among those who were saved.

Because the standard was so high, people were deeply conscious of sin, however insignificant it might appear, as this was playing into the hands of the enemy. People lived their lives under the watchful eye of the Almighty, 'to whom all hearts were open, all desires known, and from whom no secrets were hid'. To enjoy a meal made one guilty of the sin of idolatry since one was putting food before God. To give more thought to the state of one's finances than to the state of one's soul was unforgivable. The breaking of one of the least of the commandments of God was to risk the pains of hell. But God did not neglect to give people warning. All suffering (of which there was a good deal in the seventeenth century) was God's punishment for sin.[3] When John Evelyn lost two of his sons through smallpox, Jeremy Taylor, one of the kindest of men, told him to look upon the tragedy 'as a

2 J. S. McGee, *The Godly Man in Stuart England* (Yale 1976), p. 42.
3 See, for example, the Visitation of the Sick in the Prayer Book of 1662, where the visiting minister says to the sick man: 'Whatsoever your sickness is, know you certainly, that it is God's visitation.'

rod of God; and he that so smites here will spare hereafter'.[4]
Suffering of any kind, since it purified the soul and made it
more fit for heaven, was to be welcomed. So people lived their
lives duly watched by the recording angel. Every detail of
their lives was judged to be either good or bad, a sign either
of pre-election to heaven or condemnation to hell.

The issues, moreover, had been made infinitely more con-
fusing by the fact that the Church of England had, long since,
committed itself to the doctrine of predestination. Article 17
of the Thirty-nine Articles declares that predestination to life
is for those whom God has secretly chosen as vessels of honour, and that those not chosen are the 'curious and carnal
persons, lacking the Spirit of Christ' who are more or less
bound to fall into 'the wretchedness of most unclean living'.

Predestination was a Protestant reaction to popular medieval teaching which made people believe that salvation could
be won by living a good life, obeying the commands of the
Church and soliciting the prayers of the saints. The reformers
saw that this was the old heresy of Pelagianism which had
been so strongly condemned by St Augustine and by several
of the Councils, though it had reared its head from time to
time in the Middle Ages and continues even down to the
present day when many people, of different Churches, would
affirm that if a man wants to get to heaven it is up to him to
make the necessary effort. Protestant writers cut right across
this. Salvation was wholly and entirely the gift of God who
had, from the beginning of time, chosen and elected a few
people to be saved while all others were to be damned.

So much depended on this article of faith that the matter
was much discussed and debated upon. There were those
who took it so literally as to maintain that the sacrifice of
Christ was efficacious only to those already predestined to
salvation. 'They who are elected,' says the Westminster
Confession of 1646, 'being fallen in Adam are redeemed by
Christ, are effectually called unto faith in Christ by his Spirit
working in due season; are justified, adopted, sanctified, and
kept by his power through faith unto salvation.' But it immediately adds: 'Neither are any other redeemed by Christ
. . . and saved, but the elect only.' Those not predestined to
salvation, it says, 'God was pleased, according to the un-
searchable counsel of his own will, whereby he extendeth or

4 J. S. McGee, op. cit., p. 35.

withholdeth mercy as he pleaseth, for the glory of his sovereign power over his creatures, to pass by, and to ordain them to dishonour and wrath for their sin, to the praise of his glorious justice'.[5]

No one could know whether or not he or she was one of the elect; and no one could become a 'vessel made to honour' unless God had decreed from all eternity that he or she should be so, for, 'by the decree of God, for the manifestation of his glory, some men and angels are predestinated unto everlasting life, and others fore-ordained to everlasting death'. 'These angels and men,' continued the official statement, 'thus predestinated and fore-ordained, are particularly and unchangeably designed: and their number is so certain and definite that it cannot be either increased or diminished.'[6] If people led holy and righteous lives, loving God and their neighbour, then it was some indication that they were probably among those destined to salvation. On the other hand, if they fell into sin, then it was a sign that they were not of the elect. But no one was allowed to know whether he or she was a vessel of honour or a vessel of wrath. The truth was hidden in the secret counsels of God.

This was the doctrine of predestination as taught by the Calvinists, Anglicans and others; but it was not universally accepted. Hooker disliked it because it denied the need for sacramental grace which God gave to the members of his Church.[7] Others doubted it because they were coming more and more to believe that moral integrity and personal responsibility played an important part in people's lives and in their final destiny. Writing of the early years of the seventeenth century, Helen White says:

> The theory that personal conduct had any direct bearing upon the main purposes of religion would seem, at first sight, to have been eliminated in the fundamental premises of religious thought of the time.

But she adds that:

> Some of the most sustained moral endeavour that the world has ever seen was carried through by men who would have

5   G. S. Hendry, *The Westminster Confession for Today* (1960), p. 50 and see p. 128. Cf. H. Bettenson, *Documents of the Christian Church* (1943), p. 345.
6   *Westminster Confession*, iii, 3–4.
7   R. Hooker, *Ecclesiastical Polity*, V, lx, 3.

held that the slightest questioning of the theory of Election was, in itself, presumptive of eternal damnation.[8]

Officially, the doctrine of predestination was generally accepted. Only the grace of God could save a person's soul: good works would get you nowhere. As John Donne said: 'Heaven is not to be had in exchange for a Hospital or a Chantry or a Colledge erected in thy last will.'[9] But many people were beginning to think that in repudiating the necessity of 'faith, or good works or perseverance' something of great value was being lost. If each person's ultimate destiny had been determined aeons before his or her birth, what part was played by conscience, right judgement and discipline in both spiritual and moral affairs? Some may even have wondered whether it was worth going through all the privations and regulations of the good life if one's fate had long since been decided. The Calvinists had been doing their utmost to get their faith accepted on all sides; and, in the 'Lambeth Articles' of 1595 they had declared that neither faith, nor perseverance, nor good works, nor anything else, was of any value whatsoever since a person's destiny to life or damnation depended entirely upon a divine decree issued before time began.[10]

But there were others who doubted. Bancroft thought it a 'desperate doctrine' and Peter Heylyn called it a 'horrible decretum' which undermined all sense of responsibility.[11] Others tried to get to the root of what St Paul meant when he wrote to the Romans about 'vessels of wrath fitted to destruction' (9.22), and some queried the precise meaning of the word translated 'predestinate' in 8.29.[12] Against this sort of assault the Calvinists held their ground; and the clash between a strict doctrine of predestination, and a growing sense of man's freedom and responsibility, lay at the root of all religious thought in the seventeenth century.

The fact that people were prepared to question a doctrine

---

8 H. C. White, *English Devotional Literature (Prose) 1600–1640* (1931), pp. 51–2.

9 J. Donne, *Twenty-six Sermons*, no. 11.

10 E. Cardwell, *Documentary Annals of the Reformed Church of England* (1844), ii, p. 50. These Articles were never officially accepted and were eventually withdrawn.

11 H. McAdoo, *The Spirit of Anglicanism* (1965), pp. 27–9.

12 RV changed this to 'fore-ordain'; but RSV went back to 'predestinate'.

embedded in a document of such weight as the Thirty-nine
Articles is a sign of a new spirit which was growing up. People
were looking again at the Bible and wondering whether every
statement in it was to be taken as sober, scientific truth and
as expressing the will of God to their generation. What about
its cosmology now that they were coming to accept the discoveries of Copernicus and Galileo? What about the moral
laws in Leviticus which told the country squire that though
he may eat all sorts of animals he must not eat a hare? Or
what was to be made of the Sermon on the Mount, or even
of the 'hard sayings' of Christ in Luke 14? Intelligent people
were bound to wonder whether everything in the Bible and
in the formularies of the Church was to be treated with equal
credulity and submission. Was all truth of the same kind, or
was it possible to put on one side things which were essential
and treat the rest as in the nature of legitimate opinions?

Thus there grew up a way of dividing truth into what came
to be called Fundamentals and Accessories. Obviously certain
things in the Bible and the Creeds were indisputable and
essential to all orthodox belief. But there were also many
other things which were of less gravity. Even Richard Baxter
pleaded with his Calvinistic friends to 'unite in necessary
truths and tolerate tolerable failing'. 'Do not', he said, 'make
a larger creed and more necessaries than God hath done';[13]
and John Hales wrote: 'Let it not offend any that I have made
Christianity rather an inn to receive all than a private house
to receive some few.'[14]

A new spirit was, therefore, in the air. In the light of
modern knowledge and inquiry people were finding it essential to break through the fetters imposed on them by the more
rigid of the Continental reformers and their English disciples;
and, when the Synod of Dort tried to clamp down on the
most exclusive doctrines of Calvinism, Hales said: 'There I
bid John Calvin good night.'[15] He was not the only one who
was finding a strict form of Calvinism more than he could
take. A little group of intelligent men were meeting from time
to time at the house of Lord Falkland at Great Tew in Ox-
fordshire to discuss the deep issues of human life. These men

13 R. Baxter, *Gildas Silvianus: The Reformed Pastor*, in *Practical Works*, xiv
    (1830), p. 235.
14 Quoted in McAdoo, *The Spirit of Anglicanism*, p. 17.
15 More and Crosse, *Anglicanism*, p. lix.

were dissatisfied with the rigour and dogmatism of both Roman Catholicism and Calvinism, and were prepared to search for truth wherever that search led them, refusing to conform to any system which, in their opinion, narrowed and constricted the glory of God and the wonder of man's redemption.

Meanwhile at Bemerton, near Salisbury, was living a most holy man. Vicar for three years from 1630 to 1633, his name was George Herbert. He was a sick man when he went there, but his life and ministry showed the perfection of his character. At his institution he was seen to be lying prostrate before the altar, making the vows which he was to keep during his short ministry. He concluded with these words:

> And I beseech him, that my humble and charitable life may so win upon others, as to bring glory to my Jesus, whom I have this day taken to be my Master and Governor; and I am so proud of his service, that I will always observe, and obey, and do his will; and always call him Jesus my Master; and I will always contemn my birth, or any title or dignity that can be conferred upon me, when I shall compare them with my title of being a Priest and serving at the Altar of Jesus my Master.[16]

His ministry was in accordance with the Prayer Book in every way. He said Mattins and Evensong daily in his church, with the utmost devotion and not like 'those Ministers that huddle upon the Church-prayers without a visible reverence and affection', and surrounded by as many of his parishioners as could get there. The rest, we are told, 'would let their plough rest when Mr Herbert's Saint's-bell rung to prayers, that they might also offer their devotion to God with him; and would then return back to their plough'. When he was asked by a visiting priest what prayers he would say with him, he declared: 'O, sir, the prayers of my Mother, the Church of England: no other prayers are equal to them.'[17]

George Herbert is mostly remembered today as a great writer of religious verse, and for his prose treatise which he called *A Priest to the Temple: or the Country Parson*. His verse is all about religion and the Church, which he calls the Temple,

16 Isaak Walton, *Lives of John Donne, Henry Wotton, Richard Hooker, George Herbert, etc.*, ii (1898), pp. 169–70.
17 Ibid., pp. 185, 192.

and includes a poem called 'The Altar' which he prints in the shape of a stone altar (not any sort of wooden table) and ends with the words:

> O let thy blessed SACRIFICE be mine,
> And sanctify this ALTAR to be thine.[18]

His prose work, *A Priest to the Temple*, gives a wonderful picture of a country parson, 'the Deputy of Christ for the reducing of Man to the Obedience of God'.[19] He gives us a perfect account of the priest's life and of his work, in church, in the parish and at home, where everything is ordered and correct.

George Herbert was a fine example of the Anglican priest in the early years of the seventeenth century, living by the rubrics of the Prayer Book, devoted to his church and to his parishioners. Doubtless there were many others in the parishes, holy and humble men of heart, unmoved by the political troubles which surrounded them, serving their people in dignity and love.

Arminians

There has never been more than one Church of England, but there have always been two or more parties or groups within that Church, holding rather different views, critical of one another, and each struggling to gain the ascendancy over the others. This conflict was at its height in the seventeenth century when religion, more than anything else, governed people's lives.

Charles I had a very high conception of the Church, and a very high conception of the monarchy which governed the Church. Church and State had stood together for a long time, and Charles was convinced that, if the Church was there by Divine Right, so also was the King. Charles, therefore, was determined to work with the Church; and it was not long before he found a man after his own heart to serve as Archbishop of Canterbury. This was William Laud, a theologian, an ascetic, a man of courage and determination who set out to impose upon the country the type of religion which he regarded as established by law, a religion which kept strictly to the rubrics of the Prayer Book, the Canons of 1604 and

18   *The Works of George Herbert*, ed. F. E. Hutchinson (1941), p. 27.
19   Ibid., p. 225.

other official documents. He found the Church very much in need of reform; and, by means of disciplinary bodies like the Court of High Commission, he exercised a dictatorial ministry from which many suffered. He was, in many ways, without compassion, ruthless and inhuman. He would stand no opposition; and when he heard that a Puritan divine, Robert Leighton, had been sentenced to be flogged, tortured and left to rot in prison for saying rude things about the Queen, he threw his cap into the air and praised God who had delivered him from his enemies.[20]

Laud found many of the clergy ignorant, ill-trained and indolent, and he did his best to raise the standards of clerical education and efficiency. He found the churches dilapidated and ill-kept – 'lying so nastily' as he called it – and he forced the clergy and laity to see that the churches were cleaned up, repaired and decently furnished. He found the clergy disobeying the rubrics of the Prayer Book, and he threatened them with severe punishment if they did not obey. He tried to silence a number of Puritan preachers or 'lecturers' who, supported by wealthy laymen, regarded themselves as outside the disciplinary powers of the Church.

Laud's ideals were right; and many of the things he stood for are now, after 300 years, accepted as normal and desirable – the churches in a good state of repair and properly furnished; the altars at the east end and protected by a communion rail; clergy putting on their surplices and laymen taking off their hats during divine service; the removal from benefices of men who had never been ordained; the use of the cross in baptism and of the ring in marriage, and a general improvement in the manners and morals of the clergy. All this did much to bring beauty and reverence into the worship of the Church, and dignity and integrity into the lives of its ministers; and one would have expected Anglicans to approve. But Laud set about reform in the wrong way, and, as Gwatkin said, 'he seemed born to make virtue odious'.[21] He got little support; and, by his rough and ruthless methods, he put many of the clergy and most of the laity against him, and did

20 A. Tindal Hart, *The Country Clergy: in Elizabethan and Stuart Times, 1558–1660* (1958), p. 103.
21 H. M. Gwatkin, *Church and State in England to the Death of Queen Anne*, (1917), p. 288.

much to strengthen the Puritan cause which he so much disliked.

But Laud's rule did not last very long. His power, like that of the King, was challenged by those who felt it was the will of God that the Church in England should take a stiffer dose of European Protestantism, get rid of bishops and prayer books, and most of the things for which men such as Hooker and Andrewes had pleaded. Charles's failure as a monarch and Laud's failure as a prelate drove the country into civil war which led to eleven years when there was neither king nor prelate. But when Anglicanism was re-established, together with the monarch, it was the Church of Laud and his party which came back into power. It is often said that Laud failed;[22] but one has only to look at the Church of England as it is today to realize that, in fact, Laud succeeded in what he set out to do.

While Anglicans and Puritans, Cavaliers and Roundheads, were locked in conflict, when many of the clergy were living in exile or concealment, when the two most prominent men in Church and State were publicly executed, when the churches were despoiled for the third time in a hundred years and all the official services of the Church were forbidden – while all this was taking place there was, in the background, a group of writers quietly proclaiming their faith in the Church of England as it had developed from the time of Queen Elizabeth onwards. Some were bishops, some were Fellows of colleges, some were country clergy. All wrote for the benefit of their fellow-churchmen, and their works are not forgotten – Joseph Hall, John Bramhall, John Cosin, Henry Hammond, Robert Sanderson, Jeremy Taylor, Hubert Thorndike and many others. They were all convinced that Anglicanism was the perfect form of religion. With its roots firmly fixed in the catholic past, yet freed from the unnecessary and sometimes cancerous growths which appeared in the Middle Ages, while, at the same time, strongly entrenched against the extravagances of Continental Puritanism, they saw their own Church as the only existing example of what a Christian community should be. So George Herbert, after a reference to Rome ('She on the hills') and Geneva ('She in the valley'), wrote:

22   H. Trevor Roper, *Archbishop Laud* (1940), says: 'Laud failed: his failure was final.'

But, dearest Mother, what those misse,
The mean, thy praise and glorie is,
    And long may be.
Blessed be God, whose love it was
To double-moat thee with his grace
    and none but thee.[23]

Jeremy Taylor expresses his satisfaction in more detail when he writes:

We have the word of God, the Faith of the Apostles, the Creeds of the Primitive Church, the Articles of the four first General Councils, a holy Liturgy, excellent prayers, perfect sacraments, faith and repentance, the Ten Commandments and the sermons of Christ, and all the precepts and counsels of the Gospel. We teach the necessity of good works, and require and strictly exact the severity of a holy life. We live in obedience to God, and are ready to die for him, and do so when he requires us so to do. We communicate often. Our priests absolve the penitent. Our bishops ordain priests, and confirm baptised persons, and bless their people and intercede for them. And what could here be wanting for salvation?[24]

What indeed? These were the fundamentals, the attributes of a true and valid Church. Papacy they regarded as an unnecessary adjunct which did more harm than good, and much of the teaching of the Church, such as purgatory, transubstantiation and the invocation of saints, they regarded as unscriptural and delusive. In his will, John Cosin expressed his dislike of 'the corruptions and impertinent new-fangled or papistical (so commonly called) superstitions and doctrines of Rome'.[25] At the same time these men repudiated both the theology and the disciplines of the Calvinists – 'our new dictators' – since they would destroy so much that the Anglicans cherished.

As far back as 1549, when the first English Prayer Book was produced, the compilers gave as their authority 'the an-

---

23 'The British Church', in *The Works of George Herbert* (1941), pp. 109–10.
24 From 'A letter to a Gentleman seduced to the Church of Rome', in More and Crosse, *Anglicanism*, p. 15.
25 John Cosin, *A Collection of Private Devotions*, ed. P. G. Stanwood (1967), no. 21.

cient fathers' to whom they refer over and over again. Like Jewel,[26] later Anglicans were convinced that, after the first six centuries, the Church had begun to deviate and to adopt customs and dogmas which were not in accordance with Scripture and the writings of the Fathers. The writers were all familiar with the patristic texts, and regarded 'antiquity as the best Expositor of the Faith'.[27] Writing of the seventeenth century Dean Addleshaw says: 'The Anglicans are thinking and working the whole time in terms of patristic thought, more especially that of the Greek fathers';[28] and as trade with the East expanded, so grew closer communication with the Orthodox Church, 'a venerable and stately Church that preserved its immemorial doctrine and worship, and yet was thoroughly hostile to Rome'.[29] Episcopacy, Creeds, a written liturgy, a regular use of the sacraments, a dignified appearance of churches and ministers, all these had come down from the distant past and were accepted and approved by the early Christian writers, of both East and West. A Church which clung to these things could well claim to be in continuity with the apostles.

While the more advanced Puritans wanted to dispose of any kind of fixed liturgy, the Caroline divines fought hard for the Book of Common Prayer as both a proper method of worship and a test of faith. Their insistence on the necessity of episcopacy and priesthood as the basis of liturgy is shown all through the Prayer Book and Ordinal, and the Prayer Book of 1662, by greatly increasing the number of saints' days, did much to link the Church with the past.[30]

The religion taught by the high churchmen of this period was basically sacramental and eucharistic. Everything was done to give honour to the altar, described by Laud as 'the greatest place of God's residence upon earth'.[31] Silver of the finest workmanship was placed upon it,[32] and carvings and decorations were placed around it. But Laud's effort to get the communion tables moved from their customary place 'in

26 See above, p. 70.
27 John Cosin, op. cit., no. 15.
28 G. W. O. Addleshaw, *The High Church Tradition* (1941), p. 26.
29 E. W. Watson, *The Church of England* (1935), p. 160.
30 Many saints, martyrs and doctors of the early Church are included, and the latest to be commemorated is St Richard of Chichester (1253).
31 *Anglicanism*, p. 608.
32 See James Gilchrist, *Anglican Church Plate* (1967), pp. 72–3.

the body of the church' to the east wall was one of the things which caused the greatest offence, as people were convinced that this was a sign that the Church was being dragged back to Rome. But the Canons of 1640, which, though passed by Convocation, were never endorsed by Parliament, ordered the table to be placed where altars used to stand, not thereby implying 'that it is or ought to be esteemed a true and proper Altar, wherein Christ is again really sacrificed; but it is and may be called an Altar by us in that sense in which the Primitive Church called it an Altar, and in no other'.[33] But, in spite of this, the word altar is never used in the Prayer Book of 1662, except in the Psalms.

The moving of the altars, which was enforced by some of the bishops, had a theological and spiritual intent, as it reminded people of the two main doctrines of the Eucharist – its re-presentation of the sacrifice of Christ, and the mode of the Lord's presence in the consecrated elements of bread and wine.

There is no doubt that the medieval Church had expressed its belief in what came to be called 'the sacrifice of the Mass' in terms which were often misunderstood by simple and uneducated worshippers. This made the Reformers careful to eliminate any language which might be misconstrued, and to make sure that the furniture for the Holy Communion was regarded as a table at which food was consumed and not an altar at which a sacrifice was offered. Yet the sacrificial aspect was enshrined in all the English Prayer Books; and people such as Jeremy Taylor had no hesitation in calling the Anglican Eucharist 'a Commemorative Sacrifice', and in declaring that, as our great High Priest 'continually offers the same one perfect sacrifice', so his ministers on earth 'offer up the same sacrifice to God'.[34]

With the repudiation of transubstantiation in the Articles, the Anglican theologians had to find some other way in which to express their conviction of a real presence of Christ in the Eucharist. Perhaps James Ussher, in a sermon before the House of Commons in 1620, put the Anglican case as well as anyone. 'The bread and wine', he said, 'are not changed in substance from being the same with that which is served at ordinary tables. But in respect of the sacred use whereunto

33   E. Cardwell, *Synodalia*, i (1842), p. 404.
34   *Anglicanism*, p. 495.

they are consecrated, such a change is made that now they differ as much from common bread and wine, as heaven from earth.'[35]

In addition to improving the public worship of the Church, the Anglican writers and preachers did all they could to encourage people to devote much of their time to private prayer and meditation, and provided them with suitable literature. Caroline spirituality owed much to John Cosin, and his *Collection of Private Devotions*, which appeared in 1627, arousing immediate opposition from the Puritan camp. This book is believed to have been written largely for Anglican ladies at the court of Henrietta Maria, some of whom showed signs of succumbing to the attractions of Rome. Cosin, who was to introduce the use of incense in the college chapel at Peterhouse, offered them a book of devotions to show that the Church of England could provide them with literature as good as, if not better than, what was put before them by the papal emissaries and others. His book was in the form of a Primer to be used as 'an integral and homogeneous *private* complement to the *Common* prayer of the Church',[36] and it contained the Hour Services, the Seven Penitential Psalms, forms of confession and preparation for Holy Communion with intercessions of various kinds. Lay people were thus encouraged to spend much of their time in prayer and devotional reading, many of them going back to the writings of St Augustine, St Anselm, Thomas à Kempis, St Teresa, François de Sales and other standard works.

From devotional reading, men and women were exhorted to turn to prayer, not in the form of devotional raptures and mystical experiences, but in order that long periods spent in meditation on the will of God should control every detail of their daily lives. 'Prayer,' wrote Henry Isaacson, 'as a Father well saith, is a familiar conference with God. By it, we talk with him, as it were, face to face. By other of his graces, as in the Word and Sacraments, he vouchsafeth to speak to us; by this we have access and speak to him for what we stand in need of.'[37]

35   C. W. Dugmore, *Eucharistic Doctrine in England from Hooker to Waterland* (1942), p. 55; cf. *Anglicanism*, p. 489.

36   John Cosin, *A Collection of Private Devotions*, ed. P. G. Stanwood (1967), no. 33.

37   From Preface to *Institutiones Piae*, quoted in H. C. White, *English Devotional Literature (Prose) 1600–1640*, p. 153.

What people most need is guidance and strength 'that they may both perceive and know what things they ought to do, and also may have grace and power faithfully to fulfil the same'.[38] How this was to be achieved was set out in books such as Jeremy Taylor's *Holy Living* which was written in 1650, when the Church was suppressed and use of the Prayer Book had been made illegal. Taylor set a very high standard as he assured his readers (who were many) that people's lives are lived always under the closest scrutiny of God. 'That God is present in all places,' he wrote, 'that he sees every action, hears all discourses and understands every thought, is no strange thing to a Christian ear, who had been taught this doctrine, not only by right reason and the consent of all the wise men in the world, but also by God himself in holy scripture.'[39] Men and women were responsible to God for everything that they thought, said or did, and they must, therefore, exercise the utmost self-discipline if they were to avoid falling into sin. The weapons against temptation, he said, include 'cheap diet and hard lodging', and he warned his readers that 'all the instances of pleasure have a sting in the tail'.[40] People must watch their step all the time, knowing that God's eye sees not only their every action but also any intentions which may lie behind it. 'That we shall intend and design God's glory in every action we do,' he wrote, 'whether it be natural or chosen, is expressed by St Paul: "*Whether ye eat or drink, do all to the glory of God*". Which rule, when we observe, every action of nature becomes religious, and every meal is an act of worship, and shall have its reward in its proportion, as well as an act of prayer.'[41]

A person's only hope lay in prayer – regular, concentrated and prolonged. Taylor uses a medieval expression in describing prayer as 'nothing but an ascent of the mind to God'.[42] God must be continuously in the thoughts of all Christians, who will delight in 'little overflowings of spiritual joy' and 'little beams of heaven'[43] which will guide and fortify them on their way through life.

All men and women were responsible for the way in which

38 Collect for Epiphany 1 in the Book of Common Prayer.
39 J. Taylor, *Holy Living* (30th edn 1820), p. 25.
40 Ibid., pp. 60–1.
41 Ibid., pp. 15–16.
42 Ibid., p. 261.
43 Ibid., p. 275.

they conducted their spiritual affairs; but they had behind
them the prayers and disciplines of the Church. Many devout
laypeople heard Mattins and Evensong every day in their
parish church, or had the offices said in their own homes in
the presence of the entire household. They also observed the
days of fasting and abstinence (of which there are 123 each
year in the Book of Common Prayer), and were told by
Jeremy Taylor that 'fasting, when it is in order to prayer,
must be a total abstinence from all meat, or else an abatement
of the quantity: for the help which fasting does to prayer,
cannot be served by changing flesh into fish, or milk-meats
into dry-diet; but by turning much into little, or little into
none at all'.[44] A regulated, disciplined, devotional life was
thus accepted by serious churchmen, some of whom were
prepared to organize their households on a system of regular
prayer and meditation. The most famous of such domestic
communities was set up in 1626 at Little Gidding in Hun-
tingdonshire by Nicholas Ferrar, who took with him his
mother, his brother and sister-in-law with their three children,
his sister with her husband and sixteen children, together
with a number of servants. Members of this community lived
a strictly disciplined life, rising daily at 4 a.m. and continuing
in prayer at regular intervals during the day and part of the
night. So much attention was given to prayer that some members of the household said the whole of the Book of Psalms
daily on their knees.

Prayer certainly occupied a very important place in the
lives of all good churchmen. But with it went a very strong
sense of responsibility for the way in which life was lived.
Caroline piety, it has been said, impressed on people the fact
that they were 'working and playing in the ante-room of
eternity'.[45] Careful study of the Bible and of the literature
provided by the moral theologians of the time, together with
the right use of reason, helped towards the acquisition of a
sharpened conscience which would give people direction as
to what things they 'ought to do'. The standard of Christian
living set before the churchmen of the day made such great
demands on good behaviour that the Puritans accused the
high-church party of preaching salvation by merit rather than
by faith, of over-emphasizing the last six commandments at

44   Ibid., p. 248.
45   H. McAdoo, *The Structure of Caroline Moral Theology* (1949), p. 139.

the expense of the first four. Yet no one can read Taylor's *Holy Living*, or the anonymous *Whole Duty of Man* without realizing that the road to salvation was a hard road, and that any who chose to follow it would have to devote all their time, their energy and their self-discipline to fulfilling the will of God as it was made known to them.

The Godly Brethren

Anyone reading a book like More and Cross's *Anglicanism*, and thinking that this was the kind of religion universally believed and practised in England in the seventeenth century, would be mistaken. Some of the bishops, many of the clergy and most of the laity would have felt very little sympathy with the opinions of the Caroline divines on the nature and function of the Church, on Christian ministry and on the sacraments and ceremonies of worship. For they were Calvinists at heart, longing for the day when the Church of England would fall in wholeheartedly with the reformed Churches of Northern Europe. Convinced that the Reformation in England had not gone nearly far enough, they believed that there was still a lot of medieval falsehood and jetsam which needed to be thrown out before the 'coming great Church' could be established. They were horrified by the simple reforms and improvements which the Laudians were trying to make, as they had no doubt whatsoever that these were aimed at undoing the work of the English reformers and dragging the Church back into the jurisdiction of Rome. What they wanted was a Church in which the only authority was the Bible as interpreted by John Calvin and his disciples. Tradition, antiquity, the decrees of Councils and the writings of the Fathers meant little or nothing to them. 'What toys and trifles', said Richard Baxter, 'did the ancient reverend Fathers of the Church trouble their heads about and pester the Church with; and what useless stuff are many of their canons composed of.'[46] But though they disliked and distrusted any traditional ecclesiastical authority – bishops, creeds, canons and rubrics – they soon created an authority of their own, setting up what

46 *Gildas Silvianus, the Reformed Pastor*, in *Practical Works of the Rev. Richard Baxter* (1830), xiv, p. 137.

has been described as the 'hard and inquisitive discipline' of Presbyterianism.[47]

This comes out in a document such as the *Westminster Confession*, which was drawn up by a group of Puritan divines in 1643 and published in 1646. Those responsible for these articles had all been ordained as priests in the Church of England, but their outlook was Calvinistic and Presbyterian; and they were determined to impose their theories and disciplines on everyone. The Bible was their infallible authority; but the Bible was subject to a number of interpretations which were not always consistent with one another. Hence the need for authoritative statements and dictatorial exegesis, for confessions of faith, for catechisms, and for a directory of public worship. People must be told what to believe, what to do, and how to worship; and the *Westminster Confession* was designed to give precise answers to any questions which might be asked. There was no room for flexibility or private judgement in the Puritan way of life; no greater freedom than in other, more traditional, Churches. The Puritan Church was to be free from any kind of prelatical or sacerdotal interference; but this did not prevent it from setting up its own 'church officers', many of them laymen, who had power to excommunicate and to absolve people from sin. 'To these officers', said the *Westminster Confession*, 'the keys of the Kingdom of heaven are committed, by virtue whereof they have power respectively to retain and remit sins, to shut that kingdom against the impenitent, both by word and censures; and to open it unto penitent sinners, by the ministry of the Gospel, and by absolution from censures, as occasion shall require.'[48]

Behind all its disciplinary and dictatorial legislation lay the Puritan conception of the Church. Committed as they were to a rigid belief in predestination they were obliged to accept the existence of two Churches. One was invisible, consisting of all those whom God had chosen for salvation. No one knew who belonged to this Church; but of its existence they had no doubt. But they recognized also a visible Church consisting of 'all those throughout the world that profess the true

47 A. T. P. Williams, *The Anglican Tradition in the Life of England* (1947), p. 43.
48 *Westminster Confession*, xxxii, 2; cf. Baxter, op. cit., p. 197 where he pleads for 'ruling elders' in every parish to impose discipline.

religion, together with their children'.[49] The test of belonging
to the visible Church was acceptance of the Calvinistic way
of life as followed in the Churches where 'the doctrine of the
gospel is taught and embraced, ordinances administered, and
public worship performed more or less purely'.[50]

By such phrases as 'the true religion' and 'the doctrine of
the gospel' they meant the whole dogma of predestination
and the irrevocable separation of the elect from the reprobate.
Since people's ultimate fate was determined long before they
were born, and nothing could be earned by the quality of
their life on earth, it might have been thought useless to
devote a vast amount of time and energy to living up to the
high standards set before us in the Gospels. But the Puritans
never ceased to exhort men and women so to organize and
discipline their lives that, should they be among the elect,
they would be fit for the Kingdom of God. Richard Baxter's
The Saints' Everlasting Rest, first published in 1650, is a passionate plea to all to live a life of intense devotion and sanctity
in order to prepare themselves for the 'everlasting rest' which
is promised to the people of God. 'Be serious', he says, 'in
thy endeavours for heaven'; and he pleads for long and concentrated prayers, strict observance of the Sabbath, regular
family prayers, prolonged reading of the Bible, a high moral
code, and so on. A man who adopted the sort of religion
which Baxter demanded would commit himself to a very
exacting spiritual discipline, and it is hard to see how any
man could earn his living, care for his family, look after his
health, serve the community, and still find time for long vigils
and hours of prayer and self-examination. But, of course, all
this was worth doing if it ensured one's ultimate entry into
the glory of the saints.

But what about those not so destined? Baxter paints a
terrible picture of those who, however hard they had tried,
were already fore-ordained to damnation. For them the future
held nothing but everlasting torment, which, says Baxter,
means 'inconceivable torment'.[51] Not only do those souls
whom God has 'passed by' suffer indescribable pain in an
everlasting furnace, but God will, apparently, 'rejoice over
them to destroy them . . . He will laugh at their calamity, he

49 *Westminster Confession*, xxvii, 1 and 2.
50 Ibid., xxvii, 4.
51 R. Baxter, *The Saints' Everlasting Rest*, 8th edn, p. 173.

will mock when their fear cometh' for it is the breath of his indignation which will fan the flames.[52] This, Baxter said, was the inevitable and unescapable destiny of all except the few, the 'little flock' whom God, before time began, had predestinated to eternal glory. Nevertheless, Baxter makes a passionate appeal to people to live good and holy lives; and there was always, among the Puritans, a strong sense of duty and of conscience. As Helen White says: 'Within the stern bounds of Predestination these men developed the mighty energies of the moral life.'[53] Faith in ultimate glory in no way dispensed a person from the duty of seeking perfection while on earth. The one thing which was totally unacceptable was the belief that salvation could be acquired by good works.

It was on the basis of this that writers conceived the idea of the Two Tables. According to the Book of Exodus, Moses came down from Mount Sinai bearing two tablets, or tables, on which God had written what we know as the Ten Commandments. Table 1 contained the first four commandments which deal with a person's immediate duty to God, while the second table was concerned more with right human behaviour. The Puritans believed that the commandments on Table 1 were of far greater importance than the rest, since pagans and unbelievers could readily accept these as their code of conduct. But the first four commandments, which put duty to God before anything else, were the heart of true religion. Indeed, some went so far as to say that, if you kept the first commandment, you would be safe, as all the other nine stem from it. All sin, they said, was based on idolatry – on money, or food, or sexual life or even charity if it took precedence over the claims of God; and they accused the conventional Anglicans of ignoring this fundamental fact and thinking that so long as you lived a good life and went to church on Sundays, all would be right.[54] Life, they said, was not as easy as that. It was, in fact, an endless and determined fight against the Devil who could so quickly drag a person into sin if he or she were not permanently vigilant. Any minute of the day or night which was not given to God was an opportunity

52 Ibid., pp. 167, 169–70.
53 H. C. White, *English Devotional Literature (Prose) 1600–1640* (1931), p. 58.
54 On this see J. Sears McGee, *The Godly Man in Stuart England* (1976), pp. 70–95.

for the Devil to get control. Any action which was not performed for the love and to the glory of God was sinful. Good works were important; but they were of no value unless they arose out of the right motive. 'A good man made a good work, not a good work a good man.'[55] Even the most unselfish acts based on the purest of motives could lead one into sin, the sin of pride. Life was, therefore, hard; but the rewards were great.

Life for the Puritan was also lonely and individualistic. Each human being was directly responsible to God for everything that he or she did, or thought, or said. The Church as created by Christ, and maintained all through the centuries by the faithful, meant nothing to him, though he would rejoice in belonging to what they called the 'godly brethren', the 'saints', the 'people of God'.

As for worship, the Puritans strongly disapproved of any fixed form of prayer, which they thought was bound to cramp and even stifle the spirit of filial converse with God. They were bitterly opposed to the changes and improvements in church furnishing which they thought smacked of Rome and which they called 'an Italian dress for our devotions'. They disliked the Holy Table placed against the east wall, not only because it suggested a belief in the sacrifice of the Mass, but also because it made it impossible for them to sit round it as the apostles had done at the Last Supper. They disapproved of the Church's year, in spite of its biblical basis, and thought that Sunday, which they called the Sabbath, was the only day on which Christians should meet together for worship (Commandment no. 4). They regarded choirs as a distraction and they liked to think that organs and other instruments of music were papistical inventions.

As soon as they got control, the 'godly brethren' abolished the Book of Common Prayer, which, they said, 'hath proved an offence, not only to many of the godly at home, but also to the Reformed Churches abroad',[56] and substituted for it *A Directory for the Publique Worship of God* (1644). This is a book not of prayers but of rubrics and directions. It contains no set prayer, not even the Lord's Prayer in spite of its origin. Instead, it gives a great many subjects for prayer, leaving it

55 Christopher Hill, *Change and Continuity in 17th-Century England* (1974), p. 83.
56 *A Directory for the Publique Worship of God* (1644), p. 1.

to the minister to provide the actual words. The fact that the leader was sometimes incompetent, or ostentatious, or unendurably verbose was a risk which had to be run. So also was the risk that elderly clergymen, who had long been familiar with the Book of Common Prayer, should, in fact, repeat by heart the Cranmerian prayers, sometimes being congratulated afterwards for their skill in the choice of such beautiful words.

Puritanism, in spite of its rigorous attitude, did much to strengthen people's faith and give them a sure sense of God; and, as such, it has survived to the present day. It gave to the ordinary man and woman a sense of responsibility for his or her own life, a feeling that life was earnest and serious, and was not to be taken lightly. It assured them of sin, the 'sin which doth so easily beset us', giving them a constant feeling of unworthiness, of failure to live up to the high standards of the gospel. It made them feel responsible for their lives at every point, in work and in play, and it persuaded them that every minute of the day was to be given to God.

For nearly twenty years the Puritan party was in control, and the Church (as understood by Laud and the Caroline divines) was put out of action. But although the majority of the people of England were Puritan at heart, they were also monarchists. They disliked the Commonwealth; and, deep down, they had a feeling that monarchy was the God-given form of government. Thus, for the sake of restoring the King, they were prepared to face the restoration of an episcopal Church and the return of the Book of Common Prayer. Had they foreseen the price which they would, in the end, have had to pay for this, they might well have hesitated.

The Church Restored

'The importance of the Commonwealth for the history of religion in England', wrote Gwatkin, 'is not so much in its constitutional experiments and foreign policy, significant as they are, as in the developments of religious thought. Here again we see the turn of the tide, between the flow of zeal for dogma and the ebb of indifference to dogma.'[57] There is no doubt that, with the Restoration, people's minds turned less to what they believed and more to how they ought to live.

57   H. M. Gwatkin, *Church and State in England to the Death of Queen Anne* (1917), p. 339.

Predestination, which had been accepted without hesitation by most people, was quietly dropped, and with it fell Calvinism as a creed. Restoration men and women had little use for the extravagances of Calvinism and its harsh dogmas. They were horrified by Baxter's picture of God rejoicing over the sufferings of the damned. They disliked what they called the Puritans' 'saucy familiarities with God' in sermons and prayers. They were afraid of 'enthusiasm' in any form. What they wanted was a sensible, matter-of-fact kind of religion in which reason played an important part, and in which the Book of Common Prayer provided the sort of worship which they enjoyed.

This did not happen automatically. During the eleven years of the Commonwealth the Church, though suppressed, was very active. Many of its leaders went abroad and continued to act as the visible Church there, nurturing a positive hatred of Presbyterianism which they regarded as responsible for all their ills. Others remained in hiding in England, secretly saying the daily offices according to the Prayer Book, preaching, administering the sacraments, doing all that a priest ought to do. Although the Prayer Book was forbidden, John Evelyn generally had no difficulty in finding Holy Communion when he wanted it, and, in private houses and old chapels, the old religion carried on. Anglicanism was not dead, but sleeping.

Thus it was that, when the King was restored in 1660, Anglicanism was restored with him. The King himself was determined that this should be so, showering favours on Arminian clergy and introducing into his chapel the Prayer Book with twelve singing boys and a pair of organs. Meanwhile the young squires, many of whom had been tutored by Anglican clergy during the Interregnum, saw to it that Parliament passed the necessary legislation. In the Declaration of Breda, issued by Charles before his return to England, he had spoken of a 'liberty of tender consciences' from which the Presbyterians and sectaries had taken some comfort; but Parliament saw to it that only the Anglican Church was to be respected. So by the Act of Uniformity, the Conventicle Act which made it illegal to attend any service at which anything but the Prayer Book was used, and the Test Act, which made it impossible for Roman Catholics to hold any civil or military office, a firm line was drawn between churchmen and dissenters which has lasted until the present day.

So began the return of the Anglican clergy and the ejection of those who had ejected them during the Commonwealth. This was sometimes done with considerable brusqueness, as when Robert Clark, who had been deprived of his living at Andover, calmly walked into his church 'at full congregation', put aside the intruding minister with the words 'Sir, the King is come into his own, and will reign alone, and I am come to my own too, and will officiate without an assistant', and, pulling a book out of his pocket, proceeded to conduct the liturgy from the Book of Common Prayer.[58] This sort of thing naturally caused some distress; but the churchmen were determined to restore the old order; and, within a remarkably short time, Anglicanism was re-established, bishops were consecrated and clergy were ordained, churches were redecorated and refurnished in the Laudian style, and the Book of Common Prayer was once more in use.

Thus was Presbyterianism driven underground and the Church, as it had been, restored. But it was fundamentally a different kind of Church. People were tired of dogma and the battles which had been fought. 'The world', as Dr Watson said, 'had grown weary of dogmatists, and the great religious struggle was now a drawn game.'[59] Faced with the licentiousness of the court, and the fact that a good many people were living immoral lives, the religious people were more concerned with morals than with dogmatics, with living a decent life than with Calvinistic doctrine.

The books which came out, and the sermons preached, during the Restoration period were mainly concerned with people's relationship with God. They did not argue so much about salvation or what Christ had done for us. What interested them was the example which Christ had given of the perfect life. Nowhere is this more clearly set forth than in the great sermon on 'The Profitableness of Godliness' preached by Isaac Barrow, shortly after the Restoration, on the text: 'But godliness is profitable for all things'. He said:

We may consider that religion doth prescribe the truest and best rule of action, thence enlightening our mind and rectifying our practice in all matters and upon all occasions, so that whatever is performed according to it is done well

58   R. S. Bosher, *The Making of the Restoration Settlement* (1951), pp. 164–5.
59   E. W. Watson, *The Church of England* (1935), p. 176.

and wisely, with a comely grace in regard to others, with a cheerful satisfaction in our own mind, with the best assurance, that things are here capable of, to find happy success and beneficial fruit.

Later he goes on:

For heartily to love and reverence the Maker of all things, who by everything apparent before us demonstrateth himself incomprehensibly powerful, wise, and good, to be kind and charitable to our neighbours, to be just and faithful in our dealings, to be sober and modest in our minds, to be meek and gentle in our demeanours, to be staunch and temperate in our enjoyments, and the like principal rules of duty, are such that the common reason of man and continual experience do approve them as hugely conducible to the public good of man and to each man's private welfare. For certainly the happiness and misery of men are wholly or chiefly seated and founded in the mind. If that is in a good state of health, rest and cheerfulness, whatever the person's outward condition or circumstances be, he cannot be wretched; if that be distempered or disturbed, he cannot be happy.

Then, after a discourse on piety as the seat of happiness, he turns to our friendship with God which is the source of all that is good in life.

It maketh God our friend, a friend infinitely better than all friends, most affectionate and kind, most faithful and sure, most able and willing, and ever most ready to perform all friendly offices, to yield advice on all our doubts, succour in all our needs, comfort in all our troubles, satisfaction to all our desires ... The pious man hath always the all-wise God to counsel him, to guide his actions, and order his steps; he hath the Almighty to protect, support and relieve him; he hath the immense Goodness to commiserate and comfort him. Unto him he is not only encouraged, but obliged to resort in need. Upon him he may, he ought to discharge all his cares and burdens.[60]

This gives us a picture of the perfect life after which everyone should strive. It was a life without much mysticism, but with long hours of prayer, Bible-reading and self-examination.

60 More and Cross, *Anglicanism* (1935), pp. 744–60.

Sin was real, and was to be confessed earnestly and regularly. Thomas Ken, writing his instructions for the Winchester scholars, tells the boys: 'When you examine yourself, either by the following catalogue, or by that in *The Whole Duty of Man*, or by any other, pause a while on every particular; and if you find yourself not guilty, then say, glory be to thee, O Lord, for preserving me from this sin.' But if their consciences show them to be guilty, then they should write down that sin on a bit of paper so as to confess it when the time comes. He then lists the kinds of sin. 'Some there are', he says, 'who either through want of conscientious parents, or through stifling good motions, or through inconstancy, or heedlessness, or unadvisedness or vicious company, or ill nature, youthful lusts, and the like, have been from their infancy very negligent of learning, or at least of practising their duty.' Others have sinned more heinously, and have need for more intense confession. Some have very few sins to mention, but these must beware of 'presuming on their own innocence, for if we say, or think, we have no sin, we miserably deceive ourselves'.[61]

The great thing was prayer, prayer without ceasing. Ken tells the Winchester boys that 'prayer is the very life of a Christian, and therefore, we are so frequently commanded to pray without ceasing, not that we can be always on our knees, but that we would accustom ourselves to frequent thoughts of God, that wheresoever we are, he sees us; and when we think on God, we should have always an ejaculation ready to offer up to him, and by this means we may pray, not only seven times a day with David, but all the day long'.[62]

The most perfect form of prayer was in the Prayer Book which was reintroduced as soon as possible after the Restoration. At the Savoy Conference the bishops took the line that the Prayer Book was there for use, and needed very little change. Various books were available such as the Durham Book which would bring the Prayer Book nearer to the original work of 1549, but this was turned down. Baxter had produced a 'Reformed Liturgy' which was, in some ways, very good. It cut out the cross in baptism and the ring in marriage, but otherwise contained much that was valuable. Indeed it has been said that Baxter's eucharistic and liturgical

61 *The Prose Works of the Right Rev. Father in God, Thomas Ken, D.D.* (1838), pp. 380–1.
62 Ibid., p. 372.

ideas approach more closely to the historic western tradition than the ideas expressed or implied in the communion service of the contemporary Prayer Book.[63] But, at the Savoy Conference, Baxter spoilt his case by producing far too many exceptions, most of which were much too trivial to be considered; and only seventeen out of ninety-six were accepted by the bishops. So came out the Prayer Book of 1662 which remained the backbone of Anglican worship until recent years.

Of the services offered by the Prayer Book, Morning and Evening Prayers were the most important. These were said day by day in many churches, and devout lay people attended regularly. Peter Barwick, a doctor, took a house near St Paul's in order to attend the daily offices; and when it was burnt down in 1666, he took another very near Westminister Abbey.[64] Bishops were constantly exhorting their clergy to say the daily offices and the people to attend them, such attendances being 'perhaps the best and most public good that they can do'.[65] This did not apply so much to the country churches, but in the large town churches, and in the cathedrals, groups of devout men and women assembled daily to recite the Psalms, hear the whole Bible read, say the Canticles and the Apostles' Creed, and join in the ancient collects and prayers of the Church. Thus there grew up a devout laity to whom the fundamentals of religion became a part of their lives.

In cathedral and collegiate churches Holy Communion was, presumably, celebrated every Sunday, as this was laid down in the rubric of the Prayer Book, and there is evidence of daily celebrations in some churches.[66] But, in most parishes the Eucharist was regarded as fit to be held once a month or even quarterly. This was not necessarily a sign that the Church was non-sacramental, but that the Eucharist was so great a mystery that it was to be treated with great respect, and needed long preparation. Thomas Ken devoted thirty-four pages to self-examination, confession and meditation which he expected the Winchester boys to read through,

63 E. C. Ratcliffe in *The English Prayer Book, 1549–1662*, p. 79.
64 J. H. Overton, *Life in the English Church (1660–1714)* (1885), p. 79.
65 Charge of Bishop Turner of Ely in 1686, quoted in Martin Thornton, *English Spirituality* (1963), p. 266.
66 J. Wickham Legg, *English Church Life, from the Restoration to the Tractarian Movement* (1914), pp. 25–6.

slowly and devoutly, before going to communion. These contain 'Meditations on the Holy Eucharist' in which the true nature of the sacramental gifts is set out. He wrote:

> I believe thy body and blood to be as really present in the Holy Sacrament as thy divine power can make it, though the manner of thy mysterious presence I cannot comprehend. Lord, I believe that the bread that we break, and the cup that we drink, are not bare signs only, but the communication of thy body and thy blood, and pledges to assure me of it; and I verily believe that if with due preparation I come to the altar, as certainly as I receive the outward signs, so certainly shall I receive the thing signified, even thy most blessed body and blood; to receive which inestimable blessing, O merciful Lord, do thou fit and prepare me. Amen, Amen.[67]

Such faith in the real presence of Christ in the eucharistic elements was expressed by all the high-church writers of the day. So was belief in the Eucharist as a 'revival' or re-presentation of the sacrifice of Christ once for all on the cross. Anglican writers were careful not to give the impression, given sometimes by Roman Catholic writers, that the Mass was a repetition of Christ's sacrifice, and various words were used to describe the connection between the two. The Anglican doctrine of the Eucharist is perhaps nowhere better described than by John Evelyn who wrote, in 1671, to a certain Father Patrick saying that

> the doctrine of the Church of England is, or at least to my best understanding, imports, that after the prayer, or words of consecration, the symbols become changed into the body and blood of Christ, after a sacramental, spiritual and real manner; and that all initiated, or baptised persons, of competent age and capacity, who by unfeigned repentance, and a faithful consideration of the life, doctrine and passion of our Blessed Saviour, resolve to undertake his holy religion and to persist in it, are made really participants of the benefits of his body and blood for the remission of their sins, and the obtaining of all other spiritual graces, inasmuch as it is a revival of the sacrifice of Christ on the cross,

67 *Prose Works*, pp. 403–4.

once offered for sin, and for ever effectual; and a renewing of the covenant of grace to the penitent:

and that

the Church of England does for all this acknowledge it in another sense to be a sacrifice, both propitiatory and impetratory; because the oblation of it to God with and by the prayers and praises of her members, does render God propitious, by obtaining the benefits which the death of our Lord does represent.[68]

Evelyn went often to the Eucharist, but Pepys, although a regular churchgoer, never once refers to the sacrament in the nine years of his diary (1661-9). What Pepys went for was the sermon, to which he listened intently and on which he commented afterwards. But the sermons which he heard would probably be very different from those of Andrewes, Donne and even Jeremy Taylor which were long, flowery, full of poetic imagery and metaphysical thought. The more modern type of sermon was plain and edifying, seeking to restore the doctrine of the 'simple, homespun but practical version of the whole duty of man'.[69] The preachers were concerned with the good life, with Christian ethics rather than Christian dogma, with holding up before men the ideal of the Christian life in following Christ and keeping his commandments. Tillotson, who became Archbishop of Canterbury in 1691, was typical of the Restoration preachers. A man of a Puritan background, who married the niece of Oliver Cromwell, he was at first much disliked and distrusted by the restored clergy. But he won over his enemies by his great charm and attractiveness, and became a popular preacher of the new style, though, under him, the sermon 'lost its heroic note and became a moral essay, the vehicle of a sober utilitarian, prudential ethic, rather than a proclamation of the Gospel of the Kingdom of God'.[70] John Evelyn records in his diary that, on 26 February 1680, the Dean of Salisbury preached at his church for 'an hour and a half from his common-place booke, of kings and great men retiring to private situations. Scarcely anything of Scripture in it.'

Behind the preaching and the thought of the day lay the

68 John Evelyn, *Diary and Correspondence* (1870), iii, pp. 232, 236.
69 N. Sykes, *From Sheldon to Secker* (1959), p. 150.
70 Charles Smyth, *The Art of Preaching* (1940), p. 160.

appeal to reason, the basic quality of the Christian life. Reason had been one of the matters discussed by the Great Tew Circle before the Civil War and the Commonwealth; but it had been lost in the Calvinistic dogmas of predestination and justification which had prevailed for many years. It now came back in the writings of a group of men, known as the Cambridge Platonists, scholars who brought knowledge and reason to bear on their search for truth. They were puritan at heart and by upbringing, but they saw the danger of believing, as many Puritans and Roman Catholics did, that ignorance was the mother of devotion. Their religion was much wider than that of their contemporaries, and was full of mystical joy. 'To go against Reason is to go against God,' said Benjamin Whichcote, while Henry More said that 'to take away reason is to rob Christianity of that spiritual prerogative it has above all other religions in the world, namely that it dares to appeal to reason'.[71] Thus these men, and those who cared for what they stood for, saw the alliance of scientific knowledge with religion, of truth with faith, of the Royal Society with the Church.

The Prayer Book of 1662 introduced a new rubric at the end of Morning and Evening Prayer, saying 'In Quires and Places where they sing, here followeth the Anthem'. During the Commonwealth, church music had been largely abandoned; but Charles II was anxious to introduce the singing of anthems into his chapel, and this became a great feature not only in the Chapel Royal but in all cathedrals and the greater parish churches. Pelham Humfrey, John Blow and Henry Purcell all wrote splendid anthems, often with instrumental accompaniment, while men such as Bernhard Schmidt (Father Smith) and Renatus Harris built organs of great charm which were installed in some of the larger and more important places of worship. So was restored the tradition of English church music which has, since the reign of Elizabeth I, played so important a part in Anglican worship. Meanwhile, for the smaller parish churches, John Playford, in 1677, published his *Whole Book of Psalms*, a collection of metrical psalms, some with new tunes, which became the standard book for the next hundred years or so. Hymns, as opposed to psalms, had been provided as early as 1623 by George Wither whose *Hymns and Songs for the Church*, with some tunes by

71   Quoted in H. McAdoo, *The Spirit of Anglicanism* (1965), p. 103.

Orlando Gibbons, were bound up with the Psalter. But they were never popular; nor were the religious poems of George Herbert, Robert Herrick and Henry Vaughan, though some of these have found their way into modern hymn books. But the great age of Anglican hymn-writing was not yet. People were content to sing metrical psalms, in spite of the fact that most of them were doggerel. But the great thing was that they were biblical, and, apart from some of the anthems, most of worship was taken from the pages of the Scriptures.

Apart from church services, much emphasis was placed upon household religion, the head of the house acting as a kind of minister of religion for his family and servants. Even Pepys, who was not a highly religious man, held 'family prayers' every Sunday night, and thought it worth recording on the few occasions when he missed, as, for example, on 29 September 1661, when he had had too much to drink, and on 9 October 1664, when he recorded 'to bed without prayers, it being cold, and tomorrow washing-day'. Meanwhile John Evelyn, a much more religious man than Pepys, spent the whole morning of his fifty-sixth birthday 'in devotion and imploring God's protection, with solemn thanksgiving for all his signal mercies to me'; on 14 April 1685, he wrote 'according to my custom, I went to London to pass the holy week', and on 2 October of the same year wrote that the Church of England was 'of all the Christian professions on the earth the most primitive, apostolic and excellent'.

In the meantime religious books poured from the press, and large numbers of copies were sold. Among these were the works of Robert Leighton, Archbishop of Glasgow, but the most popular of all was *The Whole Duty of Man*, published anonymously but now thought to be by Richard Allestree, which stood next to the Bible and the Prayer Book as the book most read. This book was written in such a way that one chapter was to be read every Sunday and the whole book three times a year. But, popular though it was, it was not a great book, no more, in fact, than 'a well-written, old-fashioned statement of church doctrine with recommendations to live a Christian Life',[72] not to be compared with Jeremy Taylor's *Golden Grove* or *Holy Living* and *Holy Dying*. Many other books appeared, intended to explain the catechism, or the sacraments, or the daily offices; and even some books,

72 J. H. Overton, *Life in the English Church, 1660–1714* (1885), p. 263.

written before the Commonwealth, were reprinted for the use of both clergy and laity, including George Herbert's splendid account of the life and character of the country parson known as *A Priest to the Temple*, Cosin's *Devotions* and Thomas Browne's *Religio Medici*.

Many examples could be given of holy laymen and women who, on the basis of all this devotional literature, stood up for religion and morals in a world where profligacy and licentiousness were common. Women such as Margaret Godolphin fought hard to preserve her integrity and nobility of character while residing at the court of Charles II, and Lady Ranalegh acted as spiritual guide to Clarendon on Sunday afternoons. Among many of the laity there was, therefore, a profound interest in religion, and, from 1678 onwards, a number of religious societies came into existence, mostly in London. These were societies of devout young men who agreed to pray, if possible, seven times a day and keep close to the teaching of the Church of England by going daily to church and making their communion every Sunday and festival. In addition, they visited the poor, helped poor scholars at the universities, and engaged in other works of charity and mercy.

The restored Church was very much a Church. It had cast out Calvinism, and had put in its place the ancient government and forms of worship which both Eastern and Western parts of the great Church regarded as essential. So far as the ministry was concerned it had reintroduced bishops, priests and deacons with no intention of ever getting rid of them, and it had restored a form of worship which was Catholic in its essentials though reformed in its nature. As a Church it was very self-conscious of its purification from popery and its repudiation of Calvinism, and it stood as the Church of the land, of the English people, to which everyone should belong.

But, of course, they didn't. There was a large number of dissenters of various kinds, Presbyterians and Independents left over from the days of the Commonwealth, Roman Catholics, Baptists and Quakers, Sabbatarians, Ranters, Socinians, Sweet Singers of Israel, and the rest of the sectarians. All these, by the legislation often known as the Clarendon Code, were cut off from the national Church and treated as outsiders or second-rate citizens. They were unable to go to the universities, to hold office under the crown, to be magistrates or Members of Parliament. From that day to this there has been a social barrier between church people and nonconformists which lies at the root of all attempts to unite the two in modern days.

Yet some of them continued very subtly to influence Anglican thought and devotional life. Baxter's *The Saints' Everlasting Rest* was reprinted in 1662, and at least four times after that; and it was very widely read and appreciated. The *Journal* of George Fox, the founder of the Quakers, found many Anglican readers after its first publication in 1694. But by far the most influential of all these writers was John Bunyan, a Puritan and probably a Baptist, who wrote over sixty books, among them *Grace Abounding to the Chief of Sinners* in 1666 and *The Pilgrim's Progress* ten years later. The first of these books is the story of his life, his wrestling with sin and, in time, his discovery of Christ. This he felt obliged to pass on to others, though preaching was forbidden by law and Bunyan found himself often in prison.

It was while he was in prison that he saw the dream which he wrote down as *The Pilgrim's Progress*, a book which has greatly influenced Anglican thought and spirituality. Here the life of man is portrayed as he journeys towards the Promised Land, meeting with various people called Obstinate and Pliable, Mr Worldly Wiseman, Purity, Prudence, Chastity, and so on. On his journey he fights with Apollyon and passes through Vanity Fair, he is beaten and imprisoned and suffers all kinds of indignities, but eventually he reaches the Heavenly City where he is warmly welcomed by the Angelic Host.

This remarkable book has been read and loved by Anglicans everywhere. Macaulay knew it by heart. To thousands it has come next to the Bible in their thought. Yet it was written not by a churchman but by a Baptist preacher of Bedford while lying in prison for the crime of preaching the gospel of Christ.

4

THE EIGHTEENTH CENTURY

A God-fearing Community

During the eighteenth century the Church, it used to be said, was asleep. The fires of the seventeenth century had burnt themselves out and had given place to a dull, formal sort of religion in which the clergy did very little and the people were largely uninterested in what they did. As Lytton Strachey said, 'For many generations the Church of England had slept the sleep of the comfortable'.[1] But modern research has shown that this is not true. Certainly there was not much fire in preaching, not much mystical or devotional literature. But, in its quiet way, the Church was content to fight for Christian behaviour in the midst of this naughty world, and to set before men the need to live a regular, devout and decent life, founded on the precepts of Christ as recorded in the Gospels.

In every respectable household the three books most likely to be found were the Bible, the Book of Common Prayer and *The Whole Duty of Man*, the last of which, though published in 1658, became the standard book for the laity for many years. This contained no speculative theology, the emphasis being on conduct rather than on belief, on the life given to God every day. But it was written in a way which influenced people's lives. Charles Simeon, when told that he must go to communion within three weeks of entering King's College, Cambridge, in 1779, went and bought a copy of *The Whole Duty of Man* 'because it was the only religious book he had ever heard of, and read it with great diligence, fasting and crying to God for mercy'.[2]

The Church in the eighteenth century was, therefore, much more alive than is commonly supposed. After reviewing the books published by the Society for Promoting Christian

1 Lytton Strachey, *Eminent Victorians*, Penguin Edition, p. 19.
2 C. J. Stranks, *Anglican Devotion* (1961), p. 136.

Knowledge during this period, Lowther Clarke can say: 'The Church of England is generally described as having been complacent in the eighteenth century. Of this there is not the slightest sign in our sources. We get an impression of a militant Church, fighting for its life against unbelief and coarse and dissolute manners, depressed at times by the magnitude of its task, but fully conscious both of the evil it was facing and of its impotence to face it with its own strength.'[3]

The parish clergy were, for the most part, not very well educated or well trained for their work. They differed from the intellectual clergy of the seventeenth and nineteenth centuries; but, within their limits, they did what was expected of them, many of them being keen antiquarians or pursuing some academic interest, while the century produced a number of great men, including Butler, Berkeley, Swift and Waterland. In 1743 Archbishop Herring of York carried out a visitation of his large diocese. After examining the returns of this visitation the parish clergy were shown to be 'a body of dutiful and conscientious men, trying to do their work according to the standards of their day'.[4] There was perhaps not much theology at the lower level of parish life. In the upper realms men argued over Deism, Socinianism, Latitudinarianism, and such like problems, but little of this got down to the ordinary man or woman who worshipped on Sundays and lived a decent life during the week. People knew that they were sinners, but that Christ had died for their sins and expected them to live a 'godly, righteous and sober life', to abstain from sin so far as they were able, and to come to church each week for a kind of springcleaning and to show their love for their heavenly Father. Some held daily, or at least weekly, prayers in their houses, read the devotional books which came out, especially things like Bishop Wilson's *Sacra Privata*, supported the Societies for the Reformation of Manners and other good causes, and set an example to their tenants and others of the Christian life as they saw it. Thus life went on quietly in the parishes, while the bishops were pinned down to life in London and the House of Lords for seven months of each year while spending the other five in their dioceses, confirming vast numbers of children, preaching

3   W. L. Lowther Clarke, *Eighteenth-Century Piety* (1944), p. 28.
4   *Archbishop Herring's Visitation Returns*, i, p. xviii.

in their cathedrals and more important churches, and in entertaining the laity and leading churchmen.

The picture of eighteenth-century church life as it has come down to us is of a god-fearing community, not wildly enthusiastic or deeply conscious of theological differences but living in 'a moral and intellectual climate of an unusually steady and definite kind. The controversies of the previous age had become wearisome; a rational, positive, scientific temper examined theological claims with the desire to reduce them to their simplest elements; mystery was disliked and suspected ... The study of nature, and of that "natural philosophy" open to all, would lead up to God and to the acceptance of a few great moral principles, and it would be fortified by the main outlines of the Christian revelation, but the complications of the creeds and of doctrines about the Trinity of the Divine Being were superfluous'.[5]

Men and women had no doubt about the existence of God whom Locke described as a 'mathematical certainty'; so they said their prayers, read their Bibles and tried to live a Christian life. Tillotson had shown that 'the laws of God are reasonable, that is suited to our nature and advantageous to our interest'; and when asked about the asceticism and suffering of Christians in New Testament times he had replied that this sort of behaviour belonged to the times in which men and women then lived, before the kingdoms of this world had adopted Christianity, and were therefore irrelevant to the age in which people were now living.[6] 'If a man', he said, 'would but go to church with as good a will as men ordinarily do to their markets and fairs, and be in as good earnest at their devotions as men commonly are in driving a bargain; if they would but endure troubles and inconveniences in the way of religion with the same patience and constancy as they do storms and foul ways and mischances when they are travelling about their worldly occasions ... I am confident that such a one could not fail of heaven.'[7]

Religion centred upon the Book of Common Prayer which was used regularly in public and in private devotions. No one doubted its theology or its moral judgements. Morning and

5 A. T. P. Williams, *The Anglican Tradition in the Life of England* (1947), p. 59.

6 N. Sykes, *Church and State in England in the XVIIIth Century* (1934), pp. 258–9.

7 Ibid., p. 259.

Evening Prayer were said Sunday by Sunday in the parish churches, and the Eucharist once a quarter in the country but more frequently in the towns. Though not very frequent it was taken very seriously with considerable preparation by the devout. Dr Johnson communicated only once a year, on Easter Day; but his attitude towards the sacrament was profound. He went twice to church on Good Friday, spent Easter Eve in reading the Greek New Testament and in fasting, and on Easter Day he attended Mattins and Litany, meditated on certain collects and prayers, 'communicated with calmness', and went home to continue his meditations and reading of the Scriptures.[8] Others attended and communicated more frequently, but generally with devotion and preparation, regarding the Eucharist with great awe as the commemoration of the offering of Christ for the sins of the whole world.

On the theory of the real presence of Christ in the bread and wine they had no doubt. Did not the Prayer Book make this clear? Did not the Prayer of Humble Access pray that we might 'so eat the flesh of thy dear Son, Jesus Christ, and drink his blood'? Was not the catechism clear that 'the Body and Blood of Christ are verily and indeed taken and received by the faithful in the Lord's Supper'? People coming to the sacrament could have no doubt about what they were about to receive, or about what difference it would make to their spiritual life.

But on the subject of the sacrificial element in the sacrament of the Eucharist – what Roman Catholics called 'the sacrifice of the Mass' – there was more doubt. The high-church party had no scruple in declaring the Eucharist in its fully sacrificial nature. Thomas Wilson, Bishop of Sodor and Man, maintained that 'Christ offered himself a sacrifice to God, as a priest, under the symbols of bread and wine in the Last Supper, before he was apprehended. And this is the sacrifice which his priests do still offer';[9] and Archbishop Wake, in his teaching on the catechism, put the question: 'What do you think of the Sacrifice, as they call it, of the Mass?' to which the reply was 'We do not deny but that, in a larger sense, the Sacrament may be called a Sacrifice.'[10] But

8 Boswell, *Life of Johnson*, 9 and 11 April 1773.
9 C. W. Dugmore, *Eucharistic Doctrine in England from Hooker to Waterland* (1942), pp. 151–2.
10 W. K. Lowther Clarke, *Eighteenth-Century Piety*, (1944), p. 14.

this was not acceptable to the low-churchmen, some of whom were drifting into Latitudinarianism, and even into Deism. A long pamphlet warfare took place in which men such as Samuel Clarke and John Johnson joined; but in the end it was Daniel Waterland, Archdeacon of Middlesex, who found language to express the main Anglican teaching. 'The Eucharist', he said, 'is both a true and a proper sacrifice, and the noblest that can be offered, as comprehending under it many true and evangelical sacrifices, namely the sacrifice of alms and oblations; of prayer; of praise and thanksgiving; of a penitent and contrite heart, of ourselves, our souls and bodies; of Christ's mystical Body, the Church; of true converts or penitents by their pastors; and of faith, hope and self-humiliation, in commemorating the grand sacrifice, and resting finally upon it.' And again: 'The sacrifice of the Eucharist is commemorative, applicative and participative, securing to us the benefits of Christ's death as the sole ground of our pardon and acceptance with God.'[11] This sort of language saved Anglicanism from Socinianism or Arianism, and remained the teaching of the Church for many years.

Meanwhile books of devotion poured from the press. As soon as the Prayer Book was restored in 1662, or even before that, books written to help people to understand the Anglican liturgy became very popular: such as Anthony Sparrow's *A Rationale upon the Book of Common Prayer of the Church of England*; Thomas Comber's *A Companion to the Temple*; and William Nicholls's *A Comment on the Book of Common Prayer*. But the book which did most to encourage devotion was written by a layman, Robert Nelson, and called *A Companion for the Festivals and Fasts of the Church of England*. It was published in 1704 but, by 1781, had run into twenty-five editions and had been described by Dr Johnson as having had the greatest sale of any book except the Bible and as being a most valuable help to devotion. Nor did the tide slacken, for books designed to encourage the devout attitude of the laity to Holy Communion were published late in the eighteenth century – by Samuel Walker in his *A Short Instruction for the Lord's Supper* (1761) and by Thomas Haweis in his *Communicants' Spiritual Companion* (1763). All this showed that 'religious practices inculcated by Sparrow, Comber, Nicholls and Nelson, reinforcing as they did earlier High Church divines, sank deeply

11 C. W. Dugmore, op.cit., pp. 179–80.

into the soul of England and maintained a hold there through-out the eighteenth century, in spite of the chilly rationalism of official religion and the strong wind of Evangelicalism which did so much to alter the appearance of the English Church.'[12]

Perhaps the greatest book of this period is William Law's *A Serious Call to a Devout and Holy Life*. Published in 1728, it followed on his previous work, called *Christian Perfection*, which it quickly overran. Law was a non-juror in 1714 when the Hanoverians came in, and he lived partly at Cambridge, partly at Putney with the Gibbon family, and partly at King's Cliffe in Northamptonshire where he set up a house with two ladies in which they could live the sort of life described in *A Serious Call*. This was based on the teaching of Christ and the apostles, all of which was to be taken seriously. The emphasis was upon ethics and right conduct, and it was an attempt to put before men and women the importance of carrying out Christian principles of life more than of just going to church. Law saw the danger of people going regularly to church on Sundays and thinking that, by so doing, they were fulfilling all their religious duties. 'It is very observable', he wrote, 'that there is not one command in all the Gospel for public worship; and perhaps it is a duty that is least insisted upon in Scripture of any other ... Is it not therefore exceeding strange, that people should place so much piety in the attendance upon public worship, concerning which there is not one precept of our Lord's to be found, and yet neglect these common duties of our ordinary life, which are commanded in every page of the Gospel?'[13]

The fully Christian life was founded upon every command-ment of Christ which was to be taken seriously, and Law illustrates this by a series of pictures of people, some praise-worthy and others derogatory, such as Penitens, 'a busy, notable tradesman, and very prosperous in his dealings', who died in his thirty-fifth year, full of penitence and regret for the way in which he had led his life. On his deathbed he declared that 'the thing that surprises me above all wonders is this, that I never had so much as a general intention of living up to the piety of the Gospel. This never so much as

---

12   C. J. Stranks, *Anglican Devotion* (1961), p. 173.
13   William Law, *A Serious Call to a Devout and Holy Life*, ed. J. H. Overton (1898), pp. 5–6.

entered into my head, or my heart.' 'I could', he said, 'have called in as many helps, have practised as many rules, and been taught as many certain methods of holy living, as of thriving in my shop, had I but so intended and desired it.'[14] Similarly, Flavia is described as one who 'will sometimes read a book of piety, if it is a short one, if it is much commended for style and language, and if she can tell where to borrow it', while Miranda 'has but one rule that she observes in her dress, to be always clean and in the cheapest things' and does everything 'in the Name and with regard to her duty to God'.[15]

Everything in *A Serious Call* is devoted to right conduct in the face of the teaching of Christ. Law's subtle attacks on those whose lives he criticized were devastating. Of Classicus he writes: 'The two Testaments would not have had so much as a place among his books, but that they are both to be had in Greek'; and of Coecus: 'He would have been very religious, but that he always thought he was so.'[16] On the other hand he can give praise where praise is due, as in the delightful account of Paternus who advises his little boy how to live.[17] In his later life William Law became inclined to mysticism, especially that of the German Lutheran mystic, Jacob Boehme, and, as such, lost the power which he had brought to bear in *A Serious Call*; but of its kind this book was warmly received by churchmen, many of whom found it of great significance.

Meanwhile the Church went on its quiet way, without taking great interest in the two rivals – popery and nonconformity – which surrounded it. Joseph Glanville, in praising the *via media* of the Church of England, said that it had 'rejected the painted bravery of one, and provided against the sordid slovenliness of the other',[18] while Warburton could say: 'I have always regarded Popery rather as an impious and impudent combination against the sense and rights of mankind than as a species of religion.'[19] But, for the most part,

14 Ibid., pp. 23–8.
15 Ibid., pp. 69, 80.
16 Ibid., pp. 133, 188.
17 Ibid., pp. 209–16.
18 N. Sykes, *From Sheldon to Secker* (1959), p. 224.
19 N. Sykes, *Church and State in England in the XVIIIth Century* (1934), p. 425.

the average churchmen were content to stick to their own Church and their own Prayer Book as the mainspring of their devotional lives.

John Wesley

'It would be vain to pretend', wrote Dr Norman Sykes, 'that churchmanship in the Hanoverian age was of a mystical or other-worldly character; or even that within the sphere of earthly citizenship it exalted the heroic virtues and called for asceticism and self-denial. Like the epoch of which it was born, it was prosaic and calculating, conceived as a prudent investment promising assured blessings both temporal and celestial.'[20] The clergy preached to their congregations about believing in God, and about living good Christian lives in accordance with the teaching of Christ. 'The sermons of the 1720s are predominantly (if safely) controversial (against Deists, Papists or Enthusiasts) or ethical (concerned with philanthropic enterprises like the charity schools) or sonorously pastoral. They offer to the layman little clear-cut dogmatic content. They speak little to the soul concerned with the great themes of sin and salvation; they have little appreciation of the tragic element in life.'[21] In fact the great theme of the Christian religion, which is the coming into the world of God the Son, his death on the cross for man's redemption from sin, and his ultimate resurrection and ascension to manifest his glory, these matters tended to be taken for granted. The Creeds dealt with all this. What mattered was that people should take Christ seriously as our great teacher, and that we should observe his commandments to the best of our ability. No one could be asked to do more than that.

Yet, into this 'prosaic and calculating' world was born the evangelical movement which had such a profound influence on Anglican spirituality. It began with the nature of sin, which was seen to be a matter of what one is rather than of what one does. Sin is to be distinguished from sins, which make one a good or bad person. But sin is inherent in every one of us, however good we may be and however holy the life which we live. Everyone is a 'child of wrath', fit only for

20 N. Sykes, *Church and State in England in the XVIIIth Century*, p. 419.
21 J. D. Walsh in *Essays in Modern English Church History in Memory of Norman Sykes* (1966), p. 142.

eternal damnation. Good works were of no avail whatsoever. Everything rested in the hand of God, who alone could forgive people's sins and bring them salvation; and this he has done for mankind by the death of Jesus on the cross. 'God commendeth his love towards us in that, while we were yet sinners, Christ died for us.'[22] The Bible is full of this. It is, in fact, what Christianity is about, the fundamental truth which forms the basis of everything. But people must accept the fact. They must acknowledge the ultimate love of God and know that they have been saved. That was why John Wesley, after years of the Holy Club at Oxford, and a preaching expedition to America, and spending his whole time in living a Christian life in every detail, could record the fact of his 'conversion' as happening at about 8.45 p.m. on 24 May 1738 among the Moravians at Aldersgate Street in London. It was then that he knew that he was saved, that his sin was forgiven through the death of Christ on the cross; it was his faith which had assured him of this. As he wrote to his brother Samuel: 'I was not a Christian till May 24 last past. For till then sin had the dominion over me, although I fought with it continually; but surely then, from that time to this, it hath not, such is the free grace of God in Christ.'[23]

The joy and wonder which this sort of experience brought to the tormented soul was indescribable. It gave a person a sense of spiritual peace, of a new birth, of belonging to the company of the redeemed, of being a whole-hearted and complete Christian. People believed themselves to be different men and women. 'It was not to be described', wrote James Hutton, 'with what joy and wonder we then grasped the doctrines of the Saviour, his Merits and Suffering, and Justification by Faith in him; and thereby freedom from the power and guilt of sin. This was to us all something so new, unexpected, joyful, penetrating, for most of us had sorely striven and fought against sin without profit or result.'[24]

John Wesley put down his awakening to the redemption wrought for him by Christ, or what we may call his 'conversion', to 24 May 1738, but a good many others had passed through a similar experience before that, and had begun open-air preaching to convert others. Griffith Jones of Llan-

22 Romans 5.8.
23 J. H. Wesley, *Letters*, ed. J. Telford, i (1931), p. 262.
24 Quoted by Walsh in *Essays in Modern English Church History*, p. 146.

dowror was at work in 1714, and George Whitefield had 'obtained mercy from God' in 1735 and two years later was busy preaching to vast congregations in London and elsewhere. Whitefield was a Calvinist, and, although a churchman, he worked a great deal with the dissenters, especially the Countess of Huntingdon whose followers, her 'connexion', lived and worshipped mainly apart from the Anglican Church, though they had some support from the Calvinistic clergy, of whom there were many.

John Wesley was fundamentally the high-churchman, the Oxford don, who fasted every Wednesday and Friday and made his communion twice a week all through his life, although he was travelling all over the country where the Eucharist was normally celebrated only four times a year. He had been born at Epworth Rectory in 1703, the son of most devout parents who brought him up strictly in the Church tradition. He had gone to Christ Church, Oxford and had been a Fellow of Lincoln College where he and his brother, Charles, founded a small society which they called the Oxford Methodists: the members of this society met once a week to study the New Testament in Greek, and they started visiting prisoners and the sick poor. They all kept very strictly to the rules and customs of the Church, fasting twice a week and attending Holy Communion every Sunday and festival. Within a short time they were meeting six nights a week for mutual comfort and support, and they were soon joined by other devout young men including George Whitefield, the poor servitor of Pembroke College.

John Wesley was now busy reading the Fathers and Thomas à Kempis. He also read William Law's *Christian Perfection* and *A Serious Call*, both of which influenced him deeply since they put forward the case for a type of Christianity which occupied one wholly, and which influenced one's every thought and action. As Wesley said: 'These convinced one more than ever of the absolute impossibility of being half a Christian; and I determined, through his grace (the absolute necessity of which I was deeply sensible of) to be all-devoted to God, to give him all my soul, my body and my substance.'[25] Then, after a short visit to Georgia, he got in touch with the Moravians, and was led by the young man called Böhler to believe that he lacked faith in any real sense of the word. All

25 *Works of the Rev. John Wesley*, xi, p. 159.

this religion which he professed was worthless because he had no real faith and was, therefore, still an outsider, unjustified and unsanctified, a sinner and an outcast.

It was then that he went through the experience of the New Birth and visited the Moravian centres in Germany. But it was not long before he quarrelled with them. His Anglicanism turned out to be too strong; and he remained a staunch member of the Church of his birth until he died in 1791, with the words on his lips: 'I declare that I live and die a member of the Church of England, and that none who regard my judgement will ever separate from it.'

Inspired by his own experience, John Wesley set out to preach the doctrine of faith and holiness, justification and sanctification which were inseparable in fact. 'God,' he said, 'in justifying us, does something *for* us; in begetting us again he does the work *in* us.' Justification is the equivalent of pardon for all our sins, known or unknown; and the moment we are justified, sanctification begins. We are born again. We enter a new life. We are new people, God's elect, children of grace, and, as such, we must now devote ourselves to personal holiness of life. There must be no more sin. Every detail of our lives must be given to God, every minute of the day must be consciously spent in his service. Wesley felt that he must attach himself to others who had experienced this New Birth, and he must preach deliverance from sin to as many souls as he could persuade to come and hear him. He must, as he said, 'avoid that bane of piety, the company of good sort of men, lukewarm Christians (as they are called), persons that have a great concern for, but no sense of religion. God deliver me from a half-Christian.'[26] He summed up his teaching in these words: 'By salvation I mean not merely deliverance from hell, or going to heaven, but a present deliverance from sin, a restoration of the soul to its primitive health, its original purity; a recovery of the divine nature; the renewal of our souls after the image of God in righteousness and true holiness, in justice, mercy and truth.'[27]

To go out and preach, to tell others the good news of rebirth, to share the joy which he had found – this became Wesley's ambition. Finding that the parish churches were

26   *Letters*, i, p. 169.
27   From his *Further Appeal*, quoted by J. H. Overton, in *John Wesley* (1891), p. 74.

mostly hostile, he began preaching anywhere and at any hour, at 5 o'clock in the morning or in the evening when people were coming away from work, in any old building which they could find, or more probably in the open air since no building was large enough to take in the vast crowds which attended his sermons. At the age of thirty-six, to set out on journeys on horseback which took him 225,000 miles in the next fifty years, during which he preached over 40,000 sermons, many of them to congregations of above 10,000 people, is an astonishing feat. But, in addition to this, he had to organize the societies which he had set up, to deal with recalcitrant members or people simply wanting help, to write what now fill eight large volumes of letters and eight large volumes of his *Diary*, together with a vast number of tracts and booklets. His output was prodigious. But what drove him on was his desire to do the will of God, whatever the cost. As he wrote in his *Diary*: 'March 9, 1759. At the Foundery. How pleasing it would be to flesh and blood to remain at this little, quiet place, where we have at length weathered the storm. Nay, I am not to consult my own ease, but the advancing the kingdom of God.'

The effect of these sermons was twofold. In the first place, they had the most astonishing influence on those who heard them, many of whom were visited by convulsions, dropped to the ground, beat upon the floor, and cried out in despair. 'While I was speaking,' he wrote, 'one before me dropped down as dead, and presently a second and a third. Five others sank down in half an hour, most of whom were in violent agonies. The pains as of hell came about them; the snares of death overtook them. In their trouble we called upon the Lord, and he gave us an answer of peace. One indeed continued an hour in strong pain; and one or two more for three days. But the rest were greatly comforted in that hour, and went away rejoicing and praising God.'[28] There is no doubt that the sermons of John Wesley were immensely popular. Thousands of people attended them, mostly working-class, and were greatly moved by what he said. Here was true religion expounded, the religion of redemption by the blood of Jesus, of justification by faith, of the call to Christian holiness and the dedication of life.

On the other hand, there was much opposition, and that

28 *Diary* for 22 June 1739.

not only from the irreligious, the professional stirrers up of trouble, who would break up a service, cast rotten eggs and filth at the preacher, and shout him down. Much opposition came from the clergy, who failed to understand Wesley's mission and who were afraid of what they saw as 'enthusiasm'. Wesley's preaching burst upon a Church which was complacent, static and self-assured. The clergy, not unnaturally, resented the open-air preaching in their parishes, and refused to allow Wesley to enter their churches. Wesley's claim was to 'look upon all the world as my parish',[29] and to the right to do what he felt God had told him was his mission. In an interview with Bishop Butler, who told him 'You have no business here; you are not commissioned to preach in this diocese; therefore I advise you to go hence', Wesley gave a spirited reply to the effect that 'my business on earth is to do what good I can. Wherever, therefore, I think I can do most good, there must I stay as long as I think so.'[30] Many of the clergy thought that he was taking people away from the Church and setting up a rival institution, which, of course, is what, in the end, he did. But it was not his wish. Wesley was a churchman through and through. He never departed from the teaching of the Church in the smallest way, and he taught his followers to observe all the rules which the Prayer Book laid down. Unlike Whitefield, who was a Calvinist, Wesley took his teaching not from the reformers but from the Fathers of the early Church who, he thought, had laid the principles from which all Churches had, in some way, departed.

In addition to his powers as a preacher and director of souls, John Wesley was also a gifted organizer, who formed his disciples into societies, who held class meetings, watch-nights, quarterly meetings, band meetings, love feasts. He had a large body of lay assistants who were trained to preach and to visit the sick. He founded a school at Kingswood, near Bristol, where the unfortunate children were brought up on the most strict and inhuman methods. He was, in fact, a great leader of men and women, ruthless, intransigent, opinionated, who saw everything from the point of view of his mission. To his sister Martha, who had lost nine of her ten children in infancy, he wrote: 'I believe the death of your children is a great instance of the goodness of God towards you. You have often mentioned to me how much of your time they took up! Now that time is restored to you, and you have nothing to do but to serve our Lord without carefulness and without distraction till you are sanctified in body, soul and spirit.'[31] The saving of souls for Christ was what came first into his thoughts. It was for this cause that he believed himself to have been sent into the world.

The societies which he founded were, in fact, his undoing. People joined them who had no interest in church matters, especially the high-church principles which meant so much to him. Gradually they drifted away from the Church, in spite of John and Charles Wesley's beseeching them to stay. If one has lay preachers, preaching to societies of the converted, what is to prevent them from giving them communion? If one has societies in America, cut off from the home Church, with no possibility of confirmation or ordination, what can prevent men from being sent out as superintendents to do this for them? Thus it came about that Methodism, which had begun as a high-church movement within the Church, ended up as a form of dissent, the largest and most influential form of dissent in the land.

Justification by Faith

While John Wesley was riding about England, preaching to large open-air congregations, organizing his societies, and creating a whole network which was shortly to break away into Methodism, and while George Whitefield was falling more and more into the hands of the Countess of Huntingdon and her dissenting connexion, there was, in the parishes, a steadily growing evangelical movement. This was an attempt to rouse personal religion based on the sense of sin and forgiveness, of repentance and salvation through Christ. It was experiential in that every person began with a sense of the horror of sin, and an acceptance of the Lord as Saviour, and a moment of conversion when the soul knew that it was forgiven and that all its sins were blotted out by the death of Christ on the cross. This was what was known as justification by faith, and was the free gift of God through grace. This was now being proclaimed by people, mostly clergy, who were dissatisfied with the easygoing religion of most of their fellows.

31 *Letters*, ii, p. 12.

Some of them had not heard of Wesley or of Whitefield, and, if they had, they were probably opposed to them, since they would identify their religion with the dreaded 'enthusiasm' and would disapprove of their preaching in other people's parishes.

'General explanations of the Revival', wrote Walsh, 'fall into three main categories. First, its roots have been traced down into that rich alluvial deposit of High Church piety which in the 1730s was still a deep and varied stratum of Anglican spirituality. Secondly, it may be seen as a reaction to early eighteenth-century rationalism. A third organising concept interprets it as an eruption within the Church of England of the traditions of seventeenth-century Puritanism, dormant but not extinguished, and still smouldering away below the crust of conventional piety.'[32] But whatever its origin, the movement caught on and laid the foundations of what became the predominantly Anglican way of thought for many generations.

Among the leading figures in this evangelical movement were men such as Fletcher, the saintly Vicar of Madeley, of whom it has been said that 'never perhaps since the rise of Christianity has the mind which was in Christ Jesus been more faithfully copied than it was in the Vicar of Madeley'.[33] Walker of Truro, Venn of Huddersfield and Grimshaw of Haworth were all in the same tradition. These were men who stayed in their parishes, preaching the Good News as they had heard it, ministering to the people whom they were appointed to serve. John Berridge of Everton told his flock 'very plainly that they were Children of Wrath, and under the Curse of God, though they knew it not . . . labouring to beat down Self-Righteousness; labouring to shew them that they were all in a lost and perishing State, and that nothing could recover them out of this State, and make them Children of God, but Faith in the Lord Jesus Christ'.[34] Berridge did a great deal of travelling to preach the faith as he knew it; but much of his work was done among his own people and those who came to hear him. As he himself said: 'I preached of Sanctification very earnestly for six years in a former Parish,

---

32 *Essays in Modern English Church History*, p. 138.
33 Abbey and Overton, *The English Church in the Eighteenth Century*, ii (1878), p. 113.
34 Charles Smyth, *Simeon and Church Order* (1940), p. 162.

and never brought one Soul to Christ. I did the same at this Parish for two years, without any success at all; but as soon as ever I preached Jesus Christ, and Faith in his Blood, then Believers were added to the Church continually; the People flocked from all Parts to hear the glorious Sound of the Gospel, some coming six miles, others eight, and others ten, and that constantly.'[35] Moreover, as with Wesley, people broke down under the spell of his preaching and felt the power of the Holy Spirit acting upon them. A well-dressed stranger, who had come forty miles to hear Mr Berridge, suddenly 'fell backward to the wall, then forward on his knees, wringing his hands and roaring like a bull'.[36]

But, for the most part, people just wept silently as they listened to these evangelical preachers proclaiming the gospel truths which they had learnt from the Bible. A few of them were Calvinists in their teaching about predestination and the overpowering gift of grace. William Romaine was one of these; so was Augustus Toplady whose famous hymn, 'Rock of Ages', is deeply Calvinistic when it says:

> Nothing in my hand I bring,
> Simply to thy cross I cling . . .
> Helpless look to Thee for grace

showing that good works are of no avail to the sinner.

These were the men who set the fashion for an evangelical form of religion which took hold of people and became very popular. When the Methodists broke away and became a dissenting sect, it was the Evangelicals who stayed in the Church, calming down in their preaching, but still maintaining the fundamental truths which they felt to be the heart of the Christian religion.

Among the evangelical clergy Charles Wesley played an important part. He was a convinced churchman, who gave up itinerating because members of the societies which his brother John founded were hostile to the Church, and he pleaded with John not to separate. But his great contribution to the movement was the writing of hymns, of which he turned out over 6500; many of them caught on and became very popular. The real originator of the hymn was a dissenter,

35 Ibid., p. 163.
36 Ibid., p. 168.

Isaac Watts, 'the creator of the modern English hymn'[37] whose *Psalms and Hymns* (1719) became the standard book of the Congregationalists. The dissenters did not much like singing Psalms, thinking that many of them were unsuitable for Christian worship (as, indeed, they are), but his hymns, especially 'O God, our help in ages past' and 'When I survey the wondrous cross' became very popular. Meanwhile the churches went on singing the Psalms, using either the Old Version of Sternhold and Hopkins or the New Version of Tate and Brady, which appealed to them as being scriptural, whereas hymns could contain any sort of heresy unless very carefully scrutinized. The only thing they allowed were the anthems which were sung in the cathedrals and in parish churches which had choirs capable of performing them.

Of the Wesley brothers John first wrote hymns, but it was Charles who really provided the hymns which Methodists sang at their meetings. John Wesley was very keen on singing, and they needed good hymns in which the large congregations could express their feelings. It was Charles who produced them – 'Jesu, lover of my soul', 'Love divine, all loves excelling', 'Let saints on earth in concert sing', 'O thou who camest from above', 'Soldiers of Christ, arise' and many others. Many were written for the Church's year, or for the sacraments, which showed Charles's churchmanship. If Isaac Watts was the creator of the modern English hymn, Charles Wesley was perhaps the greatest of all hymn-writers. Books of hymns for the use of Methodists now began to pour from the press, and no meeting was considered to be complete without the singing of a hymn.

Meanwhile the Church was introducing more hymns into its worship, many of them coming from collections produced for the hospitals and charity children. This change, however, came slowly as people still objected to the introduction of non-biblical words into the worship of the Church. 'Why', wrote William Romaine in 1775, 'should Dr Watts, or any hymn-maker, not only take precedence of the Holy Ghost, but also thrust him entirely out of the Church?'[38] So they carried on with their psalms, the clerk reading out the words line by line so that the illiterate could sing them, and the

---

37   W. H. Frere in *Hymns Ancient and Modern: Historical Edition* (1909), p. lxxxiii.
38   Ibid., p. xcii.

organ or parish band providing interludes. But gradually the hymn replaced the psalm. To the vast output of Charles Wesley, William Cowper and John Newton produced in 1779 their book called *Olney Hymns*, which contained a number of beautiful evangelical hymns very appropriate to the world in which they lived. Cowper's 'O for a closer walk with God' and Newton's 'How sweet the name of Jesus sounds' were typical of this type of hymnody.

The introduction of hymns completely changed parish worship, making it much brighter and more personal than it had been. People rejoiced in the hymns, for which good tunes were quickly found, and formed their spiritual outlook on them. They were sung not only at church but in the homes of the people and thus added a new dimension to Christian worship and to Anglican spirituality.

5

PARTISANSHIP

The Evangelicals

While Methodism drifted into dissent, the evangelical party flourished in the Church of England, capturing the minds of many prominent laymen as well as the clergy. They adopted much of the teaching of John Wesley, proclaiming the sins of men and women and their forgiveness through the sacrifice of Christ, the necessity of conversion and moral earnestness. The religion which they sought was an individual affair. It had little conception of the Church as the Body of Christ, the spiritual home of all that put their trust in him. A person's relation with God was what mattered; that, and that alone. 'The only religion worth having, the one that must be longed for, sought for, and prayed for, with all the power of each man's being, is that which consists in entire surrender to the love of God shown to us in Christ, and in the dedicated life which springs from such committal.'[1]

Much emphasis was laid on conversion, probably at a given moment in time. Most men knew the exact hour of their conversion, their acceptance of Christ as their Saviour and Redeemer, and the new life into which they had entered. Those not converted were in the outer darkness, and must, somehow or other, be brought into the true light. Hence the enthusiasm for foreign missions and for preaching the gospel, as they saw it, to all people everywhere. This conversion was God's gift to men and women. It was based on faith – faith in the redeeming work of Christ conquering the sins of people. We are all sinners; but the load which we bear can be removed by Christ. This liberation was the heart of Christianity. It makes their religion the very centre of people's lives, the one thing which controls all that they do. As Liddon said: 'The deepest and most fervid religion in England during the first

1   C. J. Stranks, *Anglican Devotion* (1961), p. 227.

three decades of the century was that of the Evangelicals. The world to come, with its boundless issues of life and death, the infinite value of the one Atonement, the regenerating, purifying, guiding action of God the Holy Spirit in respect of the Christian soul, was preached to our grandfathers with a force and earnestness which are beyond controversy.'[2] Wilberforce spent three hours every day in prayer and meditation. Sir James Stephen not only carried a Bible in his pocket to read as he walked about, but also chose a text each morning on which he pondered all day. Every hour and every shilling belonged to God, and must eventually be accounted for. Sir Fowell Buxton invited the ploughboys and milkmaids into his house to hear him expound the Scriptures and to pray with him. Bible-reading occupied much of their time, to the exclusion of all other reading. The Revd William Cadogan, on receiving from John Wesley a complete set of his writings, threw them all into the fire, proclaiming that the Bible was the only book he wished to read.[3] They attended the church services most regularly, and many of them were present also at catechetical meetings for instruction in the religion which they held.

There were perhaps not a great many of them, but their influence on society was enormous. The Clapham Sect, which included people such as Henry Thornton, William Wilberforce, Granville Sharp, Zachary Macaulay and Lord Teignmouth, all gathered round the pulpit of Henry Venn, were enthusiastic Evangelicals, and all worked for the abolition of slavery, improvement in the factories of this land, the liberation of little boys who swept the chimneys, and the missionary societies in all parts of the earth. Their influence on the world was profound. Within half a century 'the Evangelicals, though a minority, converted the Church of England to foreign missions, effected the abolition of the Slave Trade and Slavery, and initiated Factory Legislation and humanitarian reform, healing the worst sores of the Industrial Revolution. Has any Church in Christendom accomplished so much in so short a time?'[4] asked C. E. Smyth.

They also wrote books in which they proclaimed their beliefs, or tried to remodel the society in which they lived, in

2 H. P. Liddon, *Life of E. B. Pusey*, i (1893), p. 255.
3 C. E. Smyth, *Simeon and Church Order* (1940), p. 221.
4 C. E. Smyth, quoted in Hennell, *Sons of the Prophets* (1979), p. 6.

which it was said that the poor lived as animals and the rich as devils. Earnestness of behaviour was their cry. Wilberforce's long book, which he entitled *A Practical View of the Prevailing Religious System of Professed Christians in the Higher and Middle Classes in this Country, contrasted with Real Christianity*, was an attempt to show the poverty of the religion professed by many Christians, which he felt to be formal and insincere, and to give them something much better. He pleaded with his readers to abandon the sort of religion which was no more than a habit, a matter of keeping certain rules, and to replace it with the religion of the soul, of justification, of liberation from death to life, of living with Jesus all day and every day. Wilberforce's book was meant to convert people, and to put before them the 'real Christianity' which meant so much to him. A more popular book was *The Dairyman's Daughter*, which has been described as 'only 92 pages, but an enchanting sentimental portrait of a godly, quiet, rustic arbour, with forelock-touching peasants in smocks, friendly gospel-preaching parson, simple consciousness of eternity in the fragrant, sunlit countryside of England; and with a child who proves that the expert in religion is not the professor but the pure, and that humble insight penetrates deeper than learning'.[5] This book was typical of the sort of literature which the Evangelicals produced in vast numbers, and was immensely popular though it did not go very deep.

Evangelicalism was, therefore, in the air in the first part of the nineteenth century, and quite a large number of laity adopted its teaching and tried to live the life which it propounded. Meanwhile the clergy were preaching it, Sunday by Sunday, from their pulpits, taking the Bible as their source-book and expounding it as they thought fit. The greatest of them, and the one who had the most profound influence on society and on the Church as a whole, was Charles Simeon, Vicar of Holy Trinity church at Cambridge from 1783 to his death in 1836. Born at Reading in 1759, and educated at Eton and at King's College, he had little sense of religion until he passed through a kind of conversion in 1779 when he came up to college and read, in preparation for receiving Holy Communion, *The Whole Duty of Man*, which, together with other books, altered his whole life. 'My distress of mind', he wrote afterwards, 'continued for about three months, and

5   O. Chadwick, *The Victorian Church*, i (1966), p. 451.

well might it have continued for years, since my sins were
more in number than the hairs of my head ... but God, in
infinite condescension, began at last to smile upon me, and
to give me a hope of acceptance with him ... Accordingly I
sought to lay my sins upon the sacred head of Jesus; ... and
on Sunday morning [Easter Day, 4 April] I awoke early with
those words upon my heart and lips: "Jesus Christ is risen
today: Hallelujah! Hallelujah!" From that hour peace flowed
in rich abundance into my soul; and at the Lord's table in
our chapel I had the sweetest access to God through my
blessed Saviour.'[6]

Simeon met with great opposition when he took over the
church of the Holy Trinity in Cambridge; but he gradually
wore it down by the excellence of his preaching and the care
and attention which he gave to his parishioners. In time
people flocked to hear him in church and in his evening
classes, and many undergraduates carried his teaching as
missionaries to the ends of the world. His teaching was always
on the Bible, and his printed books contain sermons on 2536
texts almost equally chosen from the Old Testament and the
New. 'Be Bible-Christians, not system Christians,' he taught;
and he lived up to it by making the Bible the book to which
he turned for inspiration, information and encouragement.
'I am willing', he said, 'that every part of God's blessed Word
should speak exactly what it was intended to speak, without
adding a single iota to it, or taking from it the smallest particle
of its legitimate import.'[7]

His themes were sin and atonement through the cross of
Christ, followed by earnestness and integrity of life. In a letter
written to him by John Berridge, in about 1792, the following
advice was given:

Lay open the universal sinfulness of nature, the darkness
of the mind, the frowardness of the temper – the earthliness
and sensuality of the affections: – Speak of the evil of sin
in its Nature, its rebellion against God as our Benefactor,
and in contempt of his authority and love: – Declare the
evil of Sin in its effects, bringing all our sickness, pains and
sorrows, all the evils we feel, and all the evils we fear: – All
inundations, fires, famines, pestilences, brawls, quarrels,

6   A. Pollard and M. Hennell, *Charles Simeon* (1959), pp. 24–5.
7   Ibid.

fightings, wars: – with Death to close those present sorrows, – and Hell to receive all that die in sin . . . Declare Man's utter helplessness to change his nature, or to make his peace. Pardon and Holiness must come from the Saviour . . . When your Hearers have been well harrowed, and the clumps begin to fall, . . . then bring out your CHRIST, and bring him out from the heart, thro' the lips, and tasting of his Grace while you publish it. Now lay open the Saviour's Almighty Power to soften the heart, and give it true repentance: to bring Pardon to the broken heart, and the Spirit of Prayer to the prayerless heart; Holiness to the filthy heart and Faith to the unbelieving heart.[8]

Simeon divided believers into two classes – the evangelical and the formal; and he was determined to see that in any parish where a 'Gospel-labourer' was at work, his influence should continue after his death or removal to another parish. He saw that there was no assurance of continuity under the present system of patronage; and so he bought advowsons and presented men of his own choice. These were mainly in the towns where he knew that they were most needed, presenting the livings to those who would see that 'the Gospel was fixed there in perpetuity'.

Though evangelical to the core, Simeon was a good churchman, who saved his fellows from drifting, like the Methodists, into dissent. He once said: 'Dissenters I never know; all who live in my parish I reckon of my parish. I won't discountenance them, for I know they have a right to go where they think they can get most good, as well as I have. But I won't countenance them, because I am of the Established Church, and ought to uphold it, convinced as I am of its excellency and sufficiency.'[9] Consequently he refused invitations to preach in other people's parishes or in barns where vast crowds were now assembled to listen to the sermons of gospel-preachers. Simeon loved the Book of Common Prayer which he regarded as the symbol of the kind of religion which he preached. 'The finest sight short of heaven', he once said, 'would be a whole congregation using the prayers of the Liturgy in the spirit of them.'[10] It is because of this that he served the Church so well, and saved it from disintegration

8   C. E. Smyth, *Simeon and Church Order* (1940), p. 277.
9   Pollard and Hennell, op.cit., p. 163.
10   Ibid., p. 3.

as thousands of its members, dissatisfied with the preaching of the 'formal professors', turned to the dissenters for the true gospel. Simeon would have none of this; and by his preaching and pastoral care, he became what Smyth called 'one of the founding fathers, or remodellers of the Church of England in the nineteenth century'.[11]

Simeon, though the greatest of the evangelical clergy, was not alone. William Cadogan of Reading and Chelsea, read the Bible in Hebrew and Greek and nothing else. He preached assiduously, often three times on a Sunday and twice during the week. Edward Bickersteth put great emphasis on hymn-singing, which, he said 'assists in maintaining spirituality of mind and constant communion with God. It greatly helps the poor to acquire the knowledge of the things of Christ. It furnishes constant subjects of devout meditation.'[12] He published his own hymn book, which he called *Christian Psalmody*, in 1833. This showed him to be far ahead of all his predecessors. He also wrote a *Treatise on Prayer and on the Lord's Supper*, in which he said that we plead the merits of the same sacrifice here that our great High Priest is continually urging for us in heaven. Then there were the three generations of the Venn family, the middle one of which, Henry, wrote a life of Francis Xavier, as a great missionary.

These were the most distinguished of the evangelical clergy. But there were many lesser men wedded to the same cause. They preached always to convert their listeners. Their sermons contained always the personal factor in religion, recognizing the fact that all people had their own problems to face and needed the redeeming love of Christ and the sacrifice of the cross to bring them pardon and deliverance from all their sins, and the new life, looking unto Jesus, which was mankind's reward. They instituted more services in their churches, with more frequent Holy Communion which was held only rarely in other parishes. They believed firmly in the second coming of Christ, and in a period of great joy when Christ would return to the earth and Satan would be defeated. Consequently they warmly supported the missionary societies who were busy sending men all over the earth to make converts to the Christian religion. They feared Rome as Anti-

11   C. E. Smyth, op. cit., p. 6.
12   Pollard and Hennell, op. cit., p. 37.

Christ and preached against it and its teaching which they regarded as abhorrent, but they sympathized with dissent.

They wrote and distributed tracts to people in railway trains or in the street. They did everything they could to propagate their doctrine. 'Are you saved?' was the question which they were liable to put to complete strangers. Moreover, they lived lives of exemplary goodness, sincerity and earnestness, having nothing to do with theatres, cards, dancing or novels, all of which they regarded as sinful. Their whole life was given to Jesus, lived under the watchful eye of God who saw and recorded every action and every thought, and to whom they would one day have to render an account. 'The Evangelicals', wrote Gladstone, the high-churchman, 'were the heralds of a real and profound revival, the revival of the spiritual life. Every Christian under their scheme had personal dealings with his God and Saviour.'[13] Or as G. W. E. Russell wrote, 'The Evangelicals were the most religious people whom I have ever known . . . I recall an abiding sense of religious responsibility, a self-sacrificing energy in works of mercy, an evangelistic zeal, an aloofness from the world, and a level of saintliness in daily life such as I do not expect again to see realized on earth.'[14]

The Churchmen

Thomas Sikes, Vicar of Guilsborough, talking to Dr Pusey in 1833, said:

> Wherever I go about the country I see among the clergy a number of very amiable and estimable men, many of them much in earnest and wishing to do good. But I have observed one universal want in their teaching: the uniform suppression of one great truth. There is no account given anywhere, so far as I can see, of the One Holy Catholic Church . . . Now this great truth is an article of the Creed; and, if so, to teach the rest of the Creed to its exclusion must be to destroy 'the analogy or proportion of the faith'. This cannot be done without the most serious consequences . . . We now hear not a breath about the Church; by and by those who live to see it will hear of nothing else . . . and

13   S. C. Carpenter, *Church and People, 1789–1889* (1933), p. 29.
14   G. W. E. Russell, *The Household of Faith* (1902), p. 231.

woe betide those, whoever they are, who shall, in the course
of Providence, have to bring it forward . . . Those who have
to explain it will hardly know where they are, or which
way to turn themselves. They will be endlessly misrep-
resented and misunderstood. There will be one great outcry
of Popery from one end of the country to the other. It will
be thrust upon minds unprepared and on an uncatechised
Church.[15]

Sikes was one of a group of men who were anxious to keep
alive the doctrine of the Church in a world in which it was
largely forgotten. Wordsworth had written about the Church
in his *Ecclesiastical Sonnets*; he had given a history from earliest
times down to his own day, and Charles Daubeny, called by
Alexander Knox 'a strange kind of clergyman from Bath'[16]
had defended the Church in his *Guide to the Church*, published
in three volumes in 1798–9; and there were others to whom
the Church meant something. Alexander Knox, who was born
at Londonderry in Ireland in 1757 and lived mostly as a
layman in Dublin, wrote in 1806:

Now I am a Churchman in grain: not a Tory Churchman,
for that is a disease in the Church, not its constitutional
turn; nor yet a Whig Churchman, for they did not value
enough the distinguishing features of our Establishment.
But, if I may so use the term, I am a primitive Churchman,
prizing in our system most cordially, what it has retained
from Christian antiquity, as well as what it has gained from
the good sense of the Reformers . . . The truth is I am not
one whit puritanic: I love Episcopacy, the surplice, festivals, the communion-table set altarwise, antiphonal
devotions.[17]

Knox was a kindly and generous man with a genuine desire
to see the best in other schools of thought. He had been a
great personal friend of John Wesley, who frequently wrote
to him as 'My dear Aleck'; and he thought much of Wesleyan
preaching which contrasted favourably with the general standard of Anglican preaching. He wrote: 'I look upon the sub-

---

15 H. P. Liddon, *The Life of E. B. Pusey*, i (1893), p. 257. Sikes had written
    a book on the Church, which he called *A Discourse on Parochial Com-
    mission*, which was published in 1812.
16 A. Knox, *Remains*, iv (1844), p. 80.
17 Ibid., iv, pp. 206–7.

stance of Methodism to be identical with the central nucleus of Christianity.'[18] Moreover, living in Ireland, he saw much of the Roman Catholic Church of which he wrote: 'The Romish Church is like a garden overrun with weeds; but there are, in this garden, some old fruit trees which bear fruit of extraordinary mellowness'; and again, 'viewed from without nothing could be more uncouth or revolting; but, under that rubbish, must be all the rich results of a providential training of Christ's mystical kingdom for fourteen centuries'.[19] But Knox's loyalty was to the Anglican Church of which he could write: 'In sober, solid verity, there never was, except when God Himself was pleased to act personally, so good-natured and delightfully wise a system as that of the Church of England . . . No Church on earth has more intrinsic excellence.' This devoted attachment to the Church is based upon two considerations: that it is truly a branch of the Catholic Church and that it has been delivered from the errors which attach to other branches. 'I am', he said, 'in the habit of maintaining that the Church of England is not Protestant, but a reformed position of the Church Catholic.'

All this was written in the early years of the nineteenth century, before the beginning of the Oxford Movement in 1833 with Keble's Assize Sermon and the first of the *Tracts for the Times*, written by Newman. People were worried about the world and the way in which things were going. The French Revolution, which had been at first welcomed by many in the Church and out of it, was later regarded as a tragedy; and men turned to the Church for consolation, for security, for peace and harmony. So there grew up a desire for no change. The Church was all that people needed. It must never be touched.

It was for such people that John Keble produced, in 1827, his book of poems called *The Christian Year*. These were based on the Collects and Readings of the Prayer Book which were taken as the source-book of all Anglican worship and devotion and which, after two poems written for Morning and Evening Prayer, went right through the Church's year, Sunday by Sunday, covering all the Festivals of the Saints, and ending with poems for Holy Communion, baptism and all the occasional offices of the Church. The book, therefore, covers the

18   Ibid., iv, p. 142.
19   Ibid., i, p. 63.

life of Christ, beginning with Advent and passing on through Christmas Day and Epiphany, to Lent and the cross, to the resurrection, to the ascension, and so to the coming of the Holy Spirit and the life of the Church. The poems proved immensely popular. Thomas Arnold thought them the finest poetry in the English language; and the book ran into countless editions, was learnt by heart by many devout Anglicans and was kept by their bedsides to be read and pondered over each night. It has been described as 'the first, the most persuasive, and, for some years after its publication, the only literary expression of the growing feeling on behalf of the Church'.[20] The poems deal ecstatically with the love and adoration of Jesus, his perpetual presence to all believers, his infinite goodness and mercy, his divine patience. Keble's morning poem which contains the well-known hymn:

> New every morning is the love
> Our wakening and uprising prove

and the evening poem with the hymn:

> Sun of my soul! Thou Saviour dear
> It is not night if Thou be near

have been part of the English language, well-known and well-loved by all. But the rest of the poems have faded away, and form no part of Anglican thought or worship today. They are mostly complicated beyond description, and seem to bear no resemblance to the subject which they are supposed to illuminate. Yet in their day they were considered exquisite, memorable, perhaps among the greatest poems in the English tongue, the very centre of Christianity, the heart of the gospel and of prayer.

The Christian Year was published in 1827 and by 1873 had run into 140 editions and become the Christian's *Vade mecum*. Meanwhile a greater man than Keble, John Henry Newman, was preaching his excellent and moving sermons, Sunday by Sunday, in the university church of St Mary's at Oxford, and attracting large numbers to hear them. Newman's great theme was the need for holiness of life. He appeals to every individual; he stresses all the time the need for a true religion. People must take themselves seriously, they must face religion for what it really is. A favourite text is the comment of Christ

20   C. J. Stranks, *Anglican Devotion* (1961), p. 246.

to the young man, 'One thing thou lackest'; and he is emphatic in going to the very roots of the Christian religion:

> A rigorous self-denial is a chief duty, nay, that it may be considered the test whether we are Christ's disciples, whether we are living in a mere dream, which we mistake for Christian faith and obedience, or are really and truly awake, alive, living in the day, on our road heavenwards . . . In what sense do *we* fulfil the words of Christ? Have we any distinct notion what is meant by the words 'taking the cross'? . . . What are we doing, which we have reason to trust is done for Christ's sake who bought us?[21]

Newman's sermons touch the very heart of the Christian religion. What is a Christian? he asks over and over again. Christianity is not just goodness, honesty, justice. All these things can be shown by Jews, infidels and heretics. To be a Christian is to love and worship Christ with everything that we have. It is to make Christ the very centre of our lives. To be a Christian, he says, is

> first of all in faith; which is placed not simply in God, but in God as manifested in Christ, according to His own words: 'Ye believe in God, believe also in me'. Next, we must adore Christ as our Lord and Master, and love Him as our most gracious Redeemer. We must have a deep sense of our guilt, and of the difficulty of securing Heaven; we must live as in His presence, daily pleading His cross and passion, thinking of His holy commandments, imitating His sinless pattern, and depending on the gracious aids of His Spirit; that we may really and truly be servants of Father, Son and Holy Ghost, in whose name we were baptised. Further we must, for His sake, aim at a noble and unusual strictness of life, perfecting holiness in His fear, destroying our sins, mastering our whole soul and bringing it into captivity to His law, denying ourselves lawful things, in order to do Him service, exercising a profound humility and an unbounded, never-failing love, giving away much of our substance in religion and charitable works, and discountenancing and shunning irreligious men. This is to be a Christian.[22]

In these sermons Newman quotes very occasionally

21 J. H. Newman, *Parochial Sermons* i (1840), pp. 75–6.
22 Ibid., i, p. 93.

Hooker, or *The Christian Year*, but almost all his quotations are from the Bible, with which he was very familiar. He takes it all quite literally, referring to events in the Old.Testament as if they had happened only yesterday, and speaking of angels and devils as existing beings fighting for the souls of men and women. He has much to say about the burden of human sin, and of the forgiveness which Christ has won for us by his sacrifice of himself on the cross. He talks about heaven, and about our meeting with God, about our going out to meet the Bridegroom, about the glory of the life which is to come. Most of the sermons deal with the same theme: people's striving after perfection, after true holiness and righteousness, of the true Christian differing so much from the natural man or woman, of the road to heaven, and of people's continued struggle to find it and to prepare themselves for the moment when they shall see God face to face and be seen by him.

While Newman was preaching these great sermons, all written in the best possible English, all appealing to the hearts of his listeners, great things were happening in the Church. It was on 14 July 1833, that Keble preached his celebrated Assize Sermon which really started off the Oxford Movement and the writing of the *Tracts for the Times* by men such as Newman, Keble and Pusey, which gave people a new idea of the meaning of the Church, so fulfilling Thomas Sikes's prophecy. Hitherto people had thought little of the Church. The great Evangelicals had taught a purely pastoral religion, a sense of sin and forgiveness, won by our faith in Christ, of justification by faith. The Church was 'the blessed company of all faithful people', but beyond that they were not prepared to take much interest. It was Rome who taught men to believe in the Church as the Mystical Body of Christ, the home of all the faithful, even as the extension and prolongation of the incarnation.

The first of the *Tracts for the Times* calls the Church 'our Holy Mother' and appeals to the clergy to exalt their office and to give honour to the bishops whose authority rests on their apostolic succession. 'Exalt our Holy Fathers, the Bishops, as the Representatives of the Apostles', wrote Newman, 'and the Angels of the Churches: and magnify your office, as being ordained by them to take part in their ministry.'[23] *Tract 2* is headed 'The Catholic Church' and declares: 'Bear with

23 *Tracts for the Times*, i, p. 4.

me, while I express my fear that we do not, as much as we ought, consider the force of that article of our Belief, "the One Catholic and Apostolic Church" ', and goes on to say that communion with that Church is necessary for salvation. *Tract 4*, written by Keble, starts by saying: 'We who believe the Nicene Creed must acknowledge it a high privilege, that we belong to the Apostolic Church', and says that we, the Anglicans, are 'the only Church in this realm which has a right to be quite sure that she has the Lord's Body to give to His people'. *Tract 7*, which is by Newman again, announces that our bishops are the heirs and representatives of the apostles, 'every link in the chain is known, from St Peter to our present Metropolitans', a statement held by the Prayer Book but rejected by all scholars today. Pusey then came in with a tract on 'The Benefits of the System of Fasting enjoyed by our Church', and another tract on 'The Scriptural Views of Holy Baptism'.

Throughout the *Tracts* there is much anti-Romanism. The writers all thought that the Roman Catholics, though given the right to hold office in the State in 1829, were not really on the same footing as the English clergy, who were the undoubted successors of the apostles. 'Remember then,' wrote Pearson in *Tract 35*,

> whether your pastors be rich or poor, honoured or despised by the world, it is only the having received this Commission that makes us bold in our God to speak unto the Gospel of God; and it is only this that can give you any security that the ministration of the Word and Sacraments shall be effectual to the saving of your souls. Learn, then, to cherish and value the blessing which God has vouchsafed to you, in having given you pastors who have received this commission. *The Dissenting teachers have it not.* They lay no claim to regular succession from the Apostles; and though the Roman Catholic clergy have been ordained by the hands of Bishops, they are mere intruders in this country, have no right to come here, and besides, have so corrupted the truth of God's word, that they are not to be listened to for a moment.

So the *Tracts*, and the teaching which went with them, brought in an entirely new conception of the Church and of the ministry. The bishops, and the rest of the clergy, were all commissioned by Christ to do his work. In their hands lay salvation, since it was they who administered to the faithful the Body and Blood of Christ. Had not Christ said: 'Except ye eat the Flesh of the Son of Man and drink his Blood, ye have no life in you.'? No longer was the Church to be regarded as part of the State. No longer could the secular powers interfere in the affairs of the Church. The Church was created by God to do his work. Membership of the Church, the true Church, the Anglican Church, ensured one's election and ultimate bliss. Those outside the Church were in utter darkness and ignorance.

Of the three great leaders in this Movement at this time, Keble lived and died peacefully at his rectory at Hursley in 1866, a humble man to the end, working quietly among his people, preaching his 'truly Christian sermons . . . affectionate, earnest, true and high'.[24] Newman went over to Rome in 1845, carrying a good many with him into what he came to regard as the only true Church. The third leader was a younger man, E. B. Pusey, who bore the burden and heat of the controversy and of the great battle between those whom he called 'High Churchmen', the defenders of the *Tracts*, those who believed in the apostolic succession of the bishops, and the rest of Englishmen who still accepted the old-fashioned evangelical attitude towards religion, based on sermons, prayer and meditation, and rather despising the Church. Pusey was one of the most sincere and devout men that the Church has ever given birth to. 'Was there', wrote S. C. Carpenter 'ever anything more wholly self-forgetting, more utterly adoring than Pusey's devotion to our Lord?'[25] He would rise every morning from his hard bed at 4.15 and say his morning devotions, including Mass, with the utmost reverence for the sacred mysteries. He made it his duty to repeat the penitential Psalms, or verses from them, when walking about. He would repeat any prayer in which he had been distracted during the church services as fervently as he could after returning home. He would pray for grace at every communion. He prayed daily to God to give him some sharp, bodily pain before he died, and the grace to bear it without complaint.[26] God, as represented in the world by Jesus, was

24 J. T. Coleridge, *Memoir of J. Keble* (1869), p. 465.
25 S. C. Carpenter, *Church and People, 1789–1889* (1933), p. 139.
26 See his Rules of Life in H. P. Liddon, *Life of E. B. Pusey*, iii (1895), pp. 104–6.

everything to him. Many thought him bigoted and cold-hearted, and he was suspended for two years from preaching within the precincts of the University of Oxford in 1843 for having preached a sermon on 'The Holy Eucharist a Comfort to the *Penitent*'. But he stood for what he believed to be true. 'Amid all the thickening assaults on faith which surround you', he said, 'and which perhaps will thicken yet more, until the days of Anti-Christ, one sure Rock there is, whereon if our feet be planted, they will never be shaken, never slide, never stumble, never falter – a personal loyalty and love for Jesus.'[27]

Keble, Newman and Pusey were the three leaders who changed the whole conception of religion and of churchmanship. There were others who helped them. Hugh James Rose, of Cambridge, was regarded as having originated the great Catholic revival. Hurrell Froude, who cried: 'Let us give up a national Church and have a real one';[28] Charles Marriott, William Palmer, James Mozley, William Perceval, who wrote some of the *Tracts for the Times*, all these were on the side of Newman, holy men, absorbed in their religion, giving all their lives to Christ and to the Church which he had founded on earth. They were all strongly anti-Rome in their thought. It was the Church of England that they loved and to which (with the exception of Newman) they devoted their lives. This was the true Church, descending in unbroken succession from the apostles, purified from the false teaching of the Middle Ages, firmly based on the writings of the early Fathers and of the Caroline divines in the seventeenth century, a Church to which every man could pay his respects and give his loyalty and obedience. Anglican religion, in the high-church party, has never been the same since the days of Newman and Pusey. Many of the things which we now take for granted, but which were unknown in their days, owe their existence to these great pioneers. As has been said of them: 'As moral guides, representing in their persons the ideals of sacramental and ascetic life which they commended, they sent out to the English religious conscience a call which sounded through the century.'[29]

27 *Sermons preached before the University of Oxford* (1872), p. 227.
28 S. C. Carpenter, op. cit., p. 125.
29 Owen Chadwick, *The Victorian Church*, i (1966), p. 231.

Post-Tractarians

The Tractarians were immensely interested in the theories of sacramental and ascetic belief and in the Church which taught them. They had little interest, however, in its outward expression. Newman was quite content for the Church to go on in its accustomed ways, with Mattins and a long sermon each Sunday morning, but Holy Communion only occasionally. The great thing for them was the Church – independent, free from the State, part of the great Catholic Church, in direct descent from the apostles. The Church must be free to be itself, untrammelled by State interference. But what went on in the churches was not really of great interest to many of them, though Pusey adopted leadership of the great reform which took place during the nineteenth century until his death in 1882.

But in the parishes things were beginning to change. Most of the churches and their services were, at the time, pretty grim. The Evangelicals were interested in people's relationship with God. Were they saved? Were they justified? Were they true followers of Christ, their Saviour? They attended church on Sundays because every good Christian did, and they listened attentively to the sermon which was preached. But they were not specially interested in what went on there, or what it looked like. But the post-Tractarians took the Church and its services seriously. If the Church of England was the Catholic Church of England, then it must look to other parts of the great Church for enlightenment. This meant Rome. There was nothing else to look to. Rome, however, was anathema to the average Englishman, and even to the Tractarians. No one wanted Rome putting its nose into our affairs. The Romans had no need to be here at all. Now that the catholicity of the Church of England had been firmly established, then Rome could keep to itself; and all good churchmen opposed the return of the Roman Catholics in 1850, the setting up of Roman dioceses in England, and the rather flamboyant attitude of Cardinal Wiseman who, in his message from the Flaminian Gate in Rome, announced that 'the greatest of blessings has just been bestowed upon our country by the restoration of its true Catholic hierarchical government, in communion with the see of Peter'.[30] Sikes had

30   R. P. Flindall, *The Church of England, 1815–1948* (1972), p. 117.

been right in prophesying that there would be one great cry of 'No popery' from one end of the country to the other.[31] But Rome was the living example of the true, apostolic Church apart from Orthodoxy, and therefore must be looked to for an example of how worship should be conducted, what a priest ought to wear, and how a church should look when properly furnished.

The post-Tractarians had no intention of becoming Roman Catholics, though Newman went over in 1845 and was followed by a good many others. Pusey and Keble and the rest stood firmly for Anglicanism, but a reformed, sacramental Anglicanism which would ensure that the Church was now to be truly catholic in every way. Pusey himself published a book called *The Real Presence* in 1857, the same year in which Keble produced his book *On Eucharistical Adoration*, which ran into three editions. So was the ground prepared for the great changes which came over Anglican worship and the appearance of the churches.

But as the movement spread to the parishes, so the outcry of others arose. They saw everything as a reintroduction of what the much-hated Church of Rome did, and did everything that they could to put the brake on. The persecution of men such as Mackonochie, Lowder and Dolling was savage, though all that they were doing was trying to bring Christianity to the poor. The Industrial Revolution had filled the towns with people who were more or less completely out of touch with the Church. Living in abject poverty and squalor, ignorant, ignored by most of the gentry, hungry and dirty, they had nothing to cheer them in their gruelling battle against filth and degradation. Charles Lowder looked after a small church in London's dockland, where a hostile parish elected an evangelical lecturer who insisted on his right to preach at the afternoon service. At all other times Lowder was in charge and tried to brighten things up. This turned the church into 'the zoo and horror and coconut-shy of London. The best days witnessed pew doors banging and feet scraping, or hissing or coughing, or syncopated responses. The worst days witnessed gleeful rows of boys shooting with peas from the gallery, fireworks, flaming speeches from tub-orators during service, bleating as of goats, spitting on choir-boys, a pair of hounds howling gin-silly round the nave,

31 See above, pp. 152–3.

cushions hurled at the altar, orange-peel and butter, kicking or hustling of the clergy.'[32] The same sort of rioting happened at other churches in London, especially at St Alban's, Holborn; St Barnabas, Pimlico; and St Paul's, Knightsbridge.

Less rioting occurred in more respectable churches where reforms were introduced in the conduct of worship and the teaching of the clergy. Gradually, changes crept in in the 'high' churches where fine services were conducted, though many of them in the Roman tradition, with everything designed to make the church look dignified and its worship of a pre-Reformation kind.

The bishops were in a sad way about it all. Most of them heartily disliked what were regarded as popish practices. They ordered the removal of candles from the altars, of vestments of every kind, including the harmless stoles, the intoning of services and the presence of robed choirs in the sanctuaries. But the Anglo-Catholics soldiered on. They were determined to bring some colour and gaiety into the sordid lives of the poor, and to reintroduce into other churches some of the splendour which had been there in the Middle Ages before the reformers had despoiled the churches of their beauty and changed the very nature of true belief.

The country, therefore, became divided between those who wanted the new ideas, and those who wished to cling to the old ways. There were the people who wanted the churches to continue to look bare, with their Sunday Mattins and long moralizing sermons. They disliked everything that smacked of Romanism, as they understood it. They stuck to occasional communions – as late as 1864 nearly a third of the parishes in the Lincoln diocese had Holy Communion only four times a year or less. Sacramentalism meant little to them. All that interested them was their relationship with God, and whether or not they were saved. But it was the innovators, the followers of the Tractarians who won in the end. Parish life could never be the same again. They had won the day.

The great changes were connected with the celebration of the Eucharist, which gradually came to be regarded as the chief service of the Church, the weekly or even daily offering of the Sacrifice of Christ on behalf of human sin and the reception by the worshipper of sacramental grace through receiving the Body and Blood of the Lord. This was now to

32   Owen Chadwick, *The Victorian Church*, i (1966), p. 499.

be performed in an entirely new way. The altar, decked with fine linen or silken frontals, now bore two or more candles, lit at every service to show the presence of Christ, the Light of the World, together with a cross as the central Christian symbol. The priest wore, in accordance with the Ornaments Rubric of the Book of Common Prayer, the traditional vestments of the Church or, at the very least, a coloured stole instead of a black scarf. Wafer-bread was now used, and a little water was mixed with the wine in the chalice. Incense was often used to symbolize the 'prayers of the saints [which] ascended up before God' (Rev. 8.4). The sign of the cross was used by priest and by worshippers, especially when the blessing was given at the end of the service. Moreover, Psalms were chanted by surpliced choirs, who also sang elaborate settings of the service, often composed by Mozart and Schubert and other continental musicians. In the service of the Church the Blessed Virgin now came into her own again, her five festivals in the calendar of the Prayer Book being rigidly and devoutly kept. Reservation of the sacrament was now observed, and the service of benediction was introduced. Figures and statues appeared in the churches, in many of which chairs or boxes were set up, attracting people to making private confessions. In many cases the churches were indistinguishable from Rome, except that the natural tongue of the English was normally used. This was the kind of service which many people liked. J. B. Dykes, coming from the rather frigid and old-fashioned north to attend such a service in a church in Brighton, wrote afterwards: 'I felt a strange mixture: delight and sorrow through all – delight at seeing such a *glorious* service in the Church of England and such signs of life! – and sorrow at comparing all this with our shortcomings in the north ... I have never enjoyed any services so much in my life. They have moved me more than I can tell. I found myself constantly in tears.'[33]

Here was to be found mystery in worship. Everything was reverent and numinous. No longer were the chancels of our churches used as storage rooms for church junk. No longer were the altars the repositories for hats and walking-sticks. Within a few years the churches were tidied up and cleaned. Altars were made to look like what they were meant to be.

33   O. Chadwick, *The Victorian Church*, ii (1970), p. 317, from *The Life of J. B. Dykes* (1897), p. 98.

The whole attitude towards worship was completely changed. And behind the changes in the appearance of the churches, and the type of service held in them, lay the conviction of many devout people that what God wanted was worship, glorification, magnificence. Nothing was too good for him. Yet he had come down and shared our human life in order that we might share with him in the glory of his resurrection and ascension, and reign with him in heaven. And he had left us the Church which was his Body and his Bride, the sacraments whereby we received grace and were fed with his Body and his Blood, and the ministry, closely descended from the apostles themselves, and appointed as his method of securing all these gifts to the faithful. 'O Lord, we beseech thee, let thy continual pity cleanse and defend thy Church' was the prayer loved by Anglicans as it came round each year.[34]

The best of the Anglo-Catholics realized that what they were doing was the natural outcome of evangelical religion with its insistence upon people's sin, and their redemption by the cross and the sacrifice of Christ. This is where the new conceptions blended with the old. Of Arthur Stanton, Mackonochie's curate and a thoroughgoing high-churchman, it was written that 'the constant – indeed the invariable – topics of his preaching were sin and forgiveness; the love of God towards the sinner and the sinner's need of the cleansed heart; the guaranteed access to the Lord through the sacrament of the altar, and the reverent love due to the Blessed Mother of God'.[35] Here we get the perfect combination of the two approaches to religion; and many other Anglo-Catholics preached the same gospel. E. B. Pusey, although the leader of the high-church movement, and one of the most disliked men in the country because of what he stood for and proclaimed, has been called 'one of the greatest English Evangelicals'.[36] There was among the high-churchmen no desire to forget the nature of man's sin, or to belittle the need of his forgiveness. The Oxford Movement had been anti-liberal and anti-Erastian, but never anti-evangelical. On the other hand, many of the Evangelicals were strongly opposed to the Anglo-Catholics for fear of undoing the work of the English reformers and dragging the country back to Rome. The

34 Collect for 16th Sunday after Trinity.
35 D. Voll, *Catholic Evangelicalism* (1963), p. 88.
36 Ibid., p. 38.

changes in worship, in the appearance of the churches and the type of services, meant nothing to them. They wanted things left as they were. Holy Communion could be held occasionally; the great thing was the Sunday sermon with its appeal to people to accept the great gifts of Christ, and to live up to the highest moral standards. So we get the rioting and confusion in the churches, the legal action in the law courts, the saintly Bishop of Lincoln being tried by the Archbishop of Canterbury for adopting, among other things, the eastward position in the Eucharist and the Revd S. F. Green languishing in Lancaster Prison for eighteen months on a similar charge. Fortunately, things gradually died down, and the government had to admit in 1904 that 'the law of public worship in the Church of England is too narrow for the religious life of the present generation'. But the post-Tractarians had made their point. All the six points on which the Bishop of Lincoln was tried are now accepted by most churches of the Anglican Communion as the most natural ways of conducting the service of the Holy Communion.[37]

Of course, other movements existed to help the Anglo-Catholics in their demands. Among these was the growth of Romanticism with its medieval interests, its pleas for a return to the times before the Reformation, to Merrie England, the maypole and country dancing. Up and down the country stood large numbers of highly medieval churches, waiting to be restored and redecorated and refurnished. In addition there were the towns where new churches were desperately needed. They must also be medieval and Gothic. So we get the foundation of the Oxford Architectural Society in 1838 and of the Cambridge Camden Society in 1839, both equally determined to erect only Gothic churches in all the towns of England, furnished and decorated in a truly early-English fashion, prepared for high ceremonial if only the vicars were prepared to introduce it.

Together with this went the printing of books to help people to understand about the past and the true nature of the Catholic Church. In 1836 money was forthcoming for a 'Li-

---

37   The six points were: mixing water with the wine, standing in the eastward position, causing the *Agnus Dei* to be sung, using the ablutions of the sacred vessels in public, putting lighted candles on the altar, using the sign of the cross in giving absolution and blessing. (See A. C. Benson, *Life of E. W. Benson*, ii (1899), p. 354.)

brary of Ancient Bishops, Fathers, Doctors, Martyrs, Confessors of Christ's Holy Catholic Church' which included forty-eight volumes under the general editorship of Charles Marriott. A similar set of volumes, called the 'Library of Anglo-Catholic Theology' was set on foot at about the same time, and published the works of the Anglican divines of the seventeenth century – Laud and Thorndike, Chillingworth and Beveridge, and many more. There were also coming into print copies of the works of the old English mystics: Julian of Norwich in 1843, Richard Rolle's *Prick of Conscience* in 1863, and the writings of Walter Hilton in 1831. People wanted to know about these medieval writers who had written so lovingly about spiritual things in the past. It mattered not that they were Roman Catholics, for people were now hungering after anything which would help them in their prayers and in their devotions. Meanwhile, English editions were published of the works of the great French writers such as François de Sales whose *Introduction to the Devout Life* became widely distributed and was read by devout Anglicans everywhere. There was also a vast output of devotional and mystical works written by Englishmen, of which T. T. Carter's *The Treasury of Devotion*, E. M. Goulburn's *The Pursuit of Holiness* and Berdmore Compton's *The Armoury of Prayer* were typical of the sort of book which people loved to have and to read and ponder over. Goulburn, who was Dean of Norwich, published in 1862 his *Thoughts on Personal Religion* which starts with the question 'Where is saintliness among us today?' and deals, among other things, with the sacraments and the 'magnificence of prayer'. There was, therefore, plenty for the devout to read, especially of a high-church complexion, Roman or Anglican, and a new spirituality gradually grew up and spread over the face of the Anglican world.

As they looked round on the Church, people realized that there was one thing lacking that they thought ought to be playing an active part in the Church's life. When Henry VIII closed all the religious houses in England in 1536 to 1539, there vanished from the scene hundreds of monasteries, occupied by monks, canons, friars and nuns, who had all played an active part in the life of the Church. Since then there had been little attempt to revive the religious life. Bramhall, a century or so later, had pointed out that when Henry closed all the monasteries 'he had a greater aim at the *goods* of the

Church than at the *good* of the Church',[38] while Thorndike thought that monastic life, if not of the *esse* of the Church is, at least, part of its perfection. Meanwhile, Nicholas Ferrar had formed his family monastery at Little Gidding where the whole Psalter was recited daily and the occupants all adopted a strict discipline in their daily life; and various attempts were made in the eighteenth century to found a house for women, though with no perpetual vows or any very definite Rule. Perhaps the nearest to the re-establishment of a religious house was William Law's call to people to 'unite themselves into little societies, professing voluntary poverty, virginity, retirement and devotion, living upon bare necessaries, that some might be relieved by charities and all be blessed with their prayers and benefited by their example . . . that they might be justly said to restore that piety which was the boast and glory of the Church when its greatest saints were alive.'[39] But nothing came of this appeal.

But there was, in the early nineteenth century, a strong feeling against the setting up of monastic houses in England. People were strongly against anything in the nature of perpetual vows, which were thought to be positively wicked. Moreover, the whole conception was thought to be Roman Catholic in origin and in its nature, and therefore to be put firmly aside. But as the feeling that the English Church, though reformed, was part of the Catholic Church of the past, and the demand for holiness of life grew, so the idea of Anglican religious orders came to be rationally considered by the Tractarians and their followers. Southey was very keen on it, and both Keble and Wordsworth gave their approval. Then, in 1837, the Lutheran deaconesses founded a house at Kaiserworth, showing that Protestants could overcome their anti-papalism and give their Church what it really needed.

So the idea developed, strengthened by the appalling horror of the slums and the need for women to form themselves into sisterhoods for the relief of the poor. These were not to be like the old nunneries of medieval England, which had all been enclosed monasteries, the inhabitants of which did little to help the poor. The new sisterhoods were to be active, like the French sisterhood founded by François de Sales or Vincent de Paul, composed of dedicated women who went among

38 J. Bramhall, *A Just Vindication of the Church of England*, i, pp. 118–20.
39 W. Law, *A Serious Call to a Devout and Holy Life* (1898), pp. 85–6.

the poor in their discomfort, who visited the sick, cared for the children, looked after the aged, and generally helped in activities in which the voluntary worker, however dedicated, could hardly be expected to take part.

Pusey was one of those who was delighted with the idea. In 1839 he wrote to Walter Hook, Vicar of Leeds, saying:

> I want very much to have one or more societies of *Soeurs de charité* formed. I think them desirable (1) in themselves as belonging to and fostering a high tone in the Church, (2) as giving a holy employment to many who yearn for something, (3) as directing zeal, which will otherwise go off in some irregular way, or go over to Rome.[40]

Hook was not very enthusiastic, but Pusey pressed on with his ideas, and in 1841 he took the three vows of religion – poverty, chastity and obedience – for Miss Marion Hughes. But still there was no community. Opinion was still violently opposed to the idea of anyone taking perpetual vows which was thought to be a purely Roman idea. So was the habit, the rules, confession, a daily Eucharist, exotic forms of service with candles and flowers on the altar and the officiating priest actually wearing vestments and adopting an eastward position. Pusey was not interested in all this. What concerned him was the charitable work which so greatly needed doing for the poor, and which he thought Sisters of Charity could so well perform.

So it was in 1845 that the first community came into existence at Park Village West, near Regent's Park in London: a group of women, under vows, working in prisons and workhouses, feeding, clothing and instructing destitute children, and even in burying the dead. It was followed, in 1848, by the Devonport Sisterhood, under Miss Sellon, and, in 1853, by the Community of St John the Baptist at Clewer, a house formed to rescue what were then known as 'fallen women'. Clewer was more Anglican and less Roman than previous attempts had been. They had the strong support of Bishop Wilberforce, and their office-book, *The Day Hours of the Church of England*, was scrupulous in keeping to the Book of Common Prayer and the Authorised Version of the Bible.

Clewer was soon followed by other houses, and the idea of perpetual vows became, in time, acceptable to those who

40   P. F. Anson, *The Call of the Cloister* (1964), p. 222.

supported them, though they were still regarded as sinful by the more Protestant churchmen. All the communities looked to Rome for shaping their Rules, their worship and their way of life. Most of them began their day at 5.00 a.m. and ended it with the recitation of Mattins at 8.00 p.m. All the canonical hours were recited in Church. Much time was spent in private prayer and meditation, mixed with various kinds of works of mercy and charity.

Meanwhile the problem of men's religious houses presented different questions, as men could not engage in the sort of work which occupied so much of the time of the women. Newman had toyed with the idea of a house at Littlemore, where, in his Anglican days, he set up something like a monastery, where a few keen men lived with him, keeping strict rules of prayer and searching for holiness and discipline of life. Various other attempts were made, but nothing really constructive was done until 1865 when R. M. Benson, who has been described as 'the personification of the devotion, reserve, austerity and self-denial of the Tractarians',[41] opened a religious house for men at Cowley, which was described as 'a Congregation of Priests and Laymen, giving up the world, living by simple rule and devoting themselves to prayer, study and mission work'. Benson was a truly holy man who, in his book *The Religious Vocation*, gave a picture of the inner life and of his vision of the Church and the world. Sanctification was his first concern – 'to sanctify ourselves through the truth, to sanctify ourselves in union with the incarnate Saviour, to sanctify ourselves in conformity with the will of God'.[42] Cowley was followed by the Order of St Paul at Alton in 1889 and the Community of the Resurrection at Mirfield in 1892.

So, after 300 years, the monastic life returned to the English scene. Gradually the old fears passed away, and men and women took their life vows with the solemnity of ordination. This was just one of the triumphs of the post-Tractarian Church, which had succeeded in entirely reforming the Church of England. They were by no means the whole Church, for many Protestants remained and fought against the changes which were coming about in our care of churches and in our worship. But it was the high-church party which

---

41   D. Voll, *Catholic Evangelicalism* (1963), p. 47.
42   A. M. Allchin, *The Silent Rebellion* (1958), p. 198, from R. M. Benson, *The Religious Vocation* (1939), p. 40.

eventually came out triumphant, and only a few parish churches today hold to the old evangelical customs which were largely swept away in the nineteenth and twentieth centuries.

Mainstream Christians

The Tractarians and the Evangelicals constituted only a minority of English Christians in the nineteenth century. Most people followed a middle course, something less detailed and strong than the Evangelicals and less complicated and demanding than the Tractarians and their followers. There were, of course, a number of evangelical churches where the gospel was preached in a somewhat Calvinistic way, with much emphasis upon sin and justification by faith. And there were the high-churches where the sacraments formed the centre of worship and a Romanesque form of religion was practised. But to most people neither of these ways was very attractive. They read their Bibles, said their prayers, tried to live a good Christian life, and attended church each Sunday for Mattins or Evensong. They were not specially interested in the Holy Communion which they went to at most on the first Sunday in each month, but which many of them attended only three times a year as the Prayer Book commanded.

Among the bishops, Charles Blomfield, Bishop of Chester from 1824 to 1828, and of London from 1828 to 1856, was typical of this type of churchman. To him the Prayer Book mattered above all else, and he ordered his clergy to obey every rubric, keeping daily services, the feasts and festivals of the Church, and doing exactly and precisely what was ordered. In his charge to the clergy of London in 1842 he approved of people bowing their heads whenever the name of Jesus occurred (was it not commanded by St Paul?); he allowed candles on the altar to be lit for Evensong (presumably to give light), and he ordered the clergyman to wear a surplice when preaching at Mattins, but only allowed a black gown at Evensong. On the other hand he condemned the placing of flowers on the Holy Table, mixing water with the wine in the chalice, beginning each service with the singing of a psalm or a hymn, and, of course, private confession, which he thought to be a wholly unnecessary and unProtestant performance. But, even so, his charge was thought to be wildly Roman in what it approved, and he was severely censured by the editor of *The Times* among other people. Nevertheless, he remained true to Anglicanism and the Prayer Book in what he said, and as such he was typical of many prominent churchmen of the time.

But there were two features which were added to people's worship, neither of which was mentioned in the Prayer Book for Mattins or Evensong – a sermon and the singing of hymns. Preaching had long been added to the morning service which included the saying of the ante-communion; but, as the latter adjunct to the service gradually fell away, so the addition of sermon and hymns was substituted.

The Sunday morning sermon was regarded by many Christians as the leading spiritual event of the week. It was discussed and commented upon at Sunday lunch, when all members of the family were expected to have listened intently, and to have brought away some message which would support them throughout the week. The preacher was, therefore, expected to give of his best. Many clergy started each Sunday evening to prepare their sermon for the following Sunday, and continued on it for most of the week. Most preachers took their task very seriously, checking biblical references, thinking out carefully their thesis, praying diligently about it, and finally writing their discourse out in full to be read from the pulpit when the time came.

Among the great Victorian preachers was F. W. Robertson of Brighton. Robertson, who was ordained in 1840, was, seven years later, appointed minister of a small, proprietory chapel in Brighton, known as Holy Trinity, where he died six years later. He was not a scientific theologian; he took the Bible as it was written; but he was able, in his preaching, to describe moments in the life of Christ, or in our human nature, which sank deep into people's minds. Preaching, for example, on sorrow and on the raising of Jairus's daughter, he said:

We are meant to sorrow; 'but not as those without hope'. The rule seems to consist in being natural. The great thing which Christ did was to call men back to simplicity and nature; not to perverted but original nature. He counted it no derogation of His manhood to be seen to weep. He thought it no shame to mingle with merry crowds. He opened his heart wide to all the genial and all the mournful impressions of this manifold life of ours. All this is what we have to do: be natural. Let God, that is, let the influences of God, freely play unthwarted upon the soul. Let there be no unnatural repression, no control of feeling by mere effort. Let there be no artificial and prolonged grief, no 'minstrels making a noise'. Let great Nature have her way.[43]

Such were the great preachers of the nineteenth century. It was Christ whom they wished to present to their people, Christ the Man, walking among men and women, living with them, entering into their joys and sorrows. Most of the sermons were on gospel texts, incidents from the life of Christ, interpreted to the modern listener. It was people in their problems and difficulties, their grief and enjoyment, that the preacher tried to help. In so doing he referred to the earthly life of Christ, the great exemplar and pattern for all human living. Sunday by Sunday the message was preached in a sermon lasting at least half an hour. It was this that kept people up to their ideals, that told them how they ought to live, that showed them, in the life of Christ, the perfect example of human life.

Hymn-singing was, for a long time, disliked by good churchmen, who thought of it as a Methodist and dissenting practice, and therefore unsuitable for a true Anglican congregation. Hymns introduced into worship a non-scriptural element, and could consequently contain material which was unorthodox or even heretical. The only things for people to sing were the Psalms, which were purely biblical and so preserved from error of any kind. For a good many years this was how things stood; but gradually hymns crept in, and after a few years they had completely won the field and had driven out the Psalms almost entirely, leaving only those which were of exceptional merit or were attached to tunes which people liked to sing. It was thus that hymns became a very real part of the Anglican spiritual tradition. People sang them in church, three or four at every service. They sang them at home, gathered round the piano on Sunday evenings. They loved the tunes rather than the words – for example, H. F. Lyte's 'Abide with me' includes the words 'Hold thou thy cross before my closing eyes', which very few middle-of-the-road Christians would ever think of saying, but did not in the least mind singing.

The creator of the modern church hymn book was Bishop

43 *Sermons*, second series (1883), pp. 37–8.

Heber who, in 1827, set out to provide a number of hymns to illustrate the Epistles and Gospels of the Prayer Book for the Church's year. This included sixty hymns of his own composition, and a number of ancient liturgical songs translated into English. This was followed in 1837 by Bishop Mant's *Ancient Hymns from the Roman Breviary for Domestic Use* and John Chandler's *Hymns of the Primitive Church* and, two years later, Isaac Williams's *Hymns translated from the Parisian Breviary*. Some years later, J. M. Neale produced his famous collection of Latin hymns which he called *A Hymnal Noted*. These hymns were acceptable to some people on the grounds of antiquity. They had long been sung by Christians who had found nothing unscriptural or unorthodox about their teaching. But even so, they were considered by most church people as foreign and unProtestant in origin, and they preferred Mrs Alexander's *Hymns for Little Children* (1848) or the great Lutheran chorales translated by Miss Winkworth in her *Lyra Germanica*, first published in 1855.

A vast number of hymn books were now in circulation and were regularly used in the service of the Church. Edward Bickersteth's *Christian Psalmody*, which came out in 1833, was one of the first, and W. J. Blew's *Church Hymn and Tune Book* followed it some twenty years later. By this time the number of hymn books was prodigious, some representing the theology of one set of people, and some of a very different class. Some of the hymns were exceptionally poor from the poetic point of view; but some, especially the translations of ancient hymns, were of a very high standard. So, in 1857, a meeting was called to discuss the publication of one book which would be used, not by every church, but by as many as possible. The committee, under the chairmanship of Sir Henry Baker, eventually produced a book, which appeared in 1860 and was called *Hymns Ancient and Modern*. The committee had deliberately chosen the best hymns, according to their judgement, from a wide range of sources: from the old Latin hymns, the best of English hymns from Watts onwards, hymns taken from Keble's *The Christian Year*, all provided with a good tune selected by William Henry Monk who himself suggested the very appropriate and attractive title of the collection. *Hymns Ancient and Modern* was supplemented by an Appendix in 1868 which increased the number of poems by 113 and by a supplement in 1889 which included a lot of hymns by Charles Wesley, the great hymn-writer of the eighteenth century.

Hymns Ancient and Modern soon became the standard hymn book for most church people. It was widely catholic in its tastes, drawing on any source which it thought proper. As such, it inspired an entirely new line in spiritual teaching. It included some of the great medieval hymns on the Eucharist, for example 'Thee we adore, O hidden Saviour, Thee' which was originally written by Thomas Aquinas in the thirteenth century but translated by Bishop Woodford and the compilers, with a plainsong melody and an alternative modern tune written by Orlando Gibbons in 1623. Another eucharistic hymn, 'O Food that weary pilgrims love', is said to have been written by a German Jesuit in the seventeenth century and was given an appropriate German tune written about 1819. But many of the hymns were modern. Newman's great poem, 'Lead, kindly light' and H. F. Lyte's 'Praise, my soul, the King of Heaven', William Bullock's 'We love the place, O God', and Isaac Watts's 'O God, our help in ages past', John Newton's 'How sweet the name of Jesus sounds' and J. B. Dykes's 'Nearer, my God, to thee' all became extremely popular, each representing something of the inner hopes and aspirations of countless worshippers.

These hymns all spoke to the soul rather than to the head. They were not meant to be theological treatises, but rather expressions of human feeling in the face of life and death, of suffering and joy, of praise and thanksgiving, and prayer offered to God from a heart overflowing with happiness. It is interesting to read that Robert Bickersteth, Bishop of Ripon from 1857 to 1884, arranged in his household that, after dinner on Sundays, everyone present was asked to repeat a hymn. These came from *The Christian Year*, from Mrs Alexander's *Hymns for Little Children*, from Lord Selborne's *Songs of Praise*, but mostly from *Hymns Ancient and Modern* and the *Hymnal Companion to the Book of Common Prayer*.[44] This shows the great love of hymns at this time, and also the fact that everyone present on such an occasion is presumed to know several hymns by heart.

But so far we have thought only of Morning and Evening Prayer and their adjuncts in the way of public worship. What of the Holy Communion? What did people think of this, the leading form of Christian worship, the only form of service

---

44 M. C. Bickersteth, *The Life and Episcopate of Robert Bickersteth* (1887), p. 129.

instituted by Christ himself, and ordered to be observed by all who called themselves his disciples? 'Do this', he said, 'in remembrance of me.'

Curiously enough, we hear very little about it in the nineteenth century. R. W. Evans gave a magnificent set of addresses to ordination candidates about 1841, which he called *The Bishopric of Souls*, in which he sets a very high standard for the young men whose job it will be 'to convert unto Christ and to establish in Christ' the souls who are to be committed to their care. 'You have fixed your position, and how gloriously, in the Church of God. You have determined your object which is the salvation of souls, and the maintenance of the honour and glory of God and our Saviour, Jesus Christ.'[45] Everything is in the highest possible order; yet, in the chapter on Sunday worship, although the men are encouraged to say the prayers with dignity and devotion, and to give much thought and care to the preparation of sermons and to their delivery, no mention whatever is made of the great sacrament of Holy Communion, which is completely ignored.

At that time, Holy Communion was held only three or four times a year, but, in the course of time, and largely through the work of the post-Tractarians, it came to be regarded as more important, though by no means essential to the Christian life. People of a devout turn of mind went to it once a month, generally staying on after Mattins on a Sunday morning in order to make their communion. This was celebrated by the priest standing at the north end of the Holy Table with no candles or flowers, and, of course, no vestments, though a coloured stole was gradually coming into use, so replacing the hood and scarf normally worn at all services. The service was thus thought of in terms of an unsung addition to the morning service, something to be indulged in occasionally, especially at Easter when the Prayer Book ordered it to be observed, but not otherwise taken very seriously. The post-Tractarians were, of course, making the Eucharist their chief service; but this was regarded by most church people as a Roman introduction, the weekly Mass, something to be objected to and to be repulsed by those who clung to the Book of Common Prayer as their only source-book and guide. So most members of the Church put all their interest

45   R. W. Evans, *The Bishopric of Souls* (1841), pp. 12, 308.

into Morning and Evening Prayer as the normal services which they attended Sunday by Sunday – the gentry in the morning and their servants in the evening.

The Bible was their main reading, and was taken in the most literal sense, as it had always been. Most church people believed that the world was made in six days, that the first two human beings were called Adam and Eve, that they sinned by disobedience to the dictates of God and were consequently cast out of the Garden of Eden, and shortly afterwards all, except Noah and his family, were drowned in the Great Flood which covered the whole of the earth. All this, and indeed everything told in the Bible, was taken to be literally true, as certain as what they read in their newspapers and history books. The great German discoveries about the way in which the Old Testament came to be written were of no interest to them whatever. Nor were the writings of English theologians in such books as *Essays and Reviews*, which was published in 1860 and caused something of a flutter in the academic field. If Benjamin Jowett, a don at Oxford, chose to say that one should read the Bible in the same way as one read any other book, or if Colenso, a bishop in South Africa, doubted the story of the Flood, then they had no right to utter such remarks and ought to be unfrocked. The Bible was people's stronghold, their infallible guide, and was in no way to be tampered with. So it was read, from cover to cover by the more devout, regularly and daily at family prayers by good church people, pondered over, and even worried over, by the more intellectual; but no one doubted its veracity.

The same thing applied to the scientific researches of men like Darwin and Huxley. Apart from a few interested persons, the majority of church people took little interest in their discoveries or in their theories. As for the fossils in the rocks, which were known to be of extreme antiquity, many people believed that God had put them there when he created the world.[46] Pusey was convinced that any critics of the Bible were essentially unbelievers, who were to be sternly refuted by all good Christians. H. P. Liddon, in his Bampton Lectures of 1866, made an attempt to prove 'that since Jesus believed Moses to be the author of the Pentateuch, or David to have

---

46 E.g. J. Keble; see J. Hunt, *Religious Thought in England in the 19th Century* (1896), p. 164. Philip Gosse believed the same (see Edmund Gosse, *Father and Son*).

written Psalm 110, or Jonah to have lived in the whale, therefore anyone who did not believe these three facts would convict his Lord of error, and therefore could not be a loyal Christian'; and it was pointed out that 'edition after edition showed how the public valued those lectures as the most cogent defence of traditional belief'.[47] There were, of course, some clever men at such places as Oxford and Cambridge who accepted them, but they were of little interest to the rank and file of the Church to whom the Bible was sacrosanct. It was the Word of God, dictated by the Holy Spirit, and could not therefore contain anything in the slightest degree erroneous.

Sunday was kept very strictly. The average churchman managed to conflate the Old Testament's Ten Commandments with the New Testament's account of the resurrection and of what St John called 'the Lord's day', and so turn Saturday into Sunday, the Sabbath Day. Sunday was therefore to be a day of rest. No one was allowed to work on that day except such people as domestic servants, who were obliged to cook the Sunday lunch and to clear up afterwards. But, for the majority of people, Sunday was a day on which work of any kind was strictly forbidden. No farmer would cut hay on a Sunday, even down to the twentieth century. No one would dream of sewing or knitting, or of playing any games on the Sabbath Day. Mrs Proudie tried to get the Archdeacon of Barchester to stop trains running on this day, though without much success. One of the chief duties of children was to learn by heart the collect for the day, a habit which was kept up for many years. As F. W. Robertson said:

> If we must choose between Puritan over-precision on the one hand, and on the other the laxity which, in many parts of the Continent, has marked the day from other days only by more riotous worldliness, and a more entire abandonment of the whole community to amusement, no Christian would hesitate; no English Christian at least; to whom that day is hallowed by all that is endearing in early associations, and who feels how much it is the very bulwark of his country's moral purity.[48]

The observance of Sunday as the modern Sabbath was, there-

47   O. Chadwick, *The Victorian Church*, ii (1970), p. 75.
48   F. W. Robertson, *Sermons preached at Brighton*, i (1893), p. 86.

fore, adopted and accepted as British and Protestant. No one who called himself a good Christian would dream of offending it.

The words of Robertson about the continental Sunday remind us of the fear of Rome which existed in the minds of most Anglicans at this time. Southey had gone so far as to call papistry 'a prodigious structure of imposition and wickedness',[49] and most people hated all that the Roman Church stood for. The Pope was Anti-Christ, that man of sin; confession was wicked, transubstantiation was a horrid thing. People were convinced that the Roman Catholics, by their 'invasion' of 1850, and by the coming over of countless Irish immigrants, threatened by famine in their own country and exploited by the English papists, had come over with the intention of undoing all the good work which had been done by the reformers and turning the country into a province of papal power. It was this fear which led to violent attacks on the post-Tractarian clergy, who were busy introducing Roman ritual and ceremonial into their churches, accompanied by much teaching of a Roman, and therefore non-British, kind. The catholicity of the Church of England meant nothing to them. The only church which they knew was their own parish church, or the church which they chose to attend. This was part of the Establishment, the purely English Church, supported by the Queen and Parliament, governed by the teaching of the English Prayer Book and the common law of the land. The rest was of no interest to them at all. 'They could not believe that the great interests of the world, of humanity, of Christianity, were bound up with such questions as episcopal succession, patristic tradition and sacramental grace.'[50] All that interested them was the great Protestant Reformation, of which they were part.

In this they showed a great enthusiasm and great keenness. Their religion meant everything to them. It governed their lives in every detail. The story of Bishop Benson's last hours with his son, Martin, at Winchester, is deeply religious in every sense of the word. They prayed together with the dying boy, he was given Holy Communion, they repeated hymns, the boy actually pointed to someone standing in the room which is thought to be Christ; all this, and the father's sub-

49 J. Hunt, op. cit., pp. 80–1.
50 J. Hunt, op. cit., p. 175.

sequent behaviour, shows the depth of their religion.[51] So it was with many devout Anglicans, as we can see from reading their lives and their letters. Religion was the very basis of their lives and governed all their thoughts.

It was, in theological terms, the religion of the incarnation rather than of the atonement. What men studied was the Word made Flesh, the natural man in Christ of Nazareth. It was to this that they turned in reading the Gospels, and it was this that lay at the heart of all their thought. They were men full of hope. They thought they could see the world getting better all the time, as more and more people came to love the Lord Jesus. The Christian socialists, the missionaries at home and abroad, and the do-gooders of every kind, thought that they were making the world the sort of place in which Christ could dwell. The old ideas of people's sins and forgiveness were gradually being laid aside and overgrown by this conviction. It has been pointed out that none of the famous hymns celebrating the passion and the resurrection were written after 1862.[52] By that time people were interested in the birth stories, in Christmas, which became by far the most important feast in the Church's year. Christmas hymns and carols abounded, the Christmas tree, and all the accompaniments of Christmas with its presents, its feasting, its good cheer, became a national festival, far more interesting to people than Good Friday and Easter, which were largely forgotten.

English Protestant religion, founded on the Prayer Book and overruled by the Establishment, with its sermons and hymns added, was the very backbone of the country, the expression of its most profound spirituality. Nothing else was needed. Let the high-churchmen have their Roman services, their vestments and incense, their rosaries and processions; they were foreign things, of no interest to the devout Christians who attended their Sunday Mattins, heard their Sunday sermon and sang their Sunday hymns. This was the root of Victorian religion.

---

51   David Newsome, *Godliness and Good Learning* (1961), pp. 187–8.
52   O. Chadwick, *The Victorian Church*, ii (1970), p. 469.

6

THE CHURCH WE KNOW

The Optimists

The last years of the nineteenth century and the opening of the twentieth was a time of great optimism. In spite of the fact that Hort had written to Benson in 1882 of 'the calm and unobtrusive alienation in thought and spirit from the great silent multitude of Englishmen'[1] people saw a great time coming, especially in England, so that, in 1891, Bishop Light-foot could write that 'the position of the English Church, standing midway between extremes in theological teaching and ecclesiastical order, points to the Church of this nation with the very finger of God Himself, as called by Him to the lofty task of reconciling a distracted Christendom and healing the wounds of the nations'.[2] Everything was of the best. The Church was in a strong position in the land, led by powerful men who counted for a lot in the life of the country and whose words were taken seriously by statesmen, businessmen, many of the intellectuals and the general public. They did not all go to church, or say their prayers, or read their Bibles. But they all looked up to the Church as a moral influence in the country and throughout the world.

In the last two decades of the nineteenth century the Church had been led by Archbishop Benson of Canterbury, perhaps no great intellectual, but a real man of God who put before people's eyes the great truths of Christianity and of the Christian way of life. Creighton, of Peterborough and then of London, and Stubbs of Chester and then of Oxford, were historians of the first rank whose books were widely read; and Lightfoot and Westcott, both bishops of Durham, were great theologians as well as men of considerable holiness of life.

1 A. T. P. Williams, *The Anglican Tradition in the Life of England* (1947), p. 111.
2 *Sermons on Special Occasions* (1891), p. 117.

Perhaps the most saintly of all the bishops was Edward King, of Lincoln, who could write to a friend:

> I am sure we must be full of hope – brave, self-sacrificing, victorious hope. To me, thank God, all these troubles of the intellect, and all our ecclesiastical and social anxieties, are full of hope. They are but, I believe, the pain and labour which will issue in the birth of more truth, more true liberty, more true union between man and nature, and man and God, a bringing us in all things near to Him.[3]

Hope – this was what filled the minds of all thoughtful people. The thought of progress was in the air, in the country, in industry, in life, knowledge and power. Everything was getting better. Even in religion people were turning hopefully towards an increase in spiritual consciousness, so that the Lambeth Conference in 1908 could declare triumphantly that 'men's minds are more and more set towards the spiritual'.[4] The bishops had little idea what was coming on the earth in the next few years.

As far as religion in England was concerned, the general standard was mainly Protestant. Every man made his own choice as to what he ought to do. Freedom was the great thing; and freedom in religion meant that there was no earthly authority which could guide one aright. The Bible was a person's guide-book, enhanced by the Sunday sermon. Otherwise people thought things out for themselves. The Church, as an authority to tell one what was right and wrong, meant nothing to them. 'What the Church says' was a Romish doctrine, completely unEnglish and unProtestant. Romanism was a foreign creed, unworthy of English people, introduced into England mostly for the sake of a handful of recusants, a whole lot of Irish immigrants, and a few converts. If the Pope was no longer to be called Anti-Christ, he was totally ignored, especially after his goings-on in 1870. He and his infallible statements meant nothing to most English people. Religion was a personal matter between the individual and God. People could believe what they liked, go to church when they liked, and do what they thought was right.

The common religion was, therefore, strongly individual and ultimately moral. It was really a question of living a

3   E. King, *Spiritual Letters* (1910), p. 33.
4   R. T. Davidson, *Five Lambeth Conferences* (1908), p. 302.

'godly, righteous and sober life', abstaining from the grosser sins, giving money to good causes, and treating Jesus as what Sir John Seeley called 'a moralist speaking with authority and perpetuating his doctrine by means of a Society'.[5] The religion of the average person was Pelagian. People did not think much about divine grace to help them on their journey. This made them unsacramental. Holy Communion, the drug of immortality, meant little to them. They might occasionally stay behind, after Mattins and the exclusion of the choir, to make their communion with a handful of other worshippers, or get up early on Sunday morning to go to an 8 o'clock celebration of the Holy Mysteries, but this was exceptional, not part of their regular spiritual life.

So much for the ordinary person. But the Catholic revival was now in full swing, and those who supported it were gradually winning their way. In many churches things which would have seemed impossible a few years ago were now becoming quite normal and common. The whole appearance of the parish church had begun to undergo a complete change. The altar was made to look like one, decorated with a coloured frontal and bearing on it a cross, candles and flowers. The celebrant wore a coloured stole or even eucharistic vestments. Some churches went much further. Incense was now used, the rosary and the Ave Maria were said, the Holy Sacrament was reserved for devotional purposes and the service of benediction was conducted at the close of Evensong. Purgatory was now taught, and the invocation of saints practised. Above all, confession was now becoming a regular thing. Bishop King had a good deal to say about it in his *Spiritual Letters*. Writing to a friend in 1874 he said, with regard to confession: 'I can only repeat the Church's advice, try and get on without it; if you can't, use it', but in 1883 he wrote to a priest: 'For myself, I go three or four times a year, not more, and I should have recommended you, therefore, something of the same kind.'[6] In either case it was coming to be regarded by the high-churchmen as a natural thing.

In their churches the Holy Communion, now called High Mass, had become the chief service of the week. Often the churches were crowded with devout worshippers, who genu-

---

5 In *Ecce Homo*, quoted by C. Gore, *The Philosophy of the Good Life* (1930), p. 174.

6 E. King, *Spiritual Letters*, pp. 104, 144.

flected, crossed themselves, bowed at the name of Jesus, knelt for a blessing if a bishop happened to be present and passed them in the church. This was not a communicating service. There were generally no communicants allowed. It was the offering by the Church of the Sacrifice of Christ on the altar. All Roman ceremonial was carried out, the servers properly robed and attending upon the priest, who wore what were called 'fiddle-back' vestments and a biretta. Preferably he was supported by two other priests to act as deacon and subdeacon. Except for the fact that the Mass was said, from the English Missal, in the language of the people, the Anglican Mass was indistinguishable from the Roman.

The priest often accepted the old medieval, pre-Reformation ideas of priesthood in their entirety, but Robert Moberly, in his book, *Ministerial Priesthood*, which came out in 1897, did much to teach Anglicans the true nature of the office. Moberly pointed out that, in the Middle Ages, the priesthood was regarded as purely mechanical and the sacraments material. But the Anglican reformers fought against this, and also against what he called 'the fierce tide of Protestantism', to produce the right result, which lay at the heart of all true thinking both about the priesthood and about the Church. Moberly wrote:

> Now the Person of Christ does not pass away from the Church. The Church is the Body of Christ. The Spirit of Christ is the Breath of Life of the Church. Whatever Christ is the Church is; as reflecting, nay in a real sense even as being, Himself. If we want to see in what the priesthood of the Church consists, or what the word priesthood ultimately means, we must examine first what it means in the Person of Christ.[7]

Later on he says:

> The ordained priests are priestly only because it is the Church's prerogative to be priestly; and because they are, by ordination, specialised and empowered to exercise ministerially and organically the prerogatives which are the prerogatives of the body as a whole. They have no greater right in the Sacraments than the laity; only they, and not the laity, have been authorised to stand before the congre-

7   R. Moberly, *Ministerial Priesthood* (1897), p. 244.

gation, and to represent the congregation in the ministerial
enactment of the Sacraments which are the Sacraments –
and the life – of both alike.[8]

The priest is the man who cares for his flock, who bears
the sin and pain of the world, who sacrifices himself at all
times for the sake of the Church of God.

To those who governed the flock, who watched for souls,
and taught them and fed them, and should 'give account'
for them, was not the Eucharistic offering an element, and
if an element, then of inherent necessity the culminating
element . . . the all dominating, all inclusive element, in
their official prerogative?[9]

And he sums up his argument with these words:

I cannot withhold my conviction that the Anglican Ordinal
has gained something far more vital and substantial than
anything it can be supposed to have lost; it has restored,
in the main, what had been gradually lost in the accretions
of the medieval Ordinal, the true *proportion* between the
outward and the inward, it has restored the essential harmony between Eucharistic Leadership – with all that it
involves – and a right conception in Christ's Church of the
meaning of ministerial priesthood as a whole.[10]

This, then, emphasized the true meaning of priesthood in the
Church. It was, as Moberly said, perfectly clear, from the
New Testament and from the history of the early Church,
that the priest was essential to the life of the Church; but not
just as a kind of performer to do something almost magical,
but as the acknowledged leader of the flock of Christ and the
appointed celebrator of the Eucharist as the very centre of
their spiritual life.

There were many priests in the Anglo-Catholic party who
accepted this attitude towards the priesthood. They were men
who were devoted to the service of the flock of Christ, with
a real love for human souls. Many of them gave the whole of
their lives to working in the slums of our great cities, among
the poor and degraded, bringing to them some idea of the
glory of God and of all his works. They said Mass daily,

8   Ibid., p. 258.
9   Ibid., p. 267.
10 Ibid., p. 289.

praying earnestly for the living and the dead, and God was never far from their thoughts. Bishop King urged on ordination candidates to begin each day by saying the *Veni Creator*, and to set aside half an hour daily for meditative reading, working through the *Memoriale Vitae Sacerdotalis* or some other devotional work.[11]

But it was not only the clergy who were caught up by this ideal. A large number of the laity were also deeply religious, in a catholic way. They went to a daily Eucharist, they prayed long hours, they read rich devotional works, whether by Anglicans or Roman Catholics, they worked among the poor, they gave to good causes. Their lives were truly dedicated to serve God and people. Perhaps nothing gives a better picture of the true Anglo-Catholic layman at prayer than the picture of old Lord Halifax, receiving the Blessed Sacrament in his home chapel. His vicar wrote:

> I do not think that where possible he ever missed assisting at daily Mass. The picture rises up before me of many an early Mass in that rather dark, private chapel at Hickleton which he loved so well. I always found that, however early I went to the chapel to say my preparation before Mass, there was always kneeling in the front row of seats on the right, and wrapped in the French cloak which he always wore, quite still, and almost invisible, the venerable figure of Lord Halifax. Perhaps there was the light of a pocket torch if he was using a book; otherwise only the gleam of the white hair of the bowed head. There was an intensity about him and the sense of entire recollection when he was praying (it was always easy to be recollected oneself if he was there): he made no movement and was utterly absorbed. During Mass he made the responses quietly but audibly; he received the Holy Communion with deep devotion, and, returning to his prayer desk, knelt again and remained quite still. I have known him not to leave the chapel for his frugal breakfast for two hours after he had received our Divine Lord.[12]

This was, perhaps, not typical. Not everyone could give up the time for such devotion. But it is the picture of a devout old man who had given his life to Christ and his Church, and

11 *Spiritual Letters*, p. 78.
12 R. Lloyd, *The Church of England in the Twentieth Century*, i (1946), p. 134.

it shows what the Catholic revival was doing for quite ordinary people.

This was still very much the age of the sermon. Preachers of all kinds thundered forth from the pulpits of the churches, proclaiming the gospel and its teaching to crowds of devout listeners. The Sunday sermon was still regarded as a serious matter, and laymen such as Sir Michael Sadler, when Vice-Chancellor of Leeds University, attended Morning Prayer at Leeds Parish Church, Sunday by Sunday, and made careful notes of what was preached even by the youngest curate. Sermons were preached in town and country churches, in cathedrals, in school and college chapels. Farrer, Dean of Canterbury, published no less than ten volumes of sermons. C. J. Vaughan, Dean of Llandaff, produced such books as *Heroes of Faith*; *Life's Work and God's Discipline*; and *Restful Thoughts in Restless Times*. H. P. Liddon's sermons at St Paul's and elsewhere, drew vast congregations and were duly printed afterwards.

> Not to be devout [he said] is not to be believing: devotion is the common sense of faith. If I see the living God – so powerful, so wise, so loving, so magnificent – I naturally speak to Him; not only because I know that He can hear me and that He will help me, but because He is there, and to speak with Him is at once the highest privilege and the best and purest instinct of my humanity.[13]

So much for prayer. Preaching at the consecration of a bishop, he said:

> For, after all, why is it that we do take Orders? Is it not because we believe and are sure that eighteen centuries ago an event occurred, compared with which all that has happened since, all that can happen in this eventful day – happen what may – is utterly insignificant? Is it not because, like St Paul at Ephesus, we believe that the Everlasting Son of God really entered into conditions of space and time, and died upon the cross for the sins of all men, and rose from the grave, and ascended, and has been pleading for us all ever since, and is doing so at this moment, and has sent us His Holy Spirit, and given us His Sacraments?[14]

13   H. P. Liddon, *Sermons on Some Words of Christ* (1895), p. 75.
14   H. P. Liddon, *Clerical Life and Work* (1894), pp. 244–5.

Meanwhile, in the USA, Phillips Brooks was preaching to vast crowds of attendant listeners and published a series of volumes of sermons. All of it is good stuff, for example this on 'The Spiritual Man':

> Spirituality is God. To be spiritual is to be in communion, in communication with God, who is the Source and Father of all spirits. When we say that every man has in him a true spiritual element, what we really mean is that every man is a child of God. The awakening of the spiritual element in any man is just his coming to know, and acting on the knowledge, that he is the child of God.[15]

He took his preaching so seriously that he wrote a delightful treatise on the art of preaching. This, called *Eight Lectures on Preaching*,[16] sets forth all that is best in the art of sermon-production. He describes the preacher with all the qualities of the true man of God – personal conviction and piety, mental and spiritual unselfishness, hopefulness, enthusiasm; 'full of the love of Christ, taking all truth and blessing as a trust, in the best sense *didactic*, hopeful, healthy . . . and going to his preaching with the enthusiasm that shows it is what God *made him for*'. The central theme is the human soul, its value to God, its need of salvation, and then the responsibility of the priest as pastor and teacher and guide. He thus brings us very near to Christ, the Good Shepherd, the lover of the souls of men and women, who longs to seek and to save that which is lost.

All these books of sermons were meant to be read, and crowds of the clergy bought them, read them, profited by them, and probably brought out the ideas in their own sermons. But the laity must also have acquired them, especially women who had long hours to fill in and who found this preaching very satisfying.

There was also a vast turnout of religious books to supply the needs of Anglicans everywhere. There were books on the Prayer Book, on the Holy Communion, on the Catechism, on the Thirty-nine Articles, and on the history of the Church, especially of the Church of England. There were books of devotion, for example R. M. Benson's *The Final Passover: A Series of Meditations upon the Passion of our Lord Jesus Christ*;

---

15 Phillips Brooks, *The Law of Growth* (1902), p. 300.
16 Published in 1881, with a new edition set out by J. R. H. Moorman in 1959.

books which dealt with doubts and uncertainties, like J. W. Diggle's *Religious Doubt: Its Nature, Treatment, Causes, Difficulties, Consequences and Dissolution*; and books intended for the clergy such as W. C. E. Newbolt's *Speculum Sacerdotum, or the Divine Model of the Priestly Life*. There were studies of the mystics, for example Ralph Inge's lectures on *Christian Mysticism* and his later books on the English mystics. People were now reading the works of medieval mystical writers, St Bernard, Ruysbroeck, St John of the Cross and St Teresa, and of course *The Imitation of Christ*. They also became greatly interested in the English mystics, Julian of Norwich, Walter Hilton, Richard Rolle and the author of *The Cloud of Unknowing*. Meanwhile, a new mystical writer of the Anglican tradition was discovered in 1895 when the poems and, later, the prose writings of Thomas Traherne were brought to the knowledge of readers who found great comfort in the *Centuries of Meditation*.

Henry Scott Holland was the writer of many books of a spiritual nature. 'Christianity', he wrote, 'has its home in the inner mysteries of the spiritual life, in the unseen struggles and aspirations of the soul.'[17] He was a thoroughgoing incarnationalist, as were also the other writers of *Lux Mundi* which was described as 'A Series of Studies in the Religion of the Incarnation'. Moberly says that the great question which everyone must answer is, 'Whom say ye that I am?',[18] and the personal intimacy of the believer with God in Christ becomes our chief concern. Charles Gore's Bampton Lectures of 1891, called *The Incarnation of the Son of God*, are full of appeals to his hearers to 'choose to be Christians'; it was no use depending on mere tradition and respectability. Christianity was fast becoming a very serious matter which people either accepted or denied. There was no other way. 'If you will be His disciple,' Gore wrote,

He will enrich your life, He will purge it of its pollution, He will conquer your lusts, He will enlighten your mind, He will deepen in you all that is generous and rich and brotherly and true and just. He will make your life worth having, yea, increasingly worth having, as you gain in experience of His power and His love even to the end. Only do not make the fatal mistake of imagining that your

17 *A Lent in London* (1895), p. 1.
18 *Lux Mundi* (1889), p. 179.

life is Christian anyhow, or that it can be Christian by any other process than by your deliberate and courageous acceptance of the law of Christ, because you desire to be His disciple.[19]

We have already mentioned hymns as providing people with their theology and spirituality. They were sung at most services in the churches and in the homes of the worshippers. Many people's ideas of God, his nature, his majesty, his will for mankind, came, not so much from sermons and books, but from the singing of hymns. *Hymns Ancient and Modern*, and, to a lesser degree, other church hymnals, were deeply loved.

But by 1903 the idea was raised of publishing a new hymn book to cut out sentimentality (of which *Hymns Ancient and Modern* contained a good deal), and to include more old hymns and a number of modern ones which were now being written. This was called the *English Hymnal*. Published in 1906, it was considerably more 'churchy', intellectual, sophisticated than anything which had gone before. A number of old hymns were included such as 'He who would valiant be' by John Bunyan; 'Dear Lord and Father of mankind' by J. G. Whittier, and Christina Rossetti's beautiful poems 'In the bleak midwinter' and 'What are these that glow from afar?' It also had no less than thirteen hymns from the *Yattendon Hymnal*, most of them translations by Robert Bridges of old Christian hymns, but a number of new poems including 'Rejoice, O land, in God thy might'. The book assured its modestly Anglo-Catholic origins by including a lot of ancient Latin hymns, office-hymns, nearly a hundred provided with plain-song music, and introits and anthems for Festivals and Saints' Days which were printed in prose with Grails, Alleluias, Tracts, Offertories and Communion suitable for use at a Sung Mass. The musical editor was Ralph Vaughan-Williams, who cleared out a good deal of rather sentimental music from the old books, and put in nearly fifty traditional English melodies, which were then very much the rage. It also contained a number of litanies, one, called 'The Story of the Cross', running into no less than twenty-four verses and ending with the saying of the three Good Friday collects.

The book was undoubtedly on the high-church side, appealing to the crowds who attended the Sunday Mass in

19   C. Gore, *Bampton Lectures* (1891), p. 215.

churches of this nature, where they would sing the plainsong and the old Latin hymns. Some of the hymns contained teaching which was not acceptable to modern ears, especially the invocation of saints, which caused the book to be condemned by Archbishop Davidson and even by Charles Gore, then Bishop of Birmingham. What they most disliked was, for example:

O Saviour, Jesu, not alone
We plead for help before thy throne:
Thy Mother's love shall aid our prayer
To win for us that healing care

a translation, by T. A. Lacey, of an old ninth-century Latin hymn. But many churches came to use the book, delighting to sing such hymns as 'Ye watchers and ye holy ones' in spite of the verse which says:

O higher than the Cherubim,
More glorious than the Seraphim,
    Lead their praises, Alleluya!
Thou Bearer of the eternal Word
Most gracious, magnify the Lord,
    Alleluya

though many of them, no doubt, thought that the fourth line referred to pious Evangelicals spreading the word of the Bible in foreign lands.

The Bible remained the book most read by devout church people, who read it quite without criticism, or even being aware of the modern approach to the Scriptures. The Revised Version had been produced, the New Testament in 1881 and the Old Testament three years later, attempting 'to introduce as few alterations as possible into the text of the Authorised Version consistently with faithfulness'. But the Revised Version was essentially the student's Bible, used by theologians in their studies, but unknown to the average English reader who clung to the older version. This was the Bible given to children, used in schools, read in the church service, whole passages being learnt by heart.

Most people kept scientific knowledge and knowledge derived from the Bible in separate compartments. They knew perfectly well that the world was not created, just as it now is, in six days, each of twenty-four hours. They knew that it was not inhabited by only two people, Adam and Eve, from whom everyone is descended. But this sort of thing did not, in the least, put them off their Bible-reading. They read it thoroughly and totally unscientifically. They quoted from it, generally completely out of context, to support their theories. Preachers took from the Authorised Version their texts and their references. The reading of the Bible, a portion every day, was a part of everyone's spiritual life, greatly enhanced by printed cards and later by the work of the Bible Reading Fellowship.

On the other hand, there was great fear among the more intelligent readers that the scientists and Bible critics had undermined the Scriptures and made it impossible to accept the old idea of inspiration and especially the truth of the Old Testament. Charles Gore, in *Lux Mundi*, dealt with this. He started by pointing out that Christianity was 'not a past event, but a present life, a life first manifested in Christ and then perpetuated in His Church'; and, with his insistence on the Church as the great central fact of all our religious belief and practice, he said that 'the Christian Church is the scene of the intensest, the most vigorous, the richest, the most "abundant" life that the universe knows, because in a pre-eminent sense it is the "Spirit-bearing body" '.[20] He then goes on to discuss the Old Testament, especially the Book of Genesis and the history of man's creation and fall. Here lay a real problem for those who accepted the literal inspiration of the Bible, and yet were puzzled by the work of the scientists. What was the intelligent reader to think? What really happened in those far-off years? If one thought the account of creation was false, what happened to the rest of the Bible and the sense of inspiration which was thought to run all through it?

Gore wrote:

Everything as we see it was made by God; that it has no being in itself but at God's will; on the other hand that everything is in its essence good, as the product of the good God: that man, besides sharing the physical nature of all creation, has a special relation to God, as made in God's image, to be God's vice-gerent: that sin, and all that it brings with it of misery and death, came not of man's nature but of his disobedience to God and rejection of the

20   *Lux Mundi*, 15th edn, (1921), p. 231.

limitations under which He put him: that in spite of all that sin brought about, God has not left man to himself, that there is a hope and a promise. These are the fundamental principles of true religion and progressive morality, and in these lies the supernatural inspiration of the Bible account of creation.[21]

This caused much distress to the devout readers of Genesis, but Gore encouraged them as much as he could. 'Critical positions', he wrote in the following year in his Preface to the tenth edition, 'are in fact compatible with the real inspiration of Holy Scripture',[22] and he had pointed out that Clement of Alexandria and Anselm of Canterbury had both treated the seven-day account of creation as allegory and not as history. But this did not satisfy older and more traditional readers, who were not really interested in what these ancient Fathers thought, but still claimed that the Bible was literally true and must be read as such. To do otherwise was to open the floodgates of disbelief, to turn the whole of the Bible into allegory, drama or myth, and to make our Lord appear false in his teaching. This was what they dreaded most, and many of them found Gore's statements unacceptable. *Lux Mundi* was regarded as a dangerous book, though it rapidly ran into fifteen editions, and was accepted by many as a firm and wise statement of what came to be regarded as the Anglo-Catholic point of view of religion and its belief in the Trinity, the Bible, the sacraments and Christian ethics.

In 1868, three years after R. M. Benson opened the first religious house for men at Cowley, Westcott preached his famous sermon at Harrow School on asceticism. He had himself been interested in the religious life since 1846, when he wrote in his diary at the age of twenty: 'How shall I account for a sudden and strange feeling with which I am filled that I ought to retire to a monastery and live in entire seclusion?'[23] Twenty-two years later he preached to the boys of Harrow showing them how, at the crisis of Christian history, different types of the ascetic life have appeared – Anthony of Egypt, Benedict, Francis of Assisi and Ignatius Loyola. Was it, he asked, time for the Church of today to revive this form of life; and he appealed to each of his hearers 'to listen humbly for

21 Ibid., p. 252.
22 Ibid., p. xiii.
23 Quoted by A. M. Allchin, *The Silent Rebellion* (1958), p. 220.

the promptings of God's spirit, if so be that He is even now calling him to take a foremost part in it'.[24] Charles Gore, then aged fifteen, was one of the boys who heard it.

We have already shown how the religious life became again part of the Anglican tradition;[25] and in the latter years of the nineteenth century houses first for women and then for men came into existence. Gradually they came to be accepted, though the question of perpetual vows was slow in coming to be recognized. People accepted the fact that vows could be made to a bishop, as these could be revoked by him if the person eventually found the life unsatisfactory. But vows to God were different, as binding in perpetuity. So the battle of indispensable vows, both for men and for women, was fought out in the last years of the century, to be finally won by those who were beginning to see what the religious life really meant in devotion to our Lord, in the daily round of prayer and meditation, in the offering of oneself, body and soul to God, to be used by him as he would think best. There could be no going back from this. Men were accustomed to take perpetual vows at their ordination; why should they not take similar vows at the time of their profession? Women took no vows of ordination, but why should they not consecrate their lives to God's service in a religious community? As Father Benson wrote at the time: 'All else is accidental. It is the contemplation of life gazing up to God, and doing battle with Satan, which is the essential characteristic of all Christian life.'[26]

So the communities flourished, receiving episcopal approval all the time. Sisterhoods were now common, and by 1900 there were thirteen of them in London alone. Most of them, like the Grey Ladies, were engaged in good works, while the men took part in parochial missions and stirred people up to a deeper Christian life. Even the nonconformists were now founding sisterhoods, especially the Salvation Army whose female members were put into Goodwill Centres, under a strict rule, though without vows, where much good work was done for the poor and distressed, of whom there were still vast crowds in the slums of London and all big cities. For men, the Community of the Resurrection was founded at Mirfield in 1892; the Society of the Sacred Mission at Kelham

24 Ibid., p. 222.
25 See above, p. 167.
26 *Followers of the Lamb* (1900), p. 8.

in 1894; the Society of the Divine Compassion, which had obvious Franciscan connections, in the same year; and Nashdom, the sole English Benedictine community, later in 1914. Meanwhile, at West Malling, an enclosed and contemplative house of nuns was set up. These, unlike all other communities, did no practical work, the sisters remaining apart, isolated from the world, celebrating the Divine Office daily in the choir, and otherwise spending their time in meditation and private prayer.

So, after more than 300 years, the religious life was restored in the English Church, and Father Congreve could write:[27]

> Our special joy is the recovery of a treasure that was supposed lost to us for ever. Here is a power of the life of Christ rediscovered among us, a long-forgotten force breaking out to our surprise in the Church. It is an encouragement to find by experience that God can do, and is doing for us still, what no one expected, or what was supposed quite impossible. In our childhood, who are old, the idea that Houses of men and women living religiously under monastic rule might ever again come to be in the English Church was quite unthinkable. Today they exist; their number is considerable, and their work and character acknowledged.

The Modern Church

The optimism of the years 1880 onwards was shattered on 4 August 1914, when England entered into the first of two major wars which rocked the country, killed off thousands of people, and altered the way of living which had survived for centuries. The first war made a great difference to the religious life of the people. Many lost their faith, or at least their churchgoing. They were bothered about God: 'Why did he allow this dreadful war to happen?' 'Why did he let my son be killed?' 'Why did he not strike the Germans as he had struck the Philistines in Old Testament days?' Meanwhile, at the front, the chaplains were finding themselves faced with enormous difficulties. The men were not interested in what they had to tell them. Their only interest was to survive and get back to their homes again. They were not impressed by

27   A. M. Allchin, op. cit., p. 231.

Winnington-Ingram's appeals to men to join in this great and noble struggle, the war of the good against the evil, the just war, the war to end war. They were not winning for themselves the martyr's crown, just a dirty death in the mud of Flanders. Services were held in the trenches and behind the lines, and a few men turned up. But indifference to religious things was the common approach of the fighting men who asked what God had to do with what they were suffering. Meanwhile, back at home, people were drifting away from the churches. They had other things to do on a Sunday morning. The Mattins parade began to look insignificant. Most of the clergy had little or no message to give them, and if they wanted to say their prayers they could do that perfectly well at home.

The second war was less destructive of religious habits, partly because there were so many fewer people who had formed any such habits, and, if they had, they went a good deal deeper than they had previously done. There was, by 1939, much less formal religion than there had been in 1914. The Church of England, though still the recognized religion of the State, to be called upon to fulfil great functions, had become more of a sect. But what the Church had lost in quantity it had made up in quality. Those who did go to church, say their prayers and read the Bible, did so with greater enthusiasm. There was now no prestige in going to church, but those who did go went out of a real desire to worship God, mainly in the sacramental life of the community. Among the more evangelical party, the Bible was read frequently. It was thought to contain everything that they needed, and to answer all their problems. The second war therefore affected the Church a good deal less than the first had done. There was, in fact, a good deal less to kill off, though it was some time before the leaders of the Church realized this.

With the two wars went a social revolution which affected the lives of most of the population. Before the first war the country was very much divided into two sections – those who had enough money to have domestic servants, go for holidays abroad, send their sons to expensive boarding schools; and 'the poor' who formed the vast majority of the population. They lived quite apart from the rest; their holidays consisted of a week at the seaside (if they could afford even that), they read no books, pawned their possessions to raise enough money to keep them going until pay-day, bought second-hand clothes, ate only the cheapest food which they could buy. But in recent times all that has changed. Though there are still some comparatively poor people, 'the poor', as a class, have more or less disappeared in the western world. They now have good wages, better and cleaner houses, furniture and clothes; they go abroad for their holidays, their womenfolk dress well and have their hair attended to every week.

How then has this social revolution affected the religious lives of the people? Arnold Bennett wrote in 1929 that 'the intelligentsia is, for the time being, godless; and as for religion the affair is over and done with'. But he was wrong. Fifty years later religion still means a great deal to some people. The Church congregations are, in fact, now steady. The numbers of men being ordained are going up, and quite a surprising number of adults are now coming forward for confirmation. Discussion on religious topics is common. People go to retreats to learn more about God. There are still many who snipe at religion, and a lot who are totally indifferent and uninterested; but there is a strong nucleus of devoted people to whom religion is the breath of life. But this is a recent development. For most of the time religion has been in the doldrums, but the Church now consists of a few devotees who attend regularly (mostly for Holy Communion), who pray and read their Bibles, and who love God and try to follow in the footsteps of his Son, Jesus Christ. The leaders of the Church have scarcely recognized the immense falling away of so many. In 1929 the Archbishops of Canterbury and York issued a Pastoral Letter in which they hoped for a renewal of church life. 'We are convinced', they said, 'that under the guidance of the Holy Spirit it may come if the whole Church will set its thought and prayer towards gaining a deeper and fuller appreciation of God, of his self-revelation in Christ, and the wonder and glory of the eternal gospel of his love and grace.'[28] Again, in 1948, after the Second World War had completed its course, the bishops of the Lambeth Conference could optimistically say: 'For those who have eyes to see there are signs that the tide of faith is beginning to come in.'

Meanwhile, instead of religion, there was a strong feeling

28 R. Lloyd, *The Church of England in the Twentieth Century*, ii (1950), p. 160.

in favour of goodness, or moral righteousness, among the people. Many people wanted to do what was right, though unaware of the grace which this needs. They specially wanted their children to grow up as good people. Religion is still taught in the schools (the only subject which has to be taught by statute), but it does not have much effect on the behaviour of many of the young. Crime figures have gone up enormously, mainly among young people, and the prisons are crowded. But this affects only a small minority. Among most people the good life is still held in honour. Even the non-religious, who would never dream of going to church or saying their prayers, care a good deal about honesty, truth, living good lives, even taking care of others. Appeals are always answered, not only by religious people. There is, in the world, a strong sense of the need to live according to a fairly high standard of behaviour, though without God.

Anglican religion is still bound to the Prayer Book, and the Bible. The Book of Common Prayer, after having been used regularly for 300 years, underwent a number of alterations in 1927–8. The Liturgical Commission had been at work for many years, since the time of the trials and persecutions of the last century. People came to see that, in the words of the Public Worship Regulation Act of 1904, 'the law of public worship in the Church of England is too narrow for the religious life of the present generation'. Something had to be done to meet the needs of the members of the Anglo-Catholic party, who had gone far beyond anything which the Church desired, and were law-breakers in a big way with their rosaries and incense, their English Missal and devotions, and all the Roman ritual and ceremonial which had crept in during the years. Eventually, in 1927, a Revised Prayer Book was brought out in the hope of finding a good ground for a general standard of worship which would be respected by all men and women. 'As men think upon God's wonderful works unveiled before them', said the Preface, 'and are quickened afresh by the power of his spirit, their hearts and minds frame for themselves new prayers and thanksgivings and seek new occasions for worship.' The new book altered some of the Occasional Offices slightly, brought in a service for the burial of a child, added a number of prayers and thanksgivings (including one for the British Empire and another for the League of Nations), but more or less let Mattins and Evensong stand as they had always stood. The chief bone of contention lay, as was to be expected, in the changes brought about in the communion service when prayers for the dead were introduced ('beseeching thee to grant them everlasting life and peace'), and an *epiclesis*, or prayer that the Holy Spirit, after the words of consecration, might 'bless and sanctify both us and these thy gifts of Bread and Wine that they may be unto us the Body and Blood of thy Son, our Saviour, Jesus Christ', which, though used in Orthodox liturgies, were no part of the Western tradition as expressed in the Roman Missal. This new Prayer Book had to be passed by Parliament in order to make it legal; but here it met its chief adversaries, mostly of the evangelical wing, who threw it out in 1927 and again, after a few alterations, in 1928. The extraordinary thing is that the new Prayer Book was used by the clergy, who entirely overlooked the illegality of what they were doing. So also did Parliament, who lost interest in the whole idea of revision. Then, in 1980, an entirely new Prayer Book was issued. This brought the language up to date, used 'you' instead of 'thou' throughout, introduced no less than six eucharistic prayers, nearly 600 pages of Sentences, Collects and Readings and a new version of the Psalms, making a total of nearly 1300 pages, rather more than twice the length of the Prayer Book of 1662. This Alternative Service Book, as its name implies, was meant to be used alongside the old Book of Common Prayer which still stands as the standard for Anglican worship.

In the same way, the Authorised Version is still the standard text of the Bible; but a large number of modern translations have been published which are gradually taking their place in the public readings and in the private devotions of the people. Apart from the Revised Standard Version, first published in America and much like the old Authorised Version, the Jerusalem Bible (of Roman Catholic origin, translated from the French), and the New English Bible are the most popular. But the New English Bible can scarcely be regarded as a satisfactory version. Great words are left out and are replaced by words of far less significance: for example, where 'righteousness and true holiness' becomes 'the just and devout life' and a great poetical phrase like 'walk as children of light' becomes 'live like men who are at home in daylight' which, to any ordinary child, means the night shift.

But people still read the Bible. The Evangelicals take it very seriously and make it the centre of their lives. They carry it about wherever they go. They know what it says, and argue from it. They believe its teaching to be true in every detail. But the regular, systematic reading of the Bible is beginning to die out, and study of the Scriptures as a whole is reduced to those who are really interested in them. It remains, however, the source-book for all theologians, the fount of revelation, the unique record of God and his dealings with people, and, as such, is read and studied.

Sunday worship has changed a great deal in recent years. The old-fashioned Morning and Evening Prayer have largely disappeared, and with them the Canticles and the Psalms. Who nowadays ever sings the Te Deum or says the Apostles' Creed? The clergy say their offices on weekdays, but as far as Sunday is concerned, these are more or less dead. Some evangelical churches keep them going, and a few country churches still have Mattins and Evensong; but, for the most part, churches have made Holy Communion the one service of the day. This came about as a result of the 'Parish and People' movement in England, and 'Associated Parishes' in the United States. There was much behind this. The sacrament is, after all, the only form of worship commanded by Jesus Christ of his followers. It is the Lord's service on the Lord's Day. Instead of being a service for a few at 8.00 a.m. or after Mattins was over, it becomes the Living Church, worshipping all together at about 9.30 on a Sunday morning. It has completely changed the Anglican attitude towards the Eucharist and made it the central feast of the Church. 'In our time', wrote Horton Davies, 'the rediscovery has been made of the Church as the people of God, the saved and saving society.'[29]

Evangelicals and Anglo-Catholics are all together on this vital change. The old high-church appeal to High Mass with no communicants is nowadays virtually no more heard. This is partly due to the Second Vatican Council and the great changes which have come about in Roman Catholic worship, with its modern services in the language of the people, its simplicity and lack of ceremonial, its worshippers communicating at all services often in both kinds, its evening Masses, its sense of familiarity and friendliness which did not exist in the old Latin Tridentine Masses. It would not be true to say that Rome is here following Canterbury, but the two have

29   Horton Davies, *Worship and Theology in England*, v (1965), p. 41.

grown together so much that strangers entering a church for the first time would have some difficulty in knowing whether what was taking place were Anglican or Roman Catholic worship.

All this has made a great difference to worship, and, incidentally, to ecumenism. But A. M. Ramsey, in a very wise article published as long ago as 1956, has a good deal to say about the parish communion. He points out three things in its favour. First of all, it gives emphasis to the Eucharist as the centre of Sunday worship. 'It is a moving thing', he says, 'to find a congregation accustomed on every Lord's Day to gather round the perpetual memorial of the death of Christ, to feed together upon his Body and Blood, and to offer themselves, their souls and bodies, through him to the Father'. Secondly, he points out that partisanship is much less now than it used to be. Evangelicals and Anglo-Catholics now do the same thing at the same hour, and party feeling is consequently greatly diminished. Thirdly, he says that the congregation now has a chance of realizing itself as a Christian family, and the church becomes the Church. On the other hand, there are dangers to be encountered. First is the lack of the doctrine of sacrifice. 'I miss too often', he says, 'in these parish communion services the due recognition, in teaching and atmosphere and choice of hymns, of the awful fact of the one, sufficient sacrifice of our Lord on Calvary.' Secondly, there is the doctrine of communion, 'the responsible act of an individual . . . an act full of awe and dread . . . the awe in the individual's approach to Holy Communion, which characterized both the Tractarians and the Evangelicals of old, stands in contrast to the ease with which our congregations come tripping to the altar week by week'. Thirdly, there is fellowship, the fellowship of those on earth with those in heaven. 'Happy are those churches which are full of reminders that the Church on earth is always a colony of Heaven, and that those who are called to be saints have fellowship with the glorious saints already.'[30] He might also have added the loss of Psalms and Canticles, the rather scrappy little sermonettes with very little teaching in them, and, perhaps above all, the disappearance of non-sacramental forms of worship so much enjoyed by those on the fringe of Christianity, who cannot commit themselves to communicating, but who enjoy the old

30 A. M. Ramsey, *Durham Essays and Addresses* (1956), pp. 15–20.

services of Mattins and Evensong with their fine readings from the Old and New Testaments, their singing of the Psalms and a good, well-thought-out, twenty-minute sermon to tell them something about God.

Two things have made this type of sermon much less common nowadays than it once was – the parish communion and broadcasting. Both of these have cut down what a preacher has to say to five or ten minutes. In fact, a really skilful preacher can get into that space a real message and some positive teaching; but where are these skilful preachers to be found nowadays? Austin Farrer is a prime example; but his sermons were all preached to a limited audience of intelligent men in a college chapel at Oxford. The result is that people are not being taught the Christian faith as they used to be. They are, curiously enough, presumed to know it, though no one knows how. They are expected to have been somehow taught what to believe about God, about the Church and sacraments, sin and forgiveness, life and death. People think that children learn these things in confirmation classes, or at school; but this is not so, with the result that there are few Christians nowadays who could 'give an answer to every man that asketh you a reason of the hope that is in you'. All that a Christian should believe is admirably set out in the 'Proposed Book of Common Prayer according to the use of the Episcopal Church' of the USA[31] in the form of an 'Outline of the Faith' which would make a fine basis of Christian preaching or teaching. But there is nothing like this in the English Prayer Book except the catechism, which is very short and nowadays so much neglected.

The other reason for killing off the long sermon is broadcasting, which works to a very close timetable and makes five-minute room for Thoughts and Prayers for the Day. These are often good, but they do not give much occasion for teaching the great doctrines of the faith. When broadcasting came about, some fifty years ago, the question of religious matters was discussed. In those days there were a few great men, such as Dom Bernard Clements OSB of All Saints, Margaret Street; and Dick Sheppard of St Martin-in-the-Fields. But they were exceptional. Many people, however, find their religious teaching on the radio nowadays, sometimes with results which are not altogether happy.

31   pp. 845–62.

There are a few churches where the old-fashioned sermon is still preached, but these sermons are not usually published. Fine sermons were delivered by E. C. Hoskyns on such subjects as eschatology and sin which give excellent teaching, though mainly to undergraduates at Cambridge,[32] and A. R. Vidler's *Windsor Sermons* are of a high standard. But the endless stream of volumes of sermons, which formed such a notable part of late Victorian and Edwardian England, has now more or less dried up. No one really wants to buy them and read them. The religious books that came out during the present century were books which struck at the heart of religion. What was it all about? Who or what was God? What do we make of the sacraments? What do we mean by sin and forgiveness? What is the Church? Who or what were the saints?

There is, of course, a vast output of religious literature, most of which is presumably bought and read. Evelyn Underhill did much to convert English people to ideas of mysticism and of worship. Gabriel Hebert introduced, with his *Liturgy and Society*, the idea of making the communion the central feature of church life. F. P. Harton, in his book *The Elements of the Spiritual Life*, has given us a long account of how God is to be approached, loved and adored. Gregory Dix OSB, in *The Shape of the Liturgy*, did much to make people understand eucharistic prayer. William Temple brought men to the heart of religion in his *Readings in St John's Gospel*. Martin Thornton in *English Spirituality* and C. J. Stranks in *Anglican Devotion* both deal with some of the great masters of the spiritual life. With these should be mentioned the work of two laymen – C. S. Lewis and Charles Williams, and the writings of the poets – T. S. Eliot, Andrew Young, R. S. Thomas, and others who all expressed their deepest joys and feelings in verse. All these writers, and many others, have, in various ways, helped people to understand the real meaning of religion.

The twentieth century is really the century of ecumenism, which is said to have begun with the Edinburgh Missionary Congress of 1910, though various attempts at church unity had been made before that. But since 1910 the idea of uniting the Churches, in accordance with the will of Christ, has been in the forefront of people's minds. The results, however, have

32   E. C. Hoskyns, *Cambridge Sermons* (1938).

been negligible, due to the fact that the Anglican Communion
is in a curious position in claiming to be part of the Catholic
Church, with its fixed liturgy, its threefold ministry and its
long association with the past, while being clearly a product
of the Reformation with a good deal of Calvinism in its official
documents. This has made its position particularly difficult,
for any approach towards Rome is sure to affect its relationship with the other Churches of the Reformation, and vice
versa.

So far as Rome is concerned, no allowance to Anglicans
has been made until very recent times. Ever since the start of
the Ecumenical Movement, the Church of Rome has stood
apart. It believes itself to be the true Church, regarding everyone else as heretical, or at least schismatic, and declaring that
the only form of unity is for those outside its jurisdiction to
come in on its terms. So those Anglicans concerned with the
promotion of unity, such men as George Bell and Arthur
Headlam, have had to concentrate on the Protestant
Churches, the Methodists, the United Reformed Church, the
Church of Scotland and the minor sects. Anglicans have succeeded in forming a union in India, but nothing else has
emerged for the simple reason that, regarding the Church of
England as catholic throughout, they do not wish to lose
anything that they think of as essential to that heritage. So
they look towards Rome, though with considerable misgiv-
ings. Archbishop Fisher paid a visit to Pope John XXIII in
1960, which was a friendly meeting of two Christian leaders,
but did not go any way towards a reunion of the Churches.
Then, two years later, came the Second Vatican Council and
with it great changes in the Roman Church, and its entry (in
a modest way) into the field of ecumenism. Archbishop Ramsey followed up the Council by a formal visit to Pope Paul
VI and the issuing of an Agreed Statement and the setting
up of a Commission to inaugurate between the Roman Catholic Church and the Anglican Communion 'a serious dialogue
which, founded on the Gospels and on the ancient common
tradition, may lead to that unity in truth, for which Christ
prayed'. This dialogue has been going on for about fifteen
years, and has produced four documents: one on the Eucharist, one on ordination and the ministry, and two on the authority of the Church. That a group of theologians can reach
universal agreement on these subjects has been a great surprise to many, but, after long discussion, the whole party –

conservative and liberal – has been able to put its signature to these documents.

This has been a great step forward in church relations between Rome and Canterbury. It has been backed up by co-operation between the Churches on an unpremeditated scale. There has been sharing of church buildings, joint services, preaching in each other's churches, friendship and co-operation at every level. The old polemic of 'No popery', which had lasted for 400 years, has faded away. Hensley Henson's declaration that 'Englishmen are not inevitably episcopalian as the Scots are inevitably presbyterian, and the Irish inevitably papists, but *are found* they are Erastian, Bibliolatrous, and always fiercely anti-Papal'[33] is no longer true, though some people still regard the Church of Rome as their natural enemy, or rival, and will have nothing to do with it. They turn naturally to the Protestants, the Nonconformists or Free Churches, with which they feel they have so much in common. Some go partly to church and partly to chapel and cannot see what keeps them apart, especially now that the Free Churches are finding a new respect for episcopacy and for a fixed, sacramental liturgy.

The Anglican Communion is therefore in a difficult position. If it goes nearer to Rome it goes away from the Protestant churches, and if it goes nearer to them it finds itself inevitably getting further from Rome and Eastern Orthodoxy. The history of ecumenism in the world today represents this dilemma. But, deep down, there is a spirit of toleration and of union, quite different from the old spirit of hatred or of indifference from which we suffered so long. There is today a new kind of ecumenism growing up. People are getting rather tired of plans and schemes for uniting the Churches. What matters most nowadays is to be a Christian, to believe in Christ as our Lord and Master, to pray to the Holy Spirit for help and guidance in all our needs. It does not much matter to these people to what Church they belong.

Meanwhile the Church of England carries on its work, still regarding itself as responsible for the spiritual welfare of the whole country. The parish, not the congregation, is still the unit, which means that every parish priest must care for everyone living in his parish. This may mean, in town parishes, upwards of 20,000 souls of whom about 500 are church-

33 H. H. Henson, *Retrospect of an Unimportant Life*, ii (1943), p. 153.

goers. What is he to do about the rest? The answer is, he must go among them and 'convert' them, that is he must try to persuade them to believe in God, to love him and to desire to worship him. Otherwise his congregation becomes no more than a sect, a little band of God-fearing people surrounded by a huge crowd of unbelievers.

This is the reason which lies behind the 'parish mission' which now plays a large part in the life of all Anglicans. Missions had been held at St James's, Wednesbury from 1854 onwards, but the great London Mission of 1874 was a combined effort on the part of a number of parishes to bring the gospel to those outside the Church. G. H. Wilkinson (1833–1907) says that he had seen the most devout church people 'content to humble themselves before their fellow-men, and to tell everybody outside how superficial, how utterly unreal, how halfhearted had been all the devotion of their life, as the world considered it, to the Lord God Almighty',[34] which shows the effect of such missions on those within the Church as well as those outside it.

The parish mission now became a very notable feature of English church life. Preparations were undertaken over a long period, and then the missioners came and spent a week or more in the parish, holding services and preaching sermons every day, visiting the houses of the parish, having special services for children, going to the church school to talk to the children there, bringing new hope and new ideas to the people of the parish. Some of the missioners were, like Brother Edward, full-time. Others were parish priests visiting each other's parishes, sometimes in small teams of three or four. Much was done by members of the religious communities.

By the end of the nineteenth century, the religious communities were well-established in the life of the Church, and had been accepted by the authorities as fulfilling a real need. The bishops at the Lambeth Conference of 1897 said that 'we recognise with thankfulness to Almighty God the manifold tokens of his blessing upon the service of the Religious Communities in our branch of the Catholic Church', and in 1913 the American Episcopal Church passed a canon for formal recognition of them, the first legislation on behalf of the religious since the Reformation. In 1935 an Advisory Council was set up in England to keep a line open between the bishops

34   D. Voll, *Catholic Evangelicalism* (1963), p. 59.

and the communities, to examine their rules and constitu-
tions, and generally to supervise their life and work. The
communities are now going through a difficult time as the
whole conception of life vows is now under consideration; but,
as Canon Allchin has said, 'When all is said, is it not true
that the qualities of truth and faithfulness, of steadfast love
and mercy, are those which characterize God above all else?
If this is so, it would seem that man, his creature, made in
his image, must in his person above all things reflect this
quality of steadfast love.'[35]

The most spectacular introduction has been the Society of
St Francis which came into being about 1921 and has since
spread all over the world. St Francis was not much known in
England until the turn of the century, when books began to
pour out, starting with Sabatier's celebrated *Vie de Saint François* in 1894. The Society of St Francis (first called the
Brotherhood of St Francis of Assisi) began in 1913, when a
man calling himself Brother Giles set out, like St Francis
himself, to live among the very poor, the tramps, who were
outside all touch with the Church or with religion, and were
wandering about the country, tramping from casual ward to
casual ward or cheap lodging-house. After some years Brother
Giles acquired a house in Dorset where he tried to reclaim
from destitution some of the younger men on the roads.
Brother Giles was forced by ill-health to give up in 1923 and
was replaced by Brother Douglas who ran the home on the
same lines, going out from time to time to share the lives of
the tramps on the roads, and looking after some of them in
the Home of St Francis. Brother Douglas and two of his
brothers took their life vows in 1931, and the Society became
recognized. Since then it has flourished, and has spread over
all the world, to the Pacific, to the USA, to Tanzania and to
Trinidad. The friars no longer have to live as tramps. Instead
they live a simple life in their thirty-two convents, conduct
parochial missions, visit prisons and hospitals, hold retreats,
look after down-and-outs in their Homes, and generally make
themselves most useful to the Church.

One of their convents is at Glasshampton, in Worcester-
shire, where Father William lived for many years as a solitary,
always hoping that other men would join him in a life of
silence and prayer. He had worked among the lepers at St

35 A. M. Allchin, *Religious Communities in the World of Today* (1970), p. 29.

Giles in Essex, and had tried various forms of the religious life until, in 1918, he went to live alone in utter poverty, hoping to build up a community of like-minded men. This never came about, though many people came there for advice and spiritual help of many kinds. But Father William remained alone in his cell for eighteen years, until he was taken to a home in 1936 and died there during the following year.

Meanwhile, in 1906, a convent of women, known as the Convent of the Incarnation, or Sisters of the Love of God, at Fairacres in Oxford, had been set up for a contemplative form of life, such as at West Malling where a Benedictine type of rule was adopted, and where the sisters lived in silence, completely cut off from the world, engaged in prayer for the needs of mankind. The Franciscans also founded, about 1940, a house of Poor Clares, with a Rule adapted from the Rule which St Francis drew up for St Clare and her 'poor ladies' in the thirteenth century.

Religious communities have also flourished in other parts of the world, especially in the United States where the Society of St John the Evangelist of Cowley founded a house at Boston, Massachusetts, as early as 1870, and the Order of the Holy Cross began in 1881. As far as women's houses are concerned, perhaps the most interesting is the Community of the Transfiguration at Glendale, in Cincinnati, Ohio, where joyousness rather than austerity is the order of the day, and where the sisters say that 'as sisters of the Transfiguration we must ever keep the vision of the King in his Beauty in our hearts, while our hands are busy ministering to his little ones'.[36] Peter Anson lists about 240 religious communities in the Anglican Communion. Some of them are brotherhoods rather than static communities. The Oratory of the Good Shepherd began in 1913 as a society of like-minded priests living in Cambridge under a Rule of Life, meeting daily for prayer, and holding gatherings from time to time when they were scattered throughout the world. The Company of Mission Priests is a body of secular clergy, living under a simple Rule, unmarried, working mostly in parishes. Other such congregations exist in the USA, one at Frostburg, Maryland, stressing what they call the Seven Notes of fellowship, liberty, stewardship, labour of the mind, the love that makes for peace, discipline and joy.[37]

36   P. F. Anson, *The Call of the Cloister* (1964), pp. 563–5.
37   Ibid., p. 182n.

Many people are far too much occupied with the world and its duties that any idea of joining a religious community is quite impossible. All they can hope for is to get away for a few days for a retreat, which means that they say their prayers, listen to addresses about God, and observe a silence from all conversation with their fellows. The retreat movement began in the nineteenth century, when R. M. Benson held his first retreat at Cowley in 1858. After this, the idea caught on, especially in the religious communities, where all that was necessary was easily found with the addition of living for a short time with a body of men or women given up to spiritual things. But there were other kinds of retreat going on – a parish priest in the north of England calling a number of factory workers together, the gathering of a few friends in the house of one of them, a London priest acquiring a country house where retreats could be held regularly.

The movement became so popular that in 1913 a society was formed calling itself the Association for Promoting Retreats for whom a Retreat House was opened in the following year. This was soon followed by other houses being made available, by religious communities opening their doors, by colleges setting aside their chapels and their living accommodation. Vast numbers of people are now thankful to get away from the car, the jet-age, the constant movement and clatter of modern life, to spend time in quiet, thinking about the things of the spirit. As Martin Thornton says of them, a lot of people 'do not undertake a disciplined three-day search for God unless they seriously hope to find him'.[38]

While the devout go off to their retreats, and while the monks and nuns sing or say their office in choir, a few people collect together in the cathedrals and some of the parish churches of the land to hear Evensong. This is sung every day by a handful of little boys and a few older men, and is perfect in every way. These choirs are exquisitely trained to sing the most difficult music, faultlessly and flawlessly. There are few there to listen to them, but that does not really matter. What matters is that God should hear, day by day, year in and year out, the perfect singing of his praises by these little groups of men and boys. It is Anglicanism at its very best.

38 M. Thornton, *English Spirituality* (1963), p. 5.

7

THE ANGLICAN SPIRITUAL TRADITION

The Anglican Spiritual Tradition is both Catholic and Protestant. It is Catholic first of all in its forms of worship. 'Anglican worship', wrote Evelyn Underhill, 'is a special
development of the traditional Christian culture, and not
merely a variant of continental Protestantism.'[1] That is to say
that it keeps to a fixed liturgy, allowing no place for extemporary prayer or self-devised services of praise and preaching
such as are common in nonconformist bodies. It is catholic
also in its maintenance of the threefold ministry of bishops,
priests and deacons. This is something which the Anglican
Communion has insisted on keeping, despite endless attempts
to abandon it in favour of some ecumenical project and to
suit the ideas of those who have long since deserted it. This
it refers back at least to Ignatius of Antioch who, about AD
110, wrote his letters in which he spoke of the threefold
ministry as being the norm in all the churches with which he
was in correspondence, and it even declares, in its Preface to
the Ordinal, that 'it is evident unto all men diligently reading
holy Scripture and ancient Authors, that from the Apostles'
time there have been these Orders of Ministers in Christ's
Church: Bishops, Priests and Decons', though this fact would
be doubted by many scholars of the present day who would
declare the absence of any clear threefold ministry in the New
Testament, but would show that it was very early present in
the Church.

The Anglican spiritual tradition is Protestant in that it
repudiates the papacy with its infallibility and universal jurisdiction, that it cuts out much of Catholic thought and worship which had developed during the Middle Ages, that it
accepts the doctrine of justification by faith, and of predestination, that it uses the vernacular in all its services. There is
also its emphasis on the reading of the Bible, and its devotion
to morality and the good Christian life.

1 Evelyn Underhill, *Worship* (1936), p. 314.

As Evelyn Underhill says: 'The student of Anglicanism can find there a complete Evangelicalism: grave, Biblical, prophetic, devoted, based on preaching of the Word, suspicious of ceremonies, acts and signs, emphasising the personal relation of the soul to God, greatly concerned with man and his needs. At the same time he can find a sacramental, objective, theocentric worship, emphasising holiness, authority and the total action of the Church, her call to adoration and vocation of sacrifice.'[2]

The basis of the Anglican spiritual tradition is the Bible, which has been known in our English translation since at least 1537 when it was first authorized. Anglicans, at any rate until recently, read the Bible assiduously. It was to be read in full in public worship at least once a year, and it has been regularly used to provide texts for sermons, which at one time lasted two or three hours and included the recitation of long passages of Scripture, and it was read deeply and devoutly in the homes of the people. People did not doubt for one moment the truth of all that appeared in the pages of the Bible from Genesis onwards. It was the Word of God, dictated by the Holy Spirit, containing all that God wishes us to know about himself, his nature, his mighty works, and his will for mankind. Few Anglicans would have let a day pass without reading the Scriptures in the Authorised Version. Many would begin with the Book of Genesis and carry on until they got to the end of Revelation, and would then start again. Texts were taken out of their context to tell us something about God or to reveal something of his will. Bibles were treated as if they were sacred things, and many English people would, to this day, refrain from putting any other book, or even papers, on top of a Bible. Possession of a Bible has been regarded as a natural thing since literacy became common. Children are given Bibles at school, or at their confirmation, ordinands are given them at their ordination to the priesthood or the episcopate, and the yearly output is prodigious even though they are not read today nearly as much as they were some years ago. Nevertheless, the Bible remains at the heart of the Anglican religious life.

Next to the Bible we have the Book of Common Prayer which is vital to all Anglican thought. This has remained virtually the same since 1549 when Cranmer produced his first book in which he said: 'Here you have an order for

2 Ibid., p. 323.

Prayer, and for the reading of the Holy Scripture, much agreeable to the mind and purpose of the old Fathers, and a great deal more profitable and commodious, than that which of late was used.'[3] In the same Preface he says that 'these many years passed, this godly and decent order of the ancient Fathers hath been so altered, broken and neglected by planting in uncertain stories, and legends, with multitude of responds, verses, vain repetitions, commemorations and synodals, that commonly when any book of the Bible was begun, after three or four chapters were read out, all the rest were unread.' Cranmer had to choose a path between retaining all these interpolations and giving way to disorder and inconvenience such as the more radical reformers desired.

The result was the Book of Common Prayer, a liturgy which was basically the old one, but reformed, updated, remodelled, cutting out all recent extravagances, and introducing a certain amount of new material to satisfy the wishes of the continental reformers. But the Prayer Book is fundamentally catholic in that it is based on the writings of the Fathers and the traditions of the Church. The English Prayer Book is not merely a permissive liturgy, to be used or abandoned according to taste; it forms, with the Bible, 'the authorised Missal and Breviary of the English branch of the Catholic Church'.[4] It contains a calendar whereby the worshipper is led through the Christian year, and kept informed of the saints; Morning and Evening Prayer, to be said daily, and which contain a confession of sin, the Psalms and Canticles, two readings from the Bible and a number of prayers; the communion service with collects, epistles and gospels for every Sunday and festival of the Church's year; services of baptism, confirmation, matrimony, visitation of the sick (with an act of penitence) and burial of the dead. Later was added the Ordinal, thus increasing the sacraments to six. It was intended to contain all that was necessary for daily worship and the Occasional Offices, a catechism setting out what a Christian should believe and be, the Ten Commandments, greatly loved by Anglicans as the basis of Christian behaviour both towards God and towards man, the Litany, the Athanasian Creed, the thanksgiving of women after childbirth,

3   Preface to the Prayer Book of 1549.
4   E. Underhill, *Worship* (1936), p. 314.

forms of prayer to be used at sea and on the anniversary of the day of accession of the reigning sovereign.

The Prayer Book is thus meant to meet every occasion, and to need nothing but the Bible to go with it. With these two books the parish priest could conduct his services every day, and, indeed, the Prayer Book has been used daily in every cathedral and in most parish churches. Although it has been more or less replaced by an Alternative Service Book it still remains the standard book, loved by most Anglicans and regarded by them as something vital to the life and spirituality of the Church. It is full of the liberal and scriptural catholicism which is the basis of all Anglican thought, and which stems down from the New Testament, through the Fathers, to the first centuries of the Church's life, before it became overloaded with medieval customs and theology which the reformers were anxious to get rid of. It provides material all of which is in the language of the people; it gives a lot for the laity in the congregation to say and to do; it holds up the ideal of 'holiness and righteousness' (which are mentioned no less than twelve times in its pages); it is truly sacramental with all the emphasis upon the Holy Communion, which it calls 'that holy sacrament', and describes the sacramental meal as 'the Body and Blood of Christ which are verily and indeed taken and received by the faithful in the Lord's Supper'.[5]

Like all Anglican theology the Prayer Book is deeply entrenched in history. This is particularly true when we look at the Calendar which, after a modest beginning, was greatly enlarged in 1662 with twenty-four red-letter days (apart from the movable feasts) and sixty-seven black-letter days. The chief festivals were feast days connected with the life of Christ and his apostles, and other New Testament characters. All were biblical, except All Saints' Day and the Feast of St Michael and All Angels. The black-letter days were given to Roman martyrs, great saints of the Church, leaders of church life in England (from St David to St Richard of Chichester) and a few biblical, or semi-biblical events and persons such as St Anne and the Invention of the Holy Cross. This meant seven or eight feast days every month, or two in every week. The red-letter days all had a collect, epistle and gospel provided for them, and although the minor festivals had no

5 The Catechism.

propers they were remembered by the pious and historically minded or were tutelary saints, patrons of churches, and so on. No Anglicans were included even in the Prayer Book of 1928, though the number of saints' days was increased considerably. It is the new Prayer Book of 1980 which has added a number of Anglicans – Thomas Cranmer, George Herbert, Lancelot Andrewes, and many more. It also, ecumenically, has brought in some Roman Catholics such as St Thomas More, St Vincent de Paul and St Francis Xavier. The United States of America Calendar has been even more adventurous with the addition of Laud, Donne, Maurice and Pusey and a lot of American bishops and priests. All this emphasis upon the saints 'prevents "earth-bound" religion and, coupled with the Kalendar, forges a sacramental relation, not only between matter and spirit but also between time and eternity; it thus perfects our prayer by making it part of the prayer of Christ to the Father'.[6]

The Virgin Mary has five days appointed for her remembrance, two of them major saints' days and three of them minor. These do not include the Assumption, though the American book makes of 15 August a feast of the Virgin. Anglican devotion to Mary has been very limited in spite of these feast days. This is due to the possibly exaggerated attention to her which the Roman Catholics have always shown, even to the extent of trying to get her declared Co-redemptrix with her Son, and Mediator of all Grace. This devotion has put off Anglicans, who always speak of her rather apologetically or ignore her altogether. But she is becoming nowadays a little more popular, as she was in the seventeenth century when Bishop Thomas Ken wrote his famous poem:

> Her Virgin-eyes saw God Incarnate born,
> When she to Bethlehem came that happy morn.
> How high her raptures then began to swell,
> None but her own omniscient Son can tell:
> . . .
>
> Heaven with transcendent joys her entrance graced
> Next to His throne her Son His Mother placed;
> And here below, now she's of Heaven possessed
> All generations are to call her blessed.[7]

6   Martin Thornton, *English Spirituality* (1963), p. 275.
7   *English Hymnal*, no. 217.

Nevertheless, the break with the past at the time of the Reformation was sudden and profound. People saw the Church giving worship to a mortal rather than to God; and while ascribing the gift of justice to the Son, turned to his Mother for mercy. Hence the need to pray to her more than to Christ. As John de Satgé says: 'He [the evangelical Christian] cannot but be impressed by what he sees in Roman churches: the blaze of candles throwing into relief shadowy figures praying before the statue of our Lady, while our Lord in the Blessed Sacrament is by comparison deserted.'[8] But he points out that the Ecumenical Movement, especially the admission of the Russian Orthodox Church to the World Council of Churches in 1961, has made people rethink their attitude to the Virgin Mary. This may be true; but the fact remains that the average Anglican, especially the layman, completely ignores the Virgin, considering her to be a Roman Catholic saint to whom he would never think of addressing a prayer. The 'Hail Mary' is used in a few high-churches, but this is thought by most of the laity to be an unnecessary bit of Roman Catholic devotion introduced, quite unnaturally, into Anglican prayer life.

The Church of England has a real claim to be at least part of the Catholic Church in England. This is emphasized in the Preface to the Prayer Book of 1662 which speaks of the 'established Doctrine or laudable Practice of the Church of *England*, or, indeed, of the whole Catholick Church of Christ'. It mentions the Catholic Church in all its Creeds, especially the Athanasian, which was required to be said monthly and began with the words: 'Whosoever will be saved: before all things it is necessary that he hold the Catholic Faith' – not the faith as taught by Luther, still less by Calvin, but the faith of the Catholic Church reaching far back into the past. The Prayer Book is the expression of this faith. 'We are fully persuaded', says the same preface, 'in our judgements (and we here profess it to the world) that the Book, as it stood before, established by law, doth not contain in it any thing contrary to the Word of God, or to sound Doctrine, or which a godly man may not with a good Conscience use and submit unto, or which is not fairly defensible against any that shall oppose the same.'

The Church of England, therefore, traces its history back into the past – to St Augustine of Canterbury, to the Celtic

8 *The Blessed Virgin Mary: Essays by Anglican Writers* (1963), p. 106.

saints and missionaries, and to the Christians among the earliest Roman conquerors, possibly including no less a person than St Joseph of Arimathea himself. It remained part of the Western Church until 1534 when Henry VIII broke with Rome and the Church of England became independent. This made little difference to doctrinal matters except for belief in the papacy, which was no part of the Catholic faith as expressed in the three Creeds of the Church. A few years later, reforms took place – the Prayer Book in English, married clergy, communion administered in both kinds (in accordance with the teaching of Christ), and the doing away with a lot of medieval doctrine and practice which had crept in. At the same time, due largely to the Council of Trent, the Canon Law was modified and brought up to date and became a very important feature in the life of the Roman Church, but was not, of course, concerned with the Church of England.

With the abandonment of the papacy, great power was given by the Church to the bishop, who became the chief source of authority in the Church. He is taken very seriously in all Anglican teaching; the Prayer Book says that where there is any doubt about how the services are to be conducted, reference should be made to the bishop of the diocese; he is to be informed of anyone refused permission to receive the sacrament; he is to give the absolution and the blessing if he is present at any service of Holy Communion; he is to be informed of any baptism to such as are of 'riper years'; he conducts all confirmations and ordinations; he is likened to the apostles, prophets, evangelists, pastors and doctors of the Church, and is ordered to be 'to the flock of Christ a shepherd, not a wolf'. All this gives great authority to the bishop whose office is drawn from the 'holy Scripture and the ancient canons' of the Church of God. This takes us back to the early Church, long before the Pope or Bishop of Rome emerged as sovereign pontiff.

This continuity with the past makes the Church of England a very learned Church, well established in the Scriptures and the Fathers. The clergy used to be called *stupor mundi*, though this title would hardly apply today, when administration and pastoral needs drive men from their books. But the close and learned study of the Bible, of the early Fathers of the Church, and of church history from the earliest times to the present day, has made the Anglican clergy, and to some extent the laity, a class of learned men. The bishops were especially chosen for their sound learning, and themselves produced books which showed how much they knew. Lightfoot, Bishop of Durham in the nineteenth century, was thought to be the most learned man in Europe, which was saying a lot in the days of the great German theologians. The universities of Oxford and Cambridge were entirely staffed by Anglican clergy until well into the nineteenth century, many of the professors being men of great authority in the field of scholasticism. Even the parish clergy were well read. They read and studied books like *Essays and Reviews, Lux Mundi* and *Essays Catholic and Critical* and the works of men such as Stubbs, Lightfoot, Westcott, Pusey and many others. The vein of sound scholarship, and of learning in all branches of theology, ran through the Church, making it an outstanding body of men to whom the world looked for guidance and inspiration.

Henry VIII, when he broke with Rome, had himself called Supreme Head, a title which his daughter, Elizabeth, changed to Supreme Governor on the ground that only Christ could be called Head of the Church on earth. But this made the Church of England, though not other parts of the Anglican Communion, very Erastian. It is the sovereign who appoints all the bishops, the deans, and a number of other dignitaries as well. He or she is crowned by the Archbishop of Canterbury in the setting of the Anglican Holy Communion. The Church of England is regarded as the religion of the State, and was for long regarded as the only religion of the English people, to which everyone was expected to conform. The sovereign is prayed for in Morning and Evening Prayer and in the communion service; and the Thirty-nine Articles state that 'the King's Majesty hath the chief power in this Realm of England, and other his Dominions, unto whom the chief Government of all Estates of this Realm, whether they be Ecclesiastical or Civil, in all causes doth pertain'. The sovereign has the prerogative given always to all 'godly Princes in holy Scriptures by God himself', and is looked up to as the Head or Governor of the Church as well as of the State. Anything said which might seem to reduce the sovereign's authority is quickly denounced, especially by the more evangelically minded of the populace. This is something which means a lot to the laity, though the clergy carry it out in theory if not so much in practice. Nevertheless, the establishment of the Church of England is regarded as one of its main features, and is highly thought of by most Anglicans.

Two documents of the Anglican Church – the Ten Commandments and the Thirty-nine Articles – are both very much loved by the laity and the evangelical wing. The Ten Commandments are losing ground liturgically as they are seldom said now in the communion service. But with the rise in violence and crime, and the low standard of morals, they are considered by many to stand for what is right. The first three, which concern our attitude towards God, are obviously extremely important. The fourth, which is about keeping the Sabbath (taken now to mean Sunday) and the remaining six, which deal with theft, murder, adultery or immorality, filial obedience, truth, and the desire to possess what really belongs to another, are regarded as the basis of all civilized life. The Decalogue has been part of the teaching of the Church for a very long time, and in the Middle Ages bishops encouraged their clergy to teach it to their people together with the Creed and the Lord's Prayer. But it has largely disappeared in Christian thought, which prefers to think in more relaxed terms nowadays.

The Thirty-nine Articles are also loved by the evangelical party in the Church. But they represent what was the teaching of the Church in the sixteenth century, and things have changed considerably since then. Predestination and election are something which not many members of the Anglican Communion would nowadays accept, nor that 'works done before the grace of Christ and the Inspiration of his Spirit are not pleasant to God' which seems to rule out all good work done by unbelievers as having 'the nature of sin'. Rome is mentioned as having erred 'not only in living and manner of Ceremonies, but also in matters of Faith', which is a hard judgement, as is the declaration that its teaching of 'Purgatory, Pardons, Worshipping and Adoration, as well of Images as of Reliques, and also invocation of Saints, is a fond thing vainly invented'. But apart from these statements, and the fact that the Bishop of Rome 'hath no jurisdiction in this realm of England', Rome is not mentioned. The part of the Articles which the Evangelicals hold firmly is the declaration that the Bible contains all things necessary to salvation, and the teaching about sin and redemption, predestination and justification, all of which are either Lutheran or Calvinist in their origin. But the Thirty-nine Articles are also ceasing to have the authority which was once theirs. They are no longer read by clergy on accepting any position in the Church, nor are they regarded as a test of loyalty and orthodoxy.

Sin is a very real part of the Anglican spiritual tradition. 'Oh, to be done with sin for ever', sighed an old lady, a good Christian and churchwoman, on her deathbed. Sin had haunted her all her life, not so much the sins which she had committed, but the fact that her life had been governed by sin. Sin meant carelessness of God, caring for the world and all that this life has to offer – wealth, health, home life, children – when everything should be centred in God. This is something which affects everyone. It is inherited, as is the sin of Adam and Eve in the Garden, who thought they knew better than God and could disobey him with impunity. It runs through all Anglican teaching from the Reformation to comparatively modern times, when, like so much else, it is beginning to fade away as people accept the teaching of the psychologists.

Sin is universal and profound. It can be forgiven only by Christ and his redeeming death on the cross. It plays an important part in the Thirty-nine Articles where it is described as 'the fault and corruption of the Nature of every man ... whereby man is very far gone from original righteousness ... and therefore deserveth God's wrath and damnation'. The Prayer Book is full of it. Morning and Evening Prayer start with a confession of sin in which the priest and the congregation say: 'We have erred and strayed from thy ways like lost sheep: we have followed too much the devices and desires of our own hearts; we have offended against thy holy laws; we have left undone those things which we ought to have done, and we have done those things which we ought not to have done; and there is no health in us.' The Holy Communion service is full of the idea of sinfulness. 'We acknowledge and bewail our manifold sins and wickedness', we cry. 'The remembrance of them is grievous unto us; the burden of them is intolerable' are words which many moderns find unacceptable, though they need to be told that the prayer is in the first person plural, and we are talking about the sin of the world, not just personal misdemeanours. Even at the last moment the canon of the Mass is broken by a form of prayer, inserted by Cranmer, in which we say that 'we are not worthy so much as to gather up the crumbs under thy table', which causes H. A. Williams to say that, although

Cranmer was an orthodox believing Christian, his liturgy is 'incomparably unChristian'.[9] This is perhaps going too far, for, after all, the canon is immediately followed by the prayer: 'O Lamb of God, which taketh away the sin of the world, have mercy on us' which Cranmer did not include in his liturgy.

Sin is a very real thing, underrated by writers of the present day. The thought of sin and its forgiveness is mentioned over and over again in the collects, where we pray that we may be delivered from our sins and wickedness (Advent 4), and that we, 'lamenting our sins and acknowledging our wickedness' (Ash Wednesday), do 'worthily deserve to be punished' (Lent 4). There is, in fact, very little joy in the collects as printed in the Prayer Book. God is the God of justice rather than of love, the God who condemns and punishes us for our sins rather than the God who exhorts us to love one another in the spirit of Christ. This means gloom rather than joy, sorrow rather than jubilation, as a fundamental part of the Christian religion. Perhaps sin is overrated; but the fact remains that man is born in sin, that he is a sinner all his life, and that he must confess his sins regularly.

The high-churchmen have taught people to confess their sins privately in the sacrament of penance, and to receive priestly absolution. This, like so much else, is becoming more common at the present time, when churches announce that confessions will be heard at certain times, and people queue up to enter the 'box' and receive absolution. This, however, is a comparatively recent phenomenon in Anglican church life. A hundred years ago Lord Shaftesbury was denouncing it in the strongest possible language. It was an unclean thing, a degradation of God's law, a scandal to Holy Scripture, something under no circumstances to be practised by any decent churchman.[10] But Anglicans do not talk like that nowadays. There is a spirit of toleration in the air, and although many would regard sacramental confession as unnecessary, and perhaps even wrong, a Roman practice which they would never themselves adopt, they do not really mind other people doing it if it does them good. It is, after all, encouraged in the Prayer Book, where anyone whose conscience is disquieted with sin is told to go to a priest and open his grief to him so

9   *Soundings* (1962), pp. 79–80.
10   R. T. Davidson and W. Benham, *Life of A. C. Tait*, ii (1891), p. 167.

that 'by the ministry of God's holy Word he may receive the
benefit of absolution'.

The Anglican spiritual tradition has always laid great emphasis on good behaviour as something most necessary to
every believer in Christ. It demands that people live a good
life, abstaining from the more conspicuous sins, giving to the
poor, trying to live exemplary lives of the kind which would
encourage their neighbours, and do good to the society of
which they are a part. But this means that they do not think
very much about God. Only about 8 per cent of the English
population go to church on a Sunday (though a good many
more in the USA), but good behaviour, family life, the training of their children, all these matter a great deal to them.

At the same time, the true Anglicans are a fine breed.
These are the people who go to church at least once a week,
almost certainly to Holy Communion which has recently become the chief service to be held every Sunday morning. They
say their prayers regularly, never allowing a day to pass
without kneeling down by their bedside to pray. The prayers
they use may perhaps be rather formal, the sort of prayers
which they were taught to say in childhood and have never
been brought up-to-date or made more mature. Mental
prayer or meditation is practised by some of the more devout,
possibly when in retreat. Bede Frost makes a great appeal for
this kind of mental prayer – being with God, attention to
him, reflection upon spiritual realities, 'an intercourse of the
spirit with God'.[11] They read their Bibles, though not as much
as they used to do. They think about God a good deal. Some
of them trust God as watching over them all the time. They
attribute everything that happens to them to God, who tells
them precisely what he wants them to do, does everything
necessary for them, and is their universal provider and guide.

Others put their trust in Christ. They follow him and try
to be like him in all that they do. They take his sayings very
seriously. They read the Gospels assiduously, and try very
hard to translate all that Christ said to modern conditions.
They learn passages by heart, and meditate upon them as
they go about their work. The Anglican Communion is full
of christocentric devotion and piety. Christ means everything
to them; and many of them can name the place and the hour
when, in St Paul's words, they 'put on Christ' and accepted

11   Bede Frost, *The Art of Mental Prayer* (new edn 1960), p. 6.

him as their Redeemer. From that moment their lives were dedicated to him, wholly in his hands.

This devotion to Christ goes with considerable liberty of conscience. Anglicans are not bound by authority except that of the Bible, which is paramount. The Church, as such, does not count for very much, and it is often disregarded. They accept none of the authority of a Pope, of Canon Law, encyclicals or decrees. Evelyn Underhill speaks of the Anglican spirit of 'reverence, sobriety, moral earnestness and sturdy realism',[12] and is right to do so, for these are the characteristics of good Anglican piety. It reverences God above all things. It also has respect for the saints, but eschews statuary and images which it thinks totally unnecessary to devotion. It loves ceremonial on big occasions like the Coronation or the Enthronement of the Archbishop of Canterbury, but it does not care for too much of it in the parish churches which most Anglicans attend.

The Anglican Church has a very strong sense of mission. The history of its work overseas is remarkable. Men and women went out and gave their lives, in Africa or the Far East, in order to win souls for Christ and to build up the Church of God, and their work and their sacrifice is now bearing fruit abundantly. But mission applies nowadays to the home field as much as to that which lives abroad. In England the parish includes everyone living within its boundaries, and a sense of responsibility for their welfare falls on the Anglican congregation which lives in a sea of unbelievers for whose souls it is ultimately responsible. Perhaps mission overstresses the appeal to people to go to church. Bede Frost says that good people are obsessed with the idea that the Christian life consists in going to church, which, he says, is 'a fond thing vainly invented by the Puritans in the seventeenth century'.[13] The really important thing is to convince them of the existence of God, of his goodness and love towards mankind, of his demands on us his children, of the joy of serving him, to bring them 'to face both the guilt and the grandeur of the human soul'.[14] This is what religion is really about; and there is no substitute for it. It is what Anglicanism,

12   E. Underhill, *Worship*, p. 327.
13   Bede Frost, *The Art of Mental Prayer*, pp. 8–9.
14   C. J. Stranks, *Anglican Devotion*, p. 272.

in the last resort, is always concerned with, the one thing that brings perpetual joy and peace to the believer.

Dr Pusey prayed as follows:

> Let me not seek out of Thee what I can only find in Thee; peace and rest and joy and bliss, which abide only in Thy abiding joy. Lift up my soul above the weary round of harassing thoughts to Thy Eternal Presence. Lift up my soul to the pure, bright, clear, serene, radiant atmosphere of Thy Presence, that there I may breathe freely, there repose in Thy Love, there be at rest from myself and from all things that weary me: and thence return, arrayed in Thy peace, to do and bear what shall please Thee.[15]

Nothing could more clearly spell out the Anglican spiritual tradition, which is well described by Martin Thornton, who writes of the English School of Spirituality as 'sane, wise, ancient, modern, sound, and simple; with roots in the New Testament and the Fathers, and of noble pedigree; with its golden periods and its full quota of saints and doctors; never obtrusive, seldom in serious error, ever holding its essential place within the glorious diversity of Catholic Christendom'.[16]

15 *Private Prayers*, 12th edn, p. 39.
16 M. Thornton, *English Spirituality* (1963), p. 14.

INDEX